In the
Vineyard of
the *Text*

In the *Vineyard* of the *Text*

A Commentary to Hugh's
Didascalicon

IVAN ILLICH

The University of Chicago Press
Chicago and London

Historian, philosopher, educator, and social critic, Ivan Illich was
born in Vienna in 1926. His many works include *Gender, Medical
Nemesis, Deschooling Society,* and *ABC: The Alphabetization of the
Popular Mind.* He is a visiting professor of philosophy at the University of Bremen and at Pennsylvania State University.

The University of Chicago Press, Chicago 60637
The University of Chicago Press, Ltd., London

02 01 00 99 98 97 96 95 94 93   1 2 3 4 5

ISBN 0-226-37235-9 (cloth)

Library of Congress Cataloging-in-Publication Data

Illich, Ivan, 1926–
    In the vineyard of the text : a commentary to Hugh's
Didascalicon / Ivan Illich.
      p.   cm.
    Includes bibliographical references.
      1. Hugh, of Saint-Victor, 1096?–1141. Didascalicon.   2. Learning
and scholarship—History—Medieval, 500–1500.   3. Manuscripts,
Medieval—History.   I. Title.
AE2.H833I43   1993
001—dc20   92-44643
                                                                CIP

⊗ The paper used in this publicaton meets the minimum require-
ments of the American National Standard for Information Sciences-
—Permanence of Paper for Printed Library Materials, ANSI Z39.48-
1984.

Contents

In the
Vineyard of
the *Text*

Introduction

This book commemorates the dawn of scholastic reading. It tells about the emergence of an approach to letters that George Steiner calls bookish, and which for eight hundred years legitimated the establishment of western scholastic institutions. Universal bookishness became the core of western secular religion, and schooling its church. Western social reality has now put aside faith in bookishness as it has put aside Christianity. Since the book has ceased to be the ultimate reason for their existence, educational institutions have proliferated. The screen, the medium, and "communication" have surreptitiously replaced the page, letters, and reading. I here deal with the beginning of the epoch of bookishness which is now closing. I do so because this is the appropriate moment to cultivate a variety of approaches to the page that have not been able to flourish under the monopoly of scholastic reading.

> *Je suis un peu lune et commis voyageur*
> *J'ai la spécialité de trouver les heures*
> *qui ont perdu leur montre*
>
> . . .
>
> *Il y a des heures qui se noient*
> *Il y en a d'autres mangées par les cannibales*
> *je connais un oiseau qui les boit*
> *on peut les faire aussi mélodies commerciales*
>
> I am a bit moon and traveling salesman
> I have the speciality of finding the hours
> which have lost their clock
>
> . . .

There are some hours which drown
there are others eaten by cannibals
I know a bird which swallows them
and one can make singing commercials of them

These lines evoke the approach I take to my subject. They are from a poem by Vicente Huidobro, the Chilean associate of Apollinaire, wounded when he ran for president of his country in 1925, later a war correspondent in Spain and France.[1]

I concentrate my attention on a fleeting but very important moment in the history of the alphabet when, after centuries of Christian reading, the page was suddenly transformed from a score for pious mumblers into an optically organized text for logical thinkers. After this date a new kind of classical reading became the dominant metaphor for the highest form of social activity.

Quite recently reading-as-a-metaphor has been broken again. The picture and its caption, the comic book, the table, box, and graph, photographs, outlines, and integration with other media demand from the user textbook habits which are contrary to those cultivated in scholastic readerships. This book contains no criticism of these new habits of media management, or the training methods by which these habits are established. It also does not in any way question the importance and beauty of bookish reading in its manifold ways. By going back to the origins of bookishness I hope to increase the distance between my reader, whom I expect to be a bookish person, and the activity in which he engages while reading me.

> Modern theories of how the universe came into being tell that an extremely delicate balance was involved. Had certain crucial temperatures and dimensions been even minutely different, the Big Bang . . . could not have occurred. The development of the modern book and of book-culture as we know it seems to have depended on a comparable fragility of crucial and interlocking factors.[2]

Classical print culture was an ephemeral phenomenon. According to Steiner, to belong to "the age of the book" meant to own the means of reading. The book was a domestic object; it was accessible at will

1. For information on Huidobro's political activity in Chile, see René de Costa, *Vicente Huidobro, The Careers of a Poet* (Oxford: Clarendon Press, 1984), pp. 2, 15, 106. The complete poem can be found in Vicente Huidobro, *Obras completas*, vol. 1 (Santiago de Chile: Zig-Zag, 1964), p. 353.

2. George Steiner, "The End of Bookishness?" in the *Times Literary Supplement,* July 8–16, 1988, p. 754.

for re-reading. The age presupposed private space and the recognition of the right to periods of silence, as well as the existence of echo-chambers such as journals, academies, or coffee circles. Book culture required a more or less agreed-upon canon of textual values and modes. And it was more than a means by which those who became expert at it could claim middle-class privileges for themselves. As long as bookish reading was the goal of initiation for Catholics, Protestants, and assimilated Jews, of clerics and enlightened anticlericals, of humanists and scientists alike, the formalities involved in this one kind of reading defined, and did not just reflect, the dimensions of social topology.

The book has now ceased to be the root-metaphor of the age; the screen has taken its place. The alphabetic text has become but one of many modes of encoding something, now called "the message." In retrospect, the combination of those elements that from Gutenberg to the transistor had fostered bookishness appears as a singularity of this one major period, characteristic of one—namely, western—society. This is so in spite of the paperback revolution, the solemn return to public poetry readings, and the sometimes magnificent flowering of alternative, home-based presses.

Bookish reading can now clearly be recognized as an epochal phenomenon and not as a logically necessary step in the progress toward the rational use of the alphabet; as one mode of interaction with the written page among several; as a particular vocation among many, to be cultivated by some, leaving other modes to others. The coexistence of distinct styles of reading would be nothing new. To make this point, I want to tell the story of reading during a distant past century of transition. With George Steiner I dream that outside the educational system which has assumed entirely different functions there might be something like *houses of reading,* not unlike the Jewish *shul,* the Islamic *medersa,* or the monastery, where the few who discover their passion for a life centered on reading would find the necessary guidance, silence, and complicity of disciplined companionship needed for the long initiation into one or the other of several "spiritualities" or styles of celebrating the book. In order that a new asceticism of reading may come to flower, we must first recognize that the bookish "classical" reading of the last 450 years is only one among several ways of using alphabetic techniques.

This is the reason why in the first six chapters I describe and interpret a technical breakthrough which took place around 1150, three hundred years before movable type came into use. This breakthrough consisted in the combination of more than a dozen technical inventions and arrangements through which the page was transformed from score to text. Not printing, as is frequently assumed, but this bundle of innovations, twelve generations earlier, is the necessary foundation for all the stages through which bookish culture has gone since. This collection of techniques and habits made it possible to imagine the "text" as something detached from the physical reality of a page. It both reflected and in turn conditioned a revolution in what learned people did when they read—and what they experienced reading to mean. In my comments on Hugh's *Didascalicon,* I propose a historical ethology of medieval reading habits, together with a historical phenomenology of reading-as-symbol in the twelfth century. I do so in the hope that the transition from monastic to scholastic reading may then throw some light on a very different transition now.

This book gathers seven lectures written in answer to three invitations: Rustum Roy's that I teach an annual course in the Science, Technology, and Society Program at Penn State University; Soedjatmoko's that I begin writing on the symbolism of western technology by placing myself at a great distance from it, by living as his guest at the United Nations University in Japan; and David Ramage's that I conduct a seminar on the history of reading in relation to wisdom at McCormick Theological Seminary at the University of Chicago. I dedicate this book to Ludolf Kuchenbuch and these three friends, on the occasion of their happy escape from further academic administration.

My lecture notes would never have turned into a book had not Ludolf Kuchenbuch invited me to participate in an academic adventure whose German name is *Schriftlichkeitsgeschichte.* This new history of Europe attempts to focus on the mutual determination of a society and its notational system. As I learned to pursue it, this is neither a history of literacy nor of the literate, neither a history of writing techniques nor of the use to which writing has been put by merchants, courts, or poets. Rather, it is a history of the relationship between the axioms of conceptual space and social reality insofar as this interrelationship is mediated and shaped by techniques that employ letters. This history focuses directly on the thing that has been shaped by letters, the *Schriftstück;* it studies the behavior this object defines, and the meanings which are given—class specifically—to this object and this behavior. We study the thing, as it has variously congealed the nature, source, and limits of an epoch's understanding of the world, society, and the self.

Our project deals with the alphabet, with the thing shaped by the alphabet, and not with the history of notation, language, structure, communication, and media. From the perspective in which we take up the historical study of letters, most of the concepts used quite naively in the now fashionable history of media appear as creatures of an alphabetic epistemology whose history is the subject we choose to investigate. By centering our analysis on the object that is shaped by letters, and on the habits and fantasies connected with its use, we turn this object into a mirror reflecting significant transformations in the mental shape of western societies, something not easily brought out by other approaches.

My choice of the early twelfth century to illustrate the impact of the alphabet in the course of a long history has been dictated by my biography: For forty years I have periodically delighted in reading the authors of this one generation, and searching for their sources. For decades a very special affection has tied me to Hugh of St. Victor, to whom I feel as grateful as I am to the very best of my still living teachers, among whom Gerhart Ladner stands out in this context. When Professor Kuchenbuch, at the University of Hagen, launched his curriculum on the impact of the alphabetized object on western cultures, it seemed logical and fitting that I comment on Hugh's *Didascalicon*. It is the first book written on the art of reading.

I have not written this book to make a learned contribution. I wrote it to offer a guide to a vantage point in the past from which I have gained new insights into the present. No one should be misled into taking my footnotes as either proof of, or invitation to, scholarship. They are here to remind the reader of the rich harvest of memorabilia—rocks, fauna, and flora—which a man has picked up on repeated walks through a certain area, and now would like to share with others. They are here mainly to encourage the reader to venture into the shelves of the library and experiment with distinct types of reading.

Writing this essay was a shared enjoyment because each sentence got its shape by being tossed back and forth between Lee Hoinacki and myself. What had started as a study in the history of technology, ended up as a new insight into the history of the heart. We came to understand Hugh's *ars legendi* as an ascetic discipline focused by a technical object. Our meditation on the survival of this mode of reading under the aegis of the *bookish text* led us to enter upon a historical study of an asceticism that faces the threat of computer "literacy."

Two friends saw to it that these ruminations became a book: Valentina Borremans who, with critical enthusiasm, urged me on from stage to stage of the manuscript; and Carl Mitcham, whose careful attention to detail, both large and small, improved the text.

 ONE

Reading toward Wisdom

Omnium expetendorum prima est sapientia. "Of all things to be sought, the first is wisdom." This is how Jerome Taylor translates the lead sentence of the *Didascalicon* of Hugh of Saint Victor, written around 1128. Taylor's introduction, translation, and notes are a masterpiece. By his careful choice of words and subtle metaphors, he provides the best available running commentary to this translation of an early twelfth-century text. His copious notes are mainly concerned with Hugh's sources. Even after twenty-five years, during which scholarly interest in Hugh of St. Victor has flourished, they require very little updating.[1]

1. Jerome Taylor, *The Didascalicon of Hugh of St. Victor: A Medieval Guide to the Arts,* translated from the Latin with an introduction and notes (New York and London: Columbia University Press, 1961). Cited as follows: *DT,* book (roman numeral), chapter (arabic numeral).

See also Michel Lemoine, *Hugo de Sancto Victore. L'art de lire: Didascalicon* (Paris: Éditions du Cerf, 1991). This French translation is an accomplished labor of love, and the preface is a terse and meaty introduction to Hugh's contemporaries at the convent of St. Victor.

Charles Henry Buttimer, *Hugonis de Sancto Victore Didascalicon, De Studio Legendi: A Critical Text,* dissertation by Brother Charles Henry Buttimer, M.A. (Washington, D.C.: The Catholic University Press, 1939). Cited as follows: *DB,* book (roman numeral), and chapter (arabic numeral).

Jacques Paul Migne, *Patrologiae cursus completus, sive bibliotheca universalis . . . omnium sanctorum patrum,* Series Latine, 221 vol. (Paris: 1844–64). I am quoting from this series abbreviating as follows: *PL* (meaning *patres latini*), volume, column, and occasionally the four quarters of the page with letters from A to D. The best edition available of Hugh's writings was reprinted here in vols. 175–77. (The *Patrologia graeca* is cited in the same manner, as *PG.*)

Versions or summaries from the Latin without references are made by the author.

Incipit

"Of all things to be sought" is the keynote phrase of Hugh's book on the art of reading. Medieval manuscripts were usually untitled. They came to be named after their opening words, called their *incipit*. Popes still use the incipit in lieu of a title when they write an encyclical letter—for instance, "Rerum novarum" (May 15, 1891), "Quadragesimo anno" (May 15, 1931), "Sollicitudo rei socialis" (February 18, 1988). When a medieval document is cited, one gives its incipit and its *explicit*, the last words. This mode of reference to a letter by its first and last line makes it sound more like a piece of music, whose first and last few notes identify it for the performer.

In Hugh's case we are lucky to possess a faithful survey of his writings.[2] In this earliest catalogue, *omnium expetendorum* is given as the incipit; I will explain later how the book got the preface which Taylor publishes with it.

Auctoritas

Titles are labels. But an incipit is like a chord. Its choice permits the author to evoke the tradition into which he wants to place his work. By the subtle variation of a frequently repeated sentence he can state the purpose that prompts him to write.

Hugh's incipit leaves no doubt that he places his book into a long "didascalic"[3] tradition whose roots go back to Greek reflections on *paideia*, or the formation of the young and their introduction into full citizenship. This tradition was brought into Latin by Varro, a man Cicero called "the most learned of Romans." Varro, librarian of Caesar and Augustus, wrote, among other things, the first normative grammar of Latin. Though a city dweller himself, he wrote four books on agriculture or gardening that Vergil used as his source for the *bucolica* (literally, cowherd's songs), a collection (*ecloga*) of poems that establishes the "back-to-the-land" theme and the search for interior landscapes in western literature. Varro was the first who defined learning as the "search for wisdom," a phrase repeated by successive gener-

2. Joseph de Ghellinck, "La Table des matières de la première édition des oeuvres de Hughes de St. Victor par Gilduin," *Recherches de sciences religieuses* 1 (1910): 270–85 and 289–96.

3. *Didascalica* is a Greek word. It might best translate "matters instructional." Originally it was used for the sessions of Greek chorus training. In Hellenistic Greek it acquired another, different meaning: the official list of playbills and athletic events that were kept in city archives. In Byzantine Greek the predominant meaning becomes "things scholastic." Medieval writers employ it self-consciously as a learned term.

ations of writers on "learned upbringing." The book in which Varro proposes this definition has been lost; his statement survives only in the references of other classical authors.

Quite explicitly, Hugh's incipit claims the heritage of Varro as it was handed down by his pupils, Cicero and Quintilian, the latter being the first learned schoolmaster who wrote on the skill of tracing letters.[4] In this tradition, the ultimate task of the pedagogue is defined as that of a guide who helps the student grasp the Good, *bonum,* which, in turn, will bring the pupil to wisdom, *sapientia.* Both words appear in Hugh's incipit: "of all things to be sought the first is that wisdom in which the form of the perfect good stands fixed," *sapientia, in qua perfecti boni forma consistit.* Like several of his contemporaries, Hugh is aware of his sources among the pre-Christian sages of Rome.

Clearly, it is not simply any good that would satisfy Hugh; his choice of words is precise. By connecting wisdom with "the form of the perfect good," he signifies that he accepts the meaning of Varro's definition, but as it was received and changed and handed on by Augustine.[5] Hugh's writings are drenched in Augustine. He lived in a community that followed Augustine's rule. He read, reread, and copied the texts of his master. Reading and writing were for him two almost indistinguishable sides of the same *studium.* How thoroughly Hugh's texts are compilations, interpretations, and rewordings of Augustine can best be seen in his work on the sacraments, which remained a torso. His final illness and death prevented him from finishing its last chapters;

4. "I quite approve of the practice . . . of stimulating children to learn by giving them ivory letters to play with . . . the sight, the handling, and the naming of which is a pleasure. . . . As soon as the child has begun to know the shapes of the various letters . . . have these cut, as accurately as possible, upon a board, so that the stylus may be guided along the grooves. . . . By increasing the frequency and speed with which the child follows these fixed outlines, we shall give steadiness to his fingers. . . . The art of writing well and quickly is not unimportant for our purposes, though it is generally disregarded by persons of quality." These passages are from Quintilian's first book on the Art of Oratory, written when he retired as a teacher around 85 A.D. Quintilian, the outstanding pedagogue, gives a relative importance to fluent writing by his "pupils of quality" which I cannot help comparing with the importance given by my best gymnasium teacher to his most gifted pupils becoming skilled in taking shorthand (stenography).

5. Ludwig Ott, "Hugo von St. Viktor und die Kirchenväter," *Divus Thomas* 3 (1949): 180–200, 293–332. Bonaventure, who was well versed in the writings of Hugh, a century after Hugh's death, marveled at the depth of his teacher's patristic knowledge. Though Hugh was, for him, "the new Augustine," he also spoke with the voices of Gregory and Pseudo-Dionysius; Augustine being his teacher in speculative theology, Gregory the Great in its practical application, and Pseudo-Dionysius in mystical contemplation (*De reductione artium ad theologiam* 5, *Opera omnia* [Claras Aquas, 1882–1902], V, 321B).

only an early draft is extant.[6] And this draft consists mostly of excerpts from Augustine which he had not yet fully digested into his own diction and style.[7]

As with Augustine, wisdom was for Hugh not something but someone.[8] Wisdom in the Augustinian tradition is the second person of the Trinity, Christ. "He is the wisdom through whom [God] has made all things . . . He is the Form, He is the Medicine, He is the Example, He is your Remedy."[9]

The wisdom Hugh seeks is Christ himself. Learning and, specifically, reading, are both simply forms of a search for Christ the Remedy, Christ the Example and Form which fallen humanity, which has lost it, hopes to recover. The need of fallen humanity for reunion with wisdom is central to Hugh's thought. This makes the concept of *remedium,* remedy or medicine, crucial for an understanding of Hugh. God became man to remedy the disorder, usually represented in visual terms as "darkness," in which humanity, through Adam's sin, has been

6. Hugh's personal method of taking notes and of constructing his books has been studied by Heinrich Weisweiler, "Die Arbeitsmethode Hugos von St. Viktor. Ein Beitrag zum Entstehen seines Hauptwerkes *De sacramentis," Scholastik* 20–24 (1949): 59–87, 232–67.

7. Joseph de Ghellinck, *L'Essor de la littérature latine au XIIe siècle* (Museum Lessianum; Desclée de Brouwer, 1957): Hugh's style is "deliciously refined, but of a modesty that contrasts with the proud diction of Abaelard. He is one of the most touchingly attractive writers of that century. . . . Certainly, his style is less vivacious than that of Abaelard, which is interwoven with quotations of classical authors, from the poets and Plato to Aristotle and the grammarians. . . . Hugh's style is of delicate liveliness in a discreet unction which allows him to depict the inner workings of the soul [*scruter les états d'âme*] in ways which were never to become common among his pupils" (p. 50). Hugh rewrites the same passage innumerable times and laboriously constructs his phrases so that his complex thought finds adequate expression in all its shadings. Quite often he succeeds in expressing himself fully, correctly, and discreetly with elegance. And he knows it; when he succeeds, he has no qualms about repeating the laboriously distilled sentence, transplanting it to a different context.

8. The major study on the relationship between science and wisdom in Hugh of St. Victor is Roger Baron, *Science et sagesse chez Hugues de Saint-Victor* (Paris: P. Lethielleux, 1957). Although the Augustinian notion of wisdom is of central importance to Hugh, wisdom holds a different place in the spirituality of the two men. Augustine's ardor in the devotion to wisdom is centered on the second person of the Trinity; for Hugh, the late Romanesque mystic, on the enfleshed divinity of his Lord. This probably led E. Gilson to the judgment, "Malgré l'intérêt des notations de Hugues, on ne trouvera pas chez lui d'analyse de la sagesse aussi poussé que celle de Saint Augustin [In spite of the interesting character of Hugh's comments, one does not find so powerful an analysis of wisdom as in St. Augustine]" (*Introduction à l'étude de Saint Augustin* [Paris, 1943], pp. 149–163).

9. This commentary on Augustine by Hugh can be found in *De tribus diebus,* which is improperly printed by Migne as *Didascalicon,* chapter 7 (*PL* 176, 834).

steeped. The ultimate remedy is God as wisdom. Arts and sciences derive their dignity from the fact that they share in being remedies for
the same purpose.[10] Hugh, by developing the concept of *remedium*,
provides for the twentieth-century thinker a unique way to address
the issue of technique or technology. Reading, as Hugh perceives and
interprets it, is an ontologically remedial technique. I intend to explore
it as such. I analyze what Hugh has to say about the techniques used in
reading in order to explore the role that alphabetic technology played
around 1130 in the shaping of these techniques.[11]

10. Most clearly wisdom inhabits the arts and sciences to which the *lector artium*
consecrates himself in his *studium. Omnium autem humanarum actionum seu stu-
diorum, quae sapientia moderatur, finis et intentio ad hoc spectare debet, ut vel naturae
nostrae reparetur integritas vel defectuum, quibus praesens subiacet vita, temperetur
necessitas (DB* I, 5, p. 12). "Of all human acts or pursuits, then, governed as these are
by Wisdom, the end and the intention ought to regard either the restoring of our nature's
integrity, or the relieving of those weaknesses to which our present life lies subject" (*DT,*
pp. 51–52).

Sermo 11; *PL* 177, 922–24: *Duodecim autem sunt quae de sanatione humani generis
nobis exponere proposuimus. Aegrotus, medicus, vulnera, medicina, vasa, antidota, di-
aeta, dispensatores, locus, tempus, sanitates, gaudia de ipsis sanitatibus recuperatis. . . .
Antidota sunt septem dona Spiritus sancti, spiritus sapientiae et intellectus, spiritus con-
silii et fortitudinis, spiritus scientiae et pietatis, spiritus timoris Domini . . . ut simus per
timorem humiles, per pietatem misericordes, per scientiam discreti, per fortitudinem
invicti, per consilium providi, per intellectum cauti, per sapientiam maturi. Timor ex-
pellit elationem, pietas crudelitatem, scientia indiscretionem, fortitudo debilitatem, consilium improvidentiam, intellectus incautelam, sapientia stultitiam. O quam bona antidota, quibus tam mala curantur apostemata!* "We want to speak about twelve things
which have to do with healing humankind. There are the sick person, the doctor,
wounds, medicine, instruments, antidotes, diet, nurses, place, time, health, and the re-
joicing which follows on the recuperation of health. . . . The antidotes are the seven gifts
of the Holy Spirit, the spirits of wisdom and understanding, the spirits of counsel and
fortitude, the spirits of knowledge and piety, the spirit of the fear of the Lord . . . that
we might be humble from fear, merciful from piety, discreet through knowledge, strong
through fortitude, helpful through counsel, cautious from understanding, mature
through wisdom. Fear expels pride, piety cruelty, knowledge indiscretion, fortitude
weakness, counsel improvidence, understanding inconsiderateness, wisdom foolishness.
Oh what good antidotes, by which such evil apostasies are cured!"

11. I am here concerned primarily with "alphabetic technology" which interacts in a
unique, epoch-specific way around 1130 with the northwest European symbolic universe, and how changes in world perception in turn facilitated and oriented the choice
of technologies. In taking this approach to the alphabet as a technology I am indebted
to Walter Ong. The simplest introduction to his thought on the matter can be found in
Walter Ong, S. J., *Orality and Literacy: The Technologization of the Word* (London:
Methuen, 1982). This is a different question from that which guided the important study
by Brian Stock, *The Implications of Literacy: Written Language and Models of Interpretation in the Eleventh and Twelfth Centuries* (Princeton: Princeton University Press,
1983). I am concerned with the historical formation of the notion of "text," and with
the discontinuity of this notion in the mid-twelfth century. For Stock "text" is an ana-

A close scrutiny shows that the incipit is not taken directly from Augustine. Its formulation stems from the *De consolatione philosophiae* of Boethius, who subtly but significantly modified Augustine.[12] "Of all things to be sought the first and the reason why all others things are pursued is the Good . . . in which rests the substance of God."[13] The philosopher who speaks of God tones down the Christocentric passion of the recent convert, Augustine.[14] Augustine writes as a former pagan who cannot forget that he recently discovered Christ as a Person. Boethius is born in 480, exactly fifty years after the death of Augustine. He is the heir of a Christian tradition of several generations. As a Roman consul, he entered into the service of King Theodoric, the Ostrogoth invader. Accused of treason, he writes his *De consolatione* while awaiting execution.[15] Unlike the passionate newcomer Augustine, who sought to detach himself from the sages of this world, Boethius turns toward them. In Plato, Aristotle, Plotinus, and Vergil he sees trailblazers who prepared the way for the coming of Christ. By doing so, he became a major source on antiquity for medieval scholars who accepted the idea that classical philosophy, especially Stoicism, was a *praeparatio evangelii,* a preface to the Gospel.[16]

---

lytic category, including a page or any structured discourse spoken aloud. Stock's interest is in studying how the elements of oral and written cultures interacted on one another, "reconstituting another society's system of communications on its own terms."

12. See Pierre Courcelle, "Étude critique sur les commentaires de la 'Consolation' de Boèce (IX–XV siècles)," *Archives d'histoire doctrinale et littéraire du moyen âge* 12, Paris (1939): 6–140.

13. Boethius: *De consolatione philosophiae,* III, 10. Cited by Taylor, *DT,* p. 175.

14. Henri-Irénée Marrou, *Saint Augustin et la fin de la culture antique,* 4th ed. (Paris: Boccard, 1958). Augustine is the first major thinker who not only did not write in Greek, but whose entire philosophical formation was exclusively Latin. His style is profoundly marked by the cultural milieu of the late Empire and its philosophers. He highly appreciates recitation and rhetoric, finds pleasure in skilled repartee, is used to reading out loud, and much more commonly listens to a *lector* in Latin. He enters the Church fully conscious of his roots in this late imperial Latin milieu.

15. Boethius was born after Constantine, from the noble family of the Anici, in Rome. He was brought up in Athens, and was thoroughly versed in Greek. After having served as a consul in 510, he was accused of subversive plotting with Byzantium for the overthrow of Theodoric, and was imprisoned under the accusation of "magic"—a nonexceptional indictment against someone with encyclopedic culture—two centuries after the official establishment of the Church in the Roman Empire.

16. Émile Mâle says that Boethius was then "venerated as the depository of antiquity's wisdom and as the educator of modern times" (*L'Art religieux du 13ᵉ siècle en France,* 4 vols, 5th ed. [Paris: Armand Colin, 1923], p. 92). During the late Middle Ages, Boethius acquired a mysterious halo not unlike that conferred by Dante upon Vergil: he was "the sage standing between two worlds." Jean de Meun added his translation of the *Consolation of Philosophy* as a postscript to the *Roman de la Rose.* Chaucer came to know him through this translation, and recognized in him the "first of all clerics."

The philosophers taught that the goal of learning was wisdom as the perfect good, and Christians accept the revelation that this perfect good consists in the Word of God made Flesh.[17]

For the contemporary reader the incipit was immediately recognized as an *auctoritas,* a sentence worthy of repetition. When Cerimon the Lord of Ephesus in Shakespeare's *Pericles* "by turning o'er authorities" has "built such strong renown as time shall ne'er decay" (*Pericles,* act 3, sc. 2, lines 33, 48), he does not say that he had subverted established power, nor that he had consulted weighty authors, but that reflecting on a number of authoritative sentences he had established his reputation of mighty wisdom. Authorities, in this now obsolete sense, are sentences which created precedents and defined reality. When Hugh picks this *auctoritas* as his keynote, he does not appeal to Boethius for his prestige. The sentence states an obvious truth precisely because it had been disembedded from the discourse of this or that particular author; it had become a free-floating statement. As such a verbal institution, the *auctoritas* quoted by Hugh became an exemplary testimony to untouchable tradition.

Studium

When we translate the incipit as "of all things to be sought, the *first* is wisdom," it would be easy to get full approval from any first-year student of Latin. *Prima* is the first. But, precisely this seeming transparency of the Latin word presents the difficulty encountered by anyone who attempts to English such a text. No doubt *omnium expetendorum prima* says "of all reachable things the (very) first." Yet, if I translate *prima* with "first," I cannot but cause misunderstanding. For us today, the first thing is that which comes at the beginning of a series or is closest at hand. We take the first of many steps when we start a book or a research project, suspecting that our endeavour will lead us on, perhaps beyond our present horizon. But the thought of an ultimate goal of all readings is not meaningful to us. Even less is there any idea that such a goal could motivate or "cause" our action whenever we open a book. We are steeped in the spirit of engineering and think of the trigger as the cause of a process. We do not think of the heart as the cause of the bullet's trajectory.

We live after Newton. When we see a stone that is falling, we perceive it as being in the grip of gravity. We find it difficult to share the perception of a medieval scholar who sees the same phenomenon as

---

17. *DT,* pp. 175–76, gives a short conspectus of Hugh's sources for this sentence and on later twelfth-century authors who relied on him as a source.

caused by the stone's desire to approach the earth; this is the *causa finalis,* the "final cause" of this movement. Instead, we perceive a force that is pushing the heavy body. The ancient *desiderium naturae,* which is a natural desire of the stone to come to rest as close as it can to the bosom of the earth, has become for us a myth. Even more thoroughly, the idea of one first or primary Final Cause, one ultimate motivating reason of all desires that are hidden in the nature of the stone or of the plant or of the reader, has become foreign to our century.[18] "End stage" in the twentieth-century mental universe connotes death. Entropy is our ultimate destiny. We experience reality as monocausal. We know only efficient causes.

This is the reason why the translation of *prima* as "the first" is at once a perfect translation and a misleading interpretation. If in modern English I want to refer to the Good, Beauty, or Truth that in the traditional sense motivates all existence I must speak of the "ultimate reason" that brings everything into existence by tugging rather than by pushing.

De studio legendi, the subtitle of the book, is just as challenging to translate. What *legere* and *lectio* meant for Hugh is the subject of the entire book. One cannot spell it out here in a few words. But when I had to translate the first term, *de studio,* I was happy that I followed my hunch to look it up in the OED rather than in the Oxford Latin Dictionary.

For the word *study,* sb. ME, the OED gives the following first and second meaning: "1. (Chiefly in translations from Latin): Affection, friendliness, devotion to another's welfare; partisan sympathy; desire, inclination; pleasure or interest felt in something—NB: all these meanings are obsolete since 1697. 2. An employment, occupation—obsolete since 1610." It would therefore be wrong to say that the book is an introduction to that which today is called "studies." It is a guide to a kind of activity which is as culturally obsolete as the *causa finalis.*[19]

Only with this qualification can the book be called a guide to higher studies. Studies pursued in a twelfth-century cloister challenged the student's heart and senses even more than his stamina and brains. Study did not refer to a liminal epoch of life, as it usually does in modern times, when we say that someone "is still a student." They encom-

18. É. Gilson, *From Aristotle to Darwin and Back Again: A Journey in Final Causality, Species, and Evolution* (Notre Dame, Indiana: University of Notre Dame Press, 1984). This is a delightful history of teleological causation (purposeful change) written by an old, learned medievalist.

19. Robert Javelet, "Sens et réalité ultime selon Hugues de Saint-Victor," *Ultimate Reality and Meaning* 3, no. 2 (1980): 84–113.

passed the person's daily and lifelong routine, his social status, and his symbolic function. No doubt this book can be talked about as a medieval precursor of the propaedeutic literature which provided curricula for first-year university students in later centuries. In this book Hugh gives advice on the division of the disciplines of his time and the methods which fit them. He also discusses at length how the fields of the knowable are to be divided. He lists the canon of classics with which he expects the students to be familiar. However, what in Hugh's view is the most central issue are the virtues needed for and developed by "reading."

Disciplina

The *studium legendi* forms the whole monk and reading will become perfect as the monk himself strives for, and finally reaches, perfection.[20]

- The beginning of discipline is humility . . . and for the reader there are three lessons taught by humility that are particularly important: First, that he hold no knowledge or writing whatsoever in contempt.[21] Second, that he not blush to learn from any man.[22] Third, that when he has at-

20. Marie-Dominique Chenu, "Notes de lexicographie philosophique médiévale: *disciplina*," *Revue des sciences philosophiques et théologiques* 25 (1936): 686–92. Henri-Irénée Marrou ("*Doctrina* et *disciplina* dans la langue des pères de l'Église," *Bulletin du Cange* 10 (1934): 5–25) deals with the semantic transformation of these two terms through their integration into the ecclesiastical Latin of the third and fourth century. *Disciplina*, a word used in classical Latin as translation for *paideia* (Greek: "upbringing"), came to mean "correction" or "guidance." *Doctrina*, that had meant "general culture," shifted toward "superior knowledge" and wisdom.
21. DB III, 13, p. 63: *Sapientior omnibus eris, si ab omnibus discere volueris. qui ab omnibus accipiunt, omnibus ditiores sunt. nullam denique scientiam vilem teneas, quia omnis scientia bona est.* "You will be wiser than all if you are willing to learn from all. Those who take from everybody, are the richest of all. Finally, hold no learning in contempt, for all learning is good" (*DT*, p. 96).
22. DB III, 13, p. 62: *Platonem audistis, audiatis et Chrysippum. in proverbio dicitur: Quod tu non nosti, fortassis novit Ofellus* [cf. Horace *Sat.* 2.2.2]. *nemo est cui omnia scire datum sit, neque quisquam rursum cui aliquid speciale a natura accepisse non contingerit. prudens igitur lector omnes libenter audit, omnia legit, non scripturam, non personam, non doctrinam spernit. indifferenter ab omnibus quod sibi deesse videt quaerit, nec quantum sciat, sed quantum ignoret, considerat. hinc illud Platonicum aiunt: Malo aliena verecunde discere, quam mea impudenter ingerere* [Isidore of Seville, *Sententiae* 2.38.3; PL 83, 639B]. "You have heard Plato!—may you hear Chrysippus too! The proverb says, 'What you do not know, maybe Ofellus knows.' There is no one to whom it is given to know all things, no one who has not received his special gift from

tained learning himself, he not look down upon anyone else.[23]

- A quiet life is just as important for discipline, whether the quiet be interior, so that the mind is not distracted with illicit desires, or exterior, so that leisure and opportunity are provided for creditable and useful studies.[24]

- Not to hanker after superfluities is of special importance for discipline. A fat belly, as the saying goes, cannot bring forth subtle sense.[25] And finally, all the world must become a foreign soil for those who want to read with perfection.[26] The Poet says:[27] "I know not by what sweetness native soil attracts a man. And suffers not that he should e'er forget." The philosopher must learn, bit by bit, to leave it.[28]

These are some of a dozen rules of a general character that Hugh gives for the shaping of those habits which the reader must acquire so that his striving lead him to wisdom, rather than to the accumulation

---

nature. The wise student, therefore, gladly hears all, reads all, and looks down upon no writing, no person, no teaching. From all indifferently he seeks what he sees he lacks, and he considers not how much he knows, but of how much he is ignorant. For this reason men repeat Plato's saying: 'I would rather learn with modesty what another man says than shamelessly push forward my own ideas'" (*DT*, p. 95).

23. *DT* III, 13, pp. 94–97.
24. *DT* III, 16, p. 99.
25. *DT* III, 18, p. 100.
26. Robert Bultot, "Cosmologie et contemptus mundi," *Recherches de théologie ancienne et médiévale*, Numéro Special 1, Mélanges de théologie de littératures médiévales offerts à Dom Hildebrand Bascuoa, O.S.B. (Louvain, 1980). The relationship between ascetical ideals and the natural "facts" founded in the epoch's science have been too little explored. The established doctrine about the four elements that compose all visible reality assigned to the "earth" the role of the heaviest, lowest, and least spiritual domain. The entire sublunar sphere is part of the "soil" on which the lover of wisdom ought to feel like a foreigner. *DB* I, 7, p. 14: *item, superlunarem, propter lucis et quietis tranquilitatem, elysium, hunc autem propter inconstantiam et confusionem rerum fluctuantium, infernum nuncupabant.* "Again, the superlunary, from the perpetual tranquility of its light and stillness, they called *elysium,* while the sublunary, from the instability and confusion of things in flux, they called the underworld or *infernum*" (*DT*, p. 54). Bultot examines the inheritance of this image of the philosopher as a stranger in the *infernum* from Macrobius through Bede to Aquinas. For literature see also *DT*, p. 190, n. 56.
27. The quotation is traced by Taylor to Ovid, *Epistulae ex Ponto* 1.3.35–36.
28. *DT* III, 19, p. 101.

of knowledge pursued for the purpose of showing off.[29] The reader is one who has made himself into an exile in order to concentrate his entire attention and desire on wisdom, which thus becomes the hoped-for home.[30]

Sapientia

In the second sentence of this first chapter Hugh begins to explain what wisdom does. The sentence begins, *sapientia illuminat hominem,* "wisdom illuminates man" . . . *ut seipsum agnoscat,* "so that he may recognize himself." Once again, in this rendering, translation and exegesis are in conflict, and the English words chosen could easily veil the sense that interpretation can reveal.

Enlightenment in Hugh's world and what is understood as enlightenment now are two different things. The difference is not merely that we flip the light switch and Hugh used wax candles. The light, which in Hugh's metaphoric usage illuminates, is the counterfoil of the eighteenth-century light of reason. The light of which Hugh speaks here brings man to a glow. Approaching wisdom makes the reader radiant. The studious striving that Hugh teaches is a commitment to engage in an activity by which the reader's own "self" will be kindled and brought to sparkle.[31]

The kind of book Hugh encountered when, back in his childhood in Flanders or his boyhood in Saxony, he was taught how to hold a reed or pen, is barely comparable to the printed objects on our shelves. It had none of the aura characteristic of that bundle of machine-rolled papers covered with printmarks and glued together at the spine that we today take for granted. The pages were still made of parchment rather than of paper. The translucent sheep- or goatskin was covered with manuscript and brought to life by miniatures painted with thin

29. G. Cremascoli (*Exire de saeculo. Esami di alcuni testi della spiritualitá benedettina e francescana [sec. 13–14],* Quaderni di Recherche Storiche sul Primo Movimento Francescano e del Monachesimo Benedettino 3 [Edizioni Rari Nantes, 1982]) notices that the obligation to leave home and follow Jesus is interpreted in a more physical sense by the early Franciscans. The members of the older orders continue to stick to a "literary" rather than a "literal" interpretation.

30. Gerhart H. Ladner, "*Homo viator:* Medieval Ideas on Alienation and Order," *Speculum* 42 (1967): 233–59. The life of the wayfarer "came to be highly esteemed as a radically Christian way of life which possesses its own *stabilitas*" (p. 242).

31. K. Emery, "Reading the World Rightly and Squarely: Bonaventure's Doctrine of the Cardinal Virtues," *Traditio* 39 (1983): 183–218. The appendix is dedicated to "Bon-

brushes. The form of Perfect Wisdom could shine through these skins, bring letters and symbols to light, and kindle the eye of the reader.[32] To face a book was comparable to the experience one can relive early in the morning in those Gothic churches in which the original windows have been preserved. When the sun rises it brings to life the colors of the stained glass which before dawn had seemed like black stuffing in stone arches.

---

aventure and Hugh of St. Victor: Scripture, Prime Matter and the Illumination of Virtue." "The successive illuminations of the world offer an instructive analogy to the gradual illumination of the *world of the human heart* by the sun of justice, which gives rise first to purifying virtues and then to contemplation."

This is how Hugh expresses himself in *De sacramentis Christianae fidei*, I, 1, cap. 12; *PL* 176, 195D–96A: *Quia omnis anima quandiu in peccato est, quasi in tenebris est quibusdam et confusione. Sed non potest evadere confusionem suam et ad ordinem justitiae formamque disponi, nisi illuminetur primum videre mala sua, et discernere lucem a tenebris, hoc est virtutes a vitiis, ut se disponat ad ordinem et conformet veritati. Hoc igitur anima in confusione jacens sine luce facere non potest; et propterea necesse est primum ut lux fiat, ut videat semetipsam, et agnoscat horrorem et turpitudinem confusionis suae, et explicet se atque coaptet ad illam rationabilem dispositionem et ordinem veritatis. Postquam autem ordinata fuerint omnia ejus, et secundum exemplar rationis formamque sapientiae disposita, tunc statim incipiet ei lucere sol justitiae; quia sic in repromissione dictum est: Beati mundo corde; quoniam ipsi Deum videbunt* [Mt. 5.8]. *Prius ergo in rationali illo mundo cordis humani creatur lux, et illuminatur confusio ut in ordinem redigatur. Post haec cum fuerint purificata interiora ejus, venit lumen solis clarum et illustrat eam. Non enim digna est contemplari lumen aeternitatis, donec munda et purificata fuerit; habent quodammodo et per materiam speciem, et per justitiam dispositionem.* "As long as a soul is in sin, it dwells in confusion and darkness. But it cannot get rid of its confusion and come to the order and form of justice unless it is first illumined to see its evils, to tell light from darkness, that is, virtues from vices, so that it might be disposed to order and conformed to truth. But a soul which has fallen into confusion cannot do this without light. Therefore, it is necessary that first there be light, so that the soul might see itself and recognize the horror and vileness of its confusion, understand itself, and then reach for the rational disposition and order of truth. After it has all aspects of itself ordered, and is disposed according to the exemplar of reason and the form of wisdom, then the sun of justice immediately begins to shine on it. For thus the promise reads: Blessed are the clean of heart for they shall see God [Mt. 5.8]. Therefore, light is first created in the rational [soul] by that cleansing of the human heart, and confusion illuminated, so that order might be restored. After all this, when its interior places are purified, the clear light of the sun comes and lights it up. For it is not worthy to contemplate the light of eternity until it is cleansed and purified; these conditions have, in a certain sense, the indeterminate character of matter and through justice receive their proper form."

32. Wisdom is, above all, in the heart. But it is also in the object. In *De unione corporis et spiritus* (*PL* 177, 287A–B), Hugh deals with the element of fire, distinguishing it from earth, water, and air because of its subtlety and mobility, and stresses its special relationship to the spirit, by calling it *sapientia vitalis*. The medieval speculations on the substantive nature of spiritual light have been poetically summed up by Dante.

Lumen

In order to better appreciate the perception of light's nature in the twelfth century it is helpful to place a miniature from a contemporary *codex* next to almost any painting of a later period. Comparing the two, one immediately notices that the beings which appear on the parchment are luminous on their own. Of course, they are not painted with luminescent paint, and they remain invisible in complete darkness. But as soon as you move them into the ambient light of a candle, the faces and clothes and symbols take on a radiance of their own.

This is in stark contrast to Renaissance art, whose creators delight in shadows and in the painting of things that are hidden in darkness. Signorelli, not to speak of Caravaggio, is proud that he knows how to paint opaque objects and, in addition, the light which makes those objects "alight." When you look at his painting you feel that light from a plane, which is distinct from the plane of the picture, strikes the picture and has the function of making the pictured world visible. These painters give the impression that they have created a dark world of things which would still be there even if the light they add were to be extinguished.

Early twelfth-century miniatures, however, continue in the tradition of the icon used in the eastern Christian Church.[33] Following this tradition, the painter neither paints nor suggests any light that strikes the object and then is reflected by it. The world is represented as if its beings all contained their own source of light. Light is immanent in this world of medieval things, and they reach the eye of the beholder as sources of their own luminosity. You feel that if this, their luminosity, were extinguished, what is in the picture would not just cease to be visible, but would cease to exist altogether. Light here is not used as a function but coincides with the *Bildwelt*—the painted realities.[34]

---

33. Gerhart H. Ladner, "The Concept of the Image in the Greek Fathers and the Byzantine Iconoclastic Controversy," in *Dumbarton Oaks Papers* 7 (1953), pp. 1–34 (German translation in *Der Mensch als Bild Gottes*, ed. Leo Scheffczyk [Darmstadt: Wissenschaftliche Buchgesellschaft, 1969], pp. 144–92); and W. Schöne, "Die Bildgeschichte der christlichen Gottesgestalten in der abendländischen Kunst," in his book, *Das Gottesbild im Abendland* (Berlin: Eckart, 1959).

34. These insights on painted light in western pictures are elaborated in great detail by Wolfgang Schöne, *Über das Licht in der Malerei* (Berlin: Mann, 1954). The luminosity of the icon has become a central subject of theological reflection in the eastern Christian, mainly Greek Orthodox tradition. On this see the brilliant study of C. von Schönborn, *L'Icône du Christ. Fondements théologiques élaborés entre le 1ᵉ et le 2ᵉ Concile de Nicée (325–987)*, 2d ed., Collection Paradosis (Fribourg: Éditions de l'Université de Fribourg, 1976); and, more generally, L. Ouspensky, *La Théologie de l'icône dans l'Église Orthodoxe* (Paris: Cerf, 1980).

In contrast to the painters of the luminous beings of the medieval world who sparkle in their *Eigenlicht* and emanate light (*Sendelicht*), the later artist paints the light which shows what is there (*Zeigelicht*), the light which comes from a painted sun or candle and illuminates these objects (*Beleuchtungslicht*). The light of medieval manuscripts "seeks" the eye, as God "reaches out" to the soul. When Hugh speaks of light which enlightens the reader he definitely speaks of the first.[35]

For Hugh the page radiates, but not only the page; the eye also sparkles.[36] Even today in ordinary speech eyes can "shine." But when you say that they do, you know you speak metaphorically. This was not so for Hugh. He conceived of the mind's operation in analogy with the perception of his own body.[37] According to the spiritual optics of the early scholastics, the *lumen oculorum*, the light which emanates from the eye, was necessary to bring the luminous objects of the world into the onlooker's sense perception. The shining eye was a condition for sight. The incipit implied that reading removed the shadow and darkness from the eyes of a fallen race. Reading, for Hugh, is a remedy because it brings light back into a world from which sin banned it. According to Hugh, Adam and Eve were created with eyes so luminous that they constantly contemplated what one now must painfully look for.

By sinning, Adam and Eve were excluded from paradise. From a world of radiance they were banished to a world of fog, and their eyes

35. For Hugh and St. Bernard and other twelfth-century philosopher-mystics, "God is longing," *Deus desiderans,* rather than *Deus in sua beatitudine,* i.e., "eternally resting," as Thomas Aquinas speaks of him.

36. Gudrun Schleusener-Eichholz, *Das Auge im Mittelalter,* 2 vols., Münsterische Mittelalterschriften 35 (Munich: Fink, 1985), is the major source on the eye and eyesight in the Middle Ages. See the section on "the luminous eye," pp. 129–87; the "blindness of the soul," pp. 532–92; the eye used as metaphor, pp. 849–87; and, above all, the inner and the outer eye, pp. 931–1010. In this last section Hugh figures prominently.

37. The lived body that is Hugh's contemporaries' experience is the prime source of analogy. *Sermo 21; PL* 177, 937A–C: *Homo quandiu in justitia perstitit, sanus fuit; sed postquam per culpam corruit, gravem languorem incidit. Et qui ante culpam in omnibus spiritualibus membris suis habuit sanitatem, post culpam in omnibus patitur infirmitatem. Clamet igitur, necesse est: sana me domine, et sanabor. Sed nunquid est dicendus homo habere membra spiritualia? Habet membra spiritualia, scilicet virtutes. Sicut enim exterius membris sibi convenientibus formatur, sic interius virtutibus sibi concordantibus mirabiliter disponitur et ordinatur; et ipsa membra corporis virtutes figurant substantiae spiritualis. Caput significat mentem. . . . Oculi designant contemplationem. Quomodo namque oculis corporis foris visibilia cernimus, sic radiis contemplationis invisibilia speculamur. Per nares discretiones accipimus. Naribus etenim odores ac fetores discernimus, et ideo per nares virtutem discretionis non inconvenienter significamus. Aures exprimunt obedientiam, eo quod audiendi obediendique sunt instrumentum.*

lost the transparency and radiating power in which they had been created and which still fits human nature and desire. Hugh presents the book as medicine for the eye. He implies that the book-page is a supreme remedy; it allows the reader, through *studium*, to regain in some part that which nature demands, but which sinful inner darkness now prevents.

The page as mirror

Hugh asks the reader to expose himself to the light emanating from the page, *ut agnoscat seipsum,* so that he may recognize himself, acknowledge his self. In the light of wisdom that brings the page to glow, the self of the reader will catch fire, and in its light the reader will recognize himself. Here again, Hugh quotes an *auctoritas:* the *gnothi seauton,* the maxim "know thyself," which is first preserved in Xenophon, remains a standing epigram throughout antiquity, and is widely quoted in the twelfth century.[38] However, the mere fact that an authoritative key sentence is quoted and requoted unchanged over a millennium and more is no guarantee that its sense has remained unaltered.

Os insinuat intelligentiam. Sicut enim cibum ore recipimus, ita virtute intelligentiae pastum divinae lectionis captamus. Dentes vero significant meditationem, quia sicut dentibus receptum cibum comminuimus, ita meditationis officio panem lectionis acceptum subtilius discutimus ac dividimus. "As long as man persisted in justice, he was well; but after falling into sin, he was afflicted with a serious illness. And the one who before sin was healthy in all his spiritual members, after sinning suffered weakness in all of them. It is necessary, therefore, to cry out: Heal me Lord, and I shall be well. But is it possible to say that a man has spiritual members? Indeed, the virtues. And just as one is formed exteriorly by fitting members, so is he marvelously shaped and ordered interiorly by appropriate virtues. And the very members of the body metaphorically manifest the virtues of a spiritual being. The head signifies the mind. . . . The eyes speak of contemplation. For as we see visible things with our bodily eyes, so through the rays of contemplation we have some idea of invisible reality. We can distinguish with our nose. For with our nostrils we can discern good from bad smells. Therefore, it is not unfitting that we signify the virtue of discernment by the nose. The ears express obedience in that they are instrumental for hearing and then obeying. The mouth suggests intelligence. For as we receive food with our mouth, so by the power of intelligence do we take in the nourishment of holy reading. And the teeth signify meditation, for as we chew up food with our teeth, so through the exercise of meditation we are able to taste the subtleties in the life-giving bread of reading."

38. Pierre Courcelle (*Connais-toi toi-même, de Socrate à Saint Bernard,* 3 vols. [Paris: Études Augustiennes, 1974]) examines the transmission of this so-called delphic maxim from its first mention in Xenophon to its reception in the school of St. Victor, with exceptional scholarship and ample quotation from the sources.

DB I, 1, p. 4: *Immortalis quippe animus sapientia illustrus respicit principium suum et quam sit indecorum agnoscit, ut extra se quidquam quaerat, cui quod ipse est, satis*

This is the reason why I am tempted to translate *seipsum,* when written by Hugh, as "thy Self" rather than "thyself."

That which we mean today when, in ordinary conversation, we speak of the "self" or the "individual," is one of the great discoveries of the twelfth century. Neither in the Greek nor in the Roman conceptual constellation was there a place into which it could have fitted. The student of the Greek Fathers or of Hellenistic philosophy is likely to be made painfully aware of the difference between their starting point and ours. Our difficulty in understanding them is largely due to the fact that they had no equivalent to our "person."[39]

A social reality in which our kind of self is taken for granted constitutes an eccentricity among cultures.[40] This eccentricity emerges noticeably during the twelfth century. Hugh's work witnesses to the first appearance of this new mode of being. As an extremely sensitive person, he experiences the new mode of selfhood characteristic of his gen-

---

esse poterat. scriptum legitur in tripode Apollinis: gnothi seauton, id est, cognosce te ipsum. "But his [man's] immortal mind, illuminated by Wisdom, beholds its own principle and recognizes how unfitting it is for it to seek anything outside itself when what it is in itself can be enough for it. It is written on the tripod of Apollo: *gnothi seauton,* that is, 'Know thyself'" (*DT,* p. 46).

39. Colin D. Morris, *The Discovery of the Individual, 1050–1200* (London: The Church Historical Society S.P.C.V., 1972), pp. 2–19. In an admirable way this book tries to put the reader in touch with the findings of recent scholarship without having recourse to the apparatus of learned study. The author explores a concept that we have come to take for granted in a society which was, "in some respects confronted with problems not wholly dissimilar from those of the twentieth century." In a major review, Yves Congar recognizes the great merits of the book, but stresses that the "individual" which the twelfth century discovers and expresses in new forms of friendship and marriage, of reading and reflection, of satire and confession, remains deeply embedded in a religious cosmos, and the new sense of individuality can be interpreted only through its organic insertion in this mental universe ("Review of *Discovery of the Individual,* by Colin D. Morris," *Revue des sciences philosophiques et théologiques* 57 [1973]: 305–7). As a result, the new sense of individuality so strong during the second half of the twelfth century is also profoundly unlike the sense of individuality which will become characteristic of later epochs of western history. For the author's response to his critics, especially Caroline Walker Bynum, see also Colin D. Morris, "Individualism and Twelfth-Century Religion: Some Further Reflections," *Journal of Ecclesiastical History* 31 (1980): 195–206.

40. Pierre Michaud-Quantin, *Études sur le vocabulaire philosophique du moyen âge* (Rome: Ateneo, 1970). The same author, in "Collectivités médiévales et institutions antiques," *Miscellanea Medievalia* 1 (1962): 240–52, examines the formation of the concept of "moral person" in connection with the innovative twelfth-century commentaries on Roman jurists, such as Ulpian; under the appearance of a return to classical Roman law, an entirely new concept of the individual and its place in the formation of community is introduced by the *auctoritas* that says *quod omnes tangit, ab omnibus debet approbari* (that which touches all, should be approved by all).

eration. As a reader who is well read in "all the literature there is," he finds ways to interpret traditional *auctoritates* and mentalities in such a way that this new selfhood could express itself within them. He wants the reader to face the page so that by the light of wisdom he shall discover his self in the mirror of the parchment.[41] In the page the reader will acknowledge himself not in the way others see him or by the titles or nicknames by which they call him, but by knowing himself by sight.

The new self

With the spirit of self-definition, estrangement acquires a new positive meaning. Hugh's call away from the "sweetness of one's native soil" and to a journey of self-discovery is but one instance of the new ethos. Bernard of Clairvaux preaches the Crusades, which are another way of expressing the same invitation: They address people at all levels of the feudal hierarchy to leave the common mind-set of the neighborhood, within which identity comes from the way others have named me and treat me, and to discover their selves in the loneliness of the long road. At Bernard's beckoning, tens of thousands leave their village communities and discover that they can survive on their own without the bonds which had sustained them and constrained them within the predetermined feudal *ordo*. Pilgrims and crusaders, traveling masons and mill mechanics, beggars and relic thieves, minstrels and wandering scholars—all these also take to the road by the end of the twelfth century.[42] Hugh's insistence on the need that the scholar be an exile-in-spirit echoes this mood. He is not the only one of his gener-

41. The twelfth and thirteenth centuries are one of those epochs in which the use of the mirror as metaphor is characterized by a significant transformation. Wilhelm Wackernagel ("Über den Spiegel im Mittelalter," *Kleinere Schriften* 1 [1872]: 128–42), and Odo Casel, O.S.B. (*Vom Spiegel als Symbol*, Nachgelassene Schriften, zusammengestellt von Julia Platz [Maria Laach: Ars Liturgica, 1961]) collect many key passages. Jurgis Baltrušaitis (*Essai sur une légende scientifique: le miroir. Révélations, science-fiction et fallacies* [Paris: Elmayan-Seuil, 1978]) relates the various medieval mirror motives to the longer traditions within which they belong. G. F. Hartlaub, *Zauber des Spiegels: Geschichte und Bedeutung des Spiegels in der Kunst* (Munich: Pieper, 1951) is the standard work on the representation of the mirror in art and on the evolution of the mirror as a metaphor in paintings since the Middle Ages.

42. Friedrich Heer, *Der Aufgang Europas: Eine Studie zu den Zusammenhängen zwischen politischer Religiosität, Frömmigkeitstil und dem Werden Europas im 12. Jahrhundert* (Vienna: Europäische Verlagsanstalt, 1949), has several gripping chapters on this "breaking out from the procrustean bed of theocratic order" during the mid-twelfth century, manifesting a period of upheaval in popular perceptual categories that can hardly be compared to any other epoch of European history (e.g., pp. 9–20).

ation to redefine the cloistered life as *peregrinatio in stabilitate,* which means spiritual pilgrimage by those who have committed themselves to local stability within a religious community.[43]

I am not suggesting that the "modern self" is born in the twelfth century, nor that the self which here emerges does not have a long ancestry.[44] We today think of each other as people with frontiers. Our personalities are as detached from each other as are our bodies. Existence in an inner distance from the community, which the pilgrim who set out to Santiago or the pupil who studied the *Didascalicon* had to discover on their own, is for us a social reality, something so obvious that we would not think of wishing it away. We are born into a world of exiles. W. H. Auden expresses it clearly:

> Some thirty inches from my nose
> The Frontier of my Person goes
> And all the untilled air between
> Is untilled *pagus* or demesne.
>
> Stranger, unless with bedroom eyes
> I beckon you to fraternize
> Beware of rudely crossing it
> I have no gun, but I can spit.[45]

This existential frontier is of the essence for a person who wants to fit into our kind of world. Once it has shaped a child's mental topology, that being will forever be a foreigner in all "worlds" except those integrated by exiles like himself.[46]

---

43. Jean Leclercq, "Mönchtum und Peregrinatio im Frühmittelalter," *Römische Quartalschrift* 55 (1960). For *stabilitas in peregrinatione,* see p. 47.

44. For literature, see Colin D. Morris, *Discovery of the Individual,* especially pp. 6–10; and Caroline Walker Bynum, "Did the Twelfth Century Discover the Individual?" *Journal of Ecclesiastical History* 31 (1980): 1–12.

45. W. H. Auden, *About the House* (London: Random House, 1966). p. 16.

46. Paul Mus ("The Problematic of Self, West and East," in *Philosophy and Culture, East and West.* 13ᵉ *conference internationale des philosophes occidentaux et orientaux, Juillet 1959,* ed. L. A. Moore [Honolulu, 1959]) stresses the fundamental distinction between the emergence of the western individual self that is "conscious of itself," and the eastern, mainly Indian, individual self that is intentional of itself within a social context. See also, from the same author, *India Seen from the East: Indian and Indigenous Cults in Champa,* Monash Papers on South East Asia 3 (Melbourne: Monash University Press, 1975); and Louis Dumont, "A Modified View of our Origins. The Christian Beginnings of Modern Individualism," *Religion* 12 (1982): 1–27. Dumont insists on the contrast between the Indian and the Christian-western valuation of the independent and autonomous individual. What distinguishes the western individual is this: under the influence of the Church the worldly institutions of Europe were built around an essentially nonsocial "moral" being.

It is commonly argued that this frontier comes into existence in Hugh's time, as one aspect of the new meaning of person, *persona*, and its social recognition.[47] For earlier medievals, *person* denotes office, function, role, variously derived from the word's origin in the Latin *persona*, a mask. For us it means the essential individual, conceived of as having a unique personality, physique, and psyche. "In the person of" still preserves the older sense by formulaic fossilization, as does *parson*—long held to be the legal *persona* who could sue and be sued in respect of a parish.[48]

What I want to stress here is a special correspondence between the emergence of selfhood understood as a person and the emergence of "the" text from the page. Hugh directs his reader to a foreign land. But he does not ask him to leave his family and accustomed landscape to move on the road from place to place toward Jerusalem or Santiago. Rather he demands that he exile himself to start on a pilgrimage that leads through the pages of a book.[49] He speaks of the Ultimate which should attract the pilgrim, not as the celestial city for pilgrims of the staff, but as the form of Supreme Goodness which motivates the pilgrims of the pen. He points out that on this road the reader is on his way into the light which will reveal his own self to him. Hugh urges his students not to read so as to appear learned, but "to seek out the sayings of wise persons, and to ardently strive to keep them ever before the eyes of their mind, as a mirror before their face."[50] *In lumine tuo uidebimus lumen* "In your light we shall see light" (Psalm 36, 9).

Hugh always speaks from an intensely visual perspective. In the search for wisdom he gives primacy to the eye. With the eye he perceives the sweetness of beauty. He speaks of the shadow out of which the philosopher has to move to approach the light, and he usually speaks of sin in terms of darkness. Enlightenment for Hugh affects three pairs of eyes: the eyes of the flesh, which discover the material things contained in the sublunar sphere of sensible objects; the eyes of

47. Peter Dronke, *Poetic Individuality in the Middle Ages. New Departures in Poetry 1000–1150* (Oxford: Clarendon Press, 1970), complemented by Peter Dronke, *Women Writers of the Middle Ages: A Critical Study of Texts from Perpetua (230) to Marguerite Porete (1310)* (Cambridge: Cambridge University Press, 1984). Dronke stresses both the continuity of romantic motives and the newness of the self-mirroring of the person at this time. The person is represented as one who reflects on himself in his suffering, as one who experiences failure, as a tragic figure.

48. See C. T. Onions, *The Oxford Dictionary of English Etymology* (New York: Oxford University Press, 1966), s.v. "parson."

49. Jean Leclercq, "Mönchtum und Peregrinatio."

50. *De modo dicendi et meditandi* (PL 176, 877B): *Dicta sapientium quaerat, et semper coram oculis mentis quasi speculum vultus sui tenere ardenter studeat.*

the mind, which contemplate the self and the world that it mirrors; and, finally, the eyes of the heart, which penetrate to the innermost reaches of God in the Light of Wisdom, God's Son, hidden, as the ultimate "book" in the lap of the Father.[51]

Amicitia

When Hugh reads, he experiences the restoration of that light of which sin has deprived us. His pilgrimage at dawn through the vineyard of the page leads toward paradise, which he conceives as a garden. The words that he plucks from the trellis of the lines are a foretaste and a promise of the sweetness that is to come. For both the hoped-for fulfillment and the means to reach it, Hugh's ultimate metaphor is friendship. *Est philosophia amor et studium et amicitia quodammodo sapientiae.*[52] "Love and pursuit and something akin to the friendship of wisdom," motivate his pilgrimage.[53] Paradoxically, the way in which twelfth-century monks speak of friendship sounds shameless to late-twentieth-century readers. The full-blooded embodiment of tender

---

51. See *De arca Noe morali,* II, 12; *PL* 176, 643D–644A (the quotation of this passage is given in Latin and English at the end of chapter 7). Hugh's language about the Second Person of the Trinity as the Book is picked up by the Franciscan school. Bonaventure, *De ligno vitae* 46 (*Opera omnia* VIII, 84B): *Sapienia scripta est in Christo Jesu tamquam in libro Vitae, in quo omnes thesauros sapientiae et scientiae recondidit Deus Pater.* "Wisdom is written in Christ Jesus as in the Book of Life, in which God the Father has hidden all the treasures of wisdom and knowledge." And *In Feria VI in Parascheve, Sermo 2* (*Opera omnia* IX, 263B, 265B): *Liber Sapientiae est Christus, qui scriptus est intus apud patrem, cum sit ars omnipotentis Dei; et foris quando carnem assumpsit. Iste liber non est apertus nisi in cruce; istum librum debemus tollere, ut intelligamus arcana sapientiae Dei. . . . multi istum librum tenent clausum, et sunt insipientes.* "The Book of Wisdom is Christ, who is inscribed interiorly with the Father, since He is the art of the omnipotent God; and exteriorly when he took on flesh. *And this book is only opened on the cross.* We should take up this book, that we might know the secrets of God's wisdom. . . . Many leave this book closed; they are the foolish."

52. Quoted from Boethius, *In Porphyrium dialogi* I, 3; *PL* 64, 10D. See *DT,* p. 195, n. 1.

53. "Epistola prima ad Ranulphum de Mauriaco," *PL* 176, 1011A–B: *Quod Charitas numquam excidit. Dilecto fratri R. Hugo peccator. Charitas numquam excidit. Audieram hoc et sciebam quod verum erat. Nunc autem, frater charissime, experimentum accessit, et scio plane, quod charitas numquam excidit. Peregre profectus eram, et veni ad vos in terram alienam; et quasi aliena non erat, quoniam inveni amicos ibi. Sed nescio, an prius fecerim an factus sim. Tamen inveni illic charitatem, et dilexi eam; et non potui fastidire, quia dulcis mihi erat, et implevi sacculum cordis mei, et dolui quod angustus inventus est. Et non valuit capere totam; tamen implevi quantum potui. Totum implevi quod habui, sed totum capere non valui, quod inveni. Accepi ergo, quantum capere potui et onustus pretio pretioso, pondus non sensi, quoniam sublevabat me sarcina mea.*

friendship of these monks for each other and their sisters, who are nuns, witnesses to a range of experience diametrically opposed to even the noblest "interpersonal relationship" found anywhere since "the *Chatterly* ban and the Beatles' first LP." [54]

Friendship is the word in Hugh for that love of wisdom[55] which is *sapientia*, or tasteful knowledge.[56] The friend is *paradisus homo*, "his very first presence is beatifying; friendship is a garden, a tree of life, wings for the flight to God . . . Sweetness, light, fire, wound . . . paradise regained." [57] When Hugh in the *Didascalicon* explains the appeal of wisdom, he cannot but use the metaphor of friendship which ultimately motivates *studium*.[58]

For a few decades, Hugh's contemporaries recovered and Christianized the Platonic doctrine in which knowledge without friendship that delights in the friend's knowledge is deficient. He himself could not avoid interpreting the ultimate aim of *studium* in terms of this experi-

---

Nunc autem, longo itinere confecto, adhuc sacculum meum plenum reperio, et non excidit quidquam ex eo: quoniam charitas numquam excidit. "Charity never ends. To my dear Brother Ranulph from Hugh, a sinner. Charity never ends. When I first heard this, I knew it was true. But now, Dearest Brother, I have the personal experience of fully knowing that charity never ends. For I was a foreigner and met you in a strange land. But the land was not really strange for I found friends there. I don't know whether I first made friends or was made one. But I found charity there and I loved it; and could not tire of it, for it was sweet to me, and I filled my heart with it, and was sad that my heart could hold so little. I could not take in all there was—but I took as much as I could. I filled up all the space I had, but I could not fit in all I found. So I accepted what I could, and weighed down with this precious gift, I did not feel any burden, because my full heart sustained me. And now, having made a long journey, I find my heart still warmed, and none of the gift has been lost: for charity never ends."

Ludwig Ott, *Untersuchungen zur theologischen Briefliteratur der Frühscholastik unter besonderer Berücksichtigung des Viktorinischen Kreises* (Münster: Aschendorff, 1932), p. 350, n. 5, gives paleographic information on this letter.

54. Sexual intercourse began
   In nineteen sixty-three
   (Which was rather late for me)—
   Between the end of the *Chatterley* ban
   And the Beatles' first LP.
Philip Larkin, *High Windows* (New York: Farrar Straus and Giroux, 1974).

55. Hugh, *In Hierarchiam coelestem* 6; *PL* 175, 1036D: *Si minus excitor ad cognitionem, incitabor ad dilectionem. Et erit interim dilectio ipsa refectio, donec ex ea oritatur contemplatio.* "If I am not so excited about knowing, yet I am strongly moved to love. And that love will refresh me until contemplation arises from it."

56. J. M. Décanet, "Amor ipse intellectus est," *Revue du moyen âge latin* (1945): 368.

57. Adèle Fiske, "Paradisus Homo amicus," *Speculum* 40 (1965): 426–59.

58. He stands in a long tradition which interprets friendship: *est autem hic amor sapientiae, intelligentis animi ab illa pura sapientia illuminatio, et quodammodo ad seip-*

ence. The light of wisdom which envelops the mind of the student calls and draws him back to himself in such a way that he affects the other always as friend. Through the visible things of the world the true reader rises to the invisible . . . traveling within his heart on an inner ladder toward a union in the arms of a delightful God.[59]

---

sam retractio atque advocatio, ut videatur sapientiae studium divinitatis et purae mentis illius amicitia (*DB* I, 2, p. 7). "This love of Wisdom, moreover, is an illumination of the apprehending mind by that pure Wisdom and, in a certain way, a drawing and a calling back to Itself of man's mind, so that the pursuit of Wisdom appears like friendship with that Divinity and pure Mind" (*DT*, p. 48).

59. *De arca Noe morali*, IV, 6; PL 176, 672C–D: *Electi autem dum temporalia Dei beneficia recolunt, ad agnitionem aeternorum proficiunt. Reprobi per visibilia ab invisibilibus cadunt; electi autem per visibilia ad invisibilia ascendunt . . . De operibus conditionis per opera restaurationis, ad conditionis et restaurationis auctorem ascendunt. Ascensus autem isti non extrinsecus, sed intrinsecus cogitandi sunt, per gradus in corde de virtute in virtutem dispositos.* "The elect, while pondering God's temporal benefits, advance to knowledge of the everlasting ones. By visible things the reprobate fall from those that are invisible; but by the visible the elect climb up to the invisible. . . . Arising from the human condition through meritorious works, they ascend to the Author of both condition and merit. But one must conceive of this ascent interiorly not exteriorly, as it proceeds from virtue to virtue through ever greater strengthening of the heart" (*Hugh of Saint-Victor, Selected Spiritual Writings*, trans. by a Religious of C.S.M.V. [New York: Harper and Row, 1962], p. 138). See also *DT*, p. 168 (n. 91) and p. 173 (n. 168). And *De Laude Charitatis* (PL 176, 972–73A: *Dic mihi, o cor humanum, utrum magis eligis, semper gaudere cum hoc saeculo, an esse semper cum Deo? quod plus diligis, hoc potius eligis. audi ergo, ut aut corrigas dilectionem, aut non differas electionem. Si mundus iste pulcher est, qualis putas est pulchritudo ubi Creator mundi est? Dilige ergo ut eligas, dilige melius ut eligas salubrius. Dilige Deum, ut eligas esse cum Deo, ergo per dilectionem eligis. Sed quo plus diligis, eo citius pervenire cupis, et festinas ut apprehendas, ergo per dilectionem curris, et per dilectionem apprehendis. Item quo plus diligis, eo avidius amplexaris, ergo per dilectionem frueris.* "Tell me, O human heart, whether you would choose to enjoy this world forever, or to be always with God? That which you love more, you will choose. Listen, therefore, that you correct your love, or not put off your choosing. If this world is beautiful, what do you imagine to be the beauty of the place where the Creator of the world is? Love, therefore, that you might choose; love better, that you might choose well. Love God that you might choose to be with God—thus you will choose from love. And when you love more, you will desire to reach your beloved more quickly, and you will hurry to get there, thus you will run through love and reach him through love. And the more you love, the more avidly will you embrace him, in the joy of love."

❧ TWO

Order, Memory, and History

Never look down on anything

"Once you have gotten your fill with little things, you may safely try the big ones."[1] Hugh quotes from Marbodus[2] to introduce one of the two passages in his entire work in which he tells something about his own youth.[3] In this splinter of an autobiography he occasionally lapses into direct speech.

> I dare to affirm before you that I myself never looked down on anything which had to do with education, but that I often learned many things which seemed to others to be a sort of joke or just nonsense. I recall that when I was still a schoolboy I worked hard to know the names of all things that my eyes fell upon or that came into my use, frankly concluding that a man cannot come to know the natures of things if he is still ignorant of their names. How many times each day would I repeat my little bits of wisdom [*sophismata*, crumbs of knowledge] which, thanks to their shortness, I had noted down in one or two words on a page, so that I might keep a mindful hold on the solutions, and even the number, of practically all the thoughts, questions, and objections which I had learned. Often I proposed cases and, when the opposing contentions were lined up against one

---

1. *DB* VI, 3, p. 114: *Parvis imbutus tentabis grandia tutus.* Taylor translates, more soberly, "Once grounded in things small, you may safely strive for all" (*DT*, p. 136).

2. Marbodus, *De ornamentis verborum*, Prologus; *PL* 171, xxxx.

3. Roger Baron, "Notes biographiques sur Hugues de Saint-Victor," *Revue d'histoire ecclésiastique* 51 (1956): 920–34.

another I diligently distinguished what would be the business of the rhetorician, what of the orator, what of the sophist. I laid out pebbles for numbers, and I marked the pavement with black coals and, by a model placed right before my eyes, I plainly showed what difference there is between an obtuse-angled, a right-angled, and an acute-angled triangle. Whether or not an equilateral parallelogram would yield the same area as a square when two of its sides were multiplied together, I learned by walking both figures and measuring them with my feet. Often I kept watch [*excubavi*] outdoors through the winter nights like one of the fixed stars, by which we measure time.[4] Often I used to bring out my strings, stretched to their number on the wooden frame, both that I might note with my ear the difference among the tones and that I might at the same time delight my soul with the sweetness of the sound. These were boyish pursuits, to be sure, yet not without their utility for me, nor does my present knowledge of them lie heavy upon my stomach. But I do not reveal these things to you in order to parade my knowledge, which is either nothing at all or very little, but in order to show you that the man who moves along step by step [*ordinate*] is the one who moves along best, not like some who fall head over heels when they wish to make a great leap ahead.[5]

Ordo

The passage from childlike searching to adult reading is governed by something that Hugh calls *ordo*. In many instances Hugh stresses the importance that the reader advance with order, *ordinate procedere debet,* or that one ought to stride forward with a harmonious gait. Hugh does not create, he follows, observes, searches the order of things.

"To order" is the interiorization of that cosmic and symbolic har-

---

4. Nocturnal horoscope. Note that Hugh had no opportunity in his lifetime to read time. The clock and its quadrant were unknown. The thirty-six fixed stars were horoscopi, time-watchers. And Hugh spent his nights star-gazing, which for him was "watching time." On the symbolic significance of stargazing for twelfth-century theologians; see Marie Thérèse de Alverny, "Astrologues et théologiens au XIIᵉ siècle," in *Mélanges offerts à Marie-Dominique Chenu,* Bibliothèque Thomistique 37. (Paris: Vrin, 1967), pp. 31–50.

5. *DB* VI, 3, pp. 114–15.

mony which God has established in the act of creation.[6] "To order" means neither to organize and systematize knowledge according to preconceived subjects, nor to manage it. The reader's order is not imposed on the story, but the story puts the reader into its order. The search for wisdom is a search for the symbols of order that we encounter on the page. Medieval poets and mystics stress the motive of the hunt,[7] pilgrims are constantly in front of a fork in the road.[8] All are in search of symbols, which they must recognize and find by finding their own place within their *ordo*.

Gerhart Ladner, whose grateful pupil I am, has called our attention to both the continuity and the break in the meaning of symbol during the twelfth century.

> It was one of the fundamental character traits of the early Christian and medieval mentalities that the signifying, symbolizing and allegorizing function was anything but arbitrary or subjective; symbols were believed to represent objectively and to express faithfully various aspects of a universe that was perceived as widely and deeply meaningful.[9]

For our generation, fed on Freud and Jung, it is almost impossible to grasp what symbol means. The Greek verb *symballein* means "to bring or throw or put together." It can mean the food which participants bring along for the festive table.[10] It is a summary, a tally or token which only in late antiquity acquires the meaning of *sēmeion,* which is sign. Significantly, *symbolon* came to mean *signum* in the writings of the late Greek Fathers, especially Pseudo-Dionysius the Areopagite, who dealt with all of creation, ourselves and the angels

6. See Gerhart H. Ladner, "Medieval and Modern Understanding of Symbolism: A Comparison," *Speculum* 54 (1979): 223–56 (now also in *Images and Ideas in the Middle Ages,* vol. 1 [Rome, 1983]; page numbers cited in this chapter refer to *Speculum* article); and for comments on the influence exercised on western ideas about symbolism by Muslim perceptions of order, Marie Thérèse d'Alverny, "L'Homme comme symbole. Le microcosme," *Simboli e simbologia nell'alto Medioevo, 3–9 aprile, 1975,* Settimane di studio 26, vol. 1 Spoleto: Centro Italiano per i studi sull'Alto Medio Evo, 1976. Pp. 123–83.

7. Friedrich Ohly, "Die Suche in Dichtungen des Mittelalters," *Zeitschrift für deutsche Altertumskunde* 94 (1965): 171–84.

8. Wolfgang Harms, *Homo viator in bivio: Studien zur Bildlichkeit des Weges,* Medium Aevum 21 (Munich: Fink, 1970).

9. Ladner, "Medieval and Modern," p. 243.

10. W. Müri, *Symbolon: wort- und sachgeschichtliche Studie,* Beilage zum Jahresbericht über das Städtische Gymnasium in Bern (Bern, 1931).

included, as symbols or signs which God created so that we may come to know him through them. But

> God is so high above human conception, [that] it may be more revealing to express the divine and heavenly by phenomena taken from the lower reaches of the created cosmos than it is to choose symbols that superficially seem closer to Him. Thus, using biblical symbolism, . . . not only the light of the sun or the stars, but also a wild animal, such as a lion, or a stone rejected by a builder, may be symbols of Christ.[11]

Hugh's mind was shaped almost as much by his reading and commenting on Dionysius as it was by his acquaintance with Augustine. Translating Dionysius perfectly he says, "a symbol is a collecting of visible forms for the demonstration of invisible things."[12] "A collecting" renders both the classical Greek sense of the word *symbolon* and suggests what symbols were understood to be in his own time: "bridges between the experience of the senses and that which lies or reaches beyond."[13] In contrast to modern interpretations of symbolism, that coordinate or even identify symbols with myths, for Hugh they are

> facts and events, phenomena in and beyond nature and history, in such a way that they lead to the meta-physical and meta-historical realms encompassed by faith and theology.[14]

Only when the given-ness of cosmic order is understood does Hugh's difficulty in explaining methodological order cease to sound childish. The reader must learn to distinguish order from order. The chronological sequence in which Cicero wrote his books is a different kind of order than the sequence in which the archivist happens to have bound them between two covers. The historical order, Hugh insists with his students, must be distinguished from the order in which we come to learn. Careful reading always picks and chooses bits that then must be bundled, sifted, and arranged. But this process of ordering will be effective only when the reader remembers one fundamental point: all things and events of this world acquire their meaning from

11. Ladner, "Medieval and Modern," p. 241, summarizing a passage from Pseudo-Dionysius, *De Coelesti hierarchia*, cap. 2; *PG* 3, 137 and 144.

12. *Symbolum est collatio formarum visibilium ad invisibilium demonstrationem* (*In hierarchiam coelestem* 2 [ad cap 1]; *PL* 175, 941B).

13. Ladner, "Medieval and Modern," p. 241.

14. Ibid., p. 252.

the place at which they are inserted in the history of creation and salvation. It is the reader's task to insert all that he reads at the respective
point where it belongs in the *historia* between Genesis and the Apocalypse.[15] Only by doing this will he advance toward wisdom through
reading.[16]

Artes

The *Didascalicon* is written for beginners. It provides them with rules
for ordered progress. The first half (chapters 1–3) deals with the seven
liberal arts,[17] the second (chapters 4–6) with the reading of Holy Scrip-

---

15. *DB* V, 2, p. 96: *Divina Scriptura ita per Dei sapientiam convenienter suis partibus
aptata est atque disposita, ut quidquid in ea continetur, aut vice chordarum spiritualis
intelligentiae suavitatem personet, aut per historiae seriem, et literae soliditatem mysteri-
orum dicta sparsim posita continens, et quasi in unum connectens, ad modum ligni
concavi super extensas chordas simul copulet, earumque sonum recipiens in se, dulci-
orem auribus referat, quem non solum chorda edidit, set et lignum modulo corporis sui
formavit . . . saepe tamen in una eademque littera omnia simul reperiri possunt, sicut
historiae veritas et mysticum aliquid per allegoriam insinuet, et quid agendum sit pariter
per tropologiam demonstret.* "All of Sacred Scripture is so suitably adjusted and arranged in all its parts through the Wisdom of God that whatever is contained in it either
resounds with the sweetness of spiritual understanding in the manner of strings; or,
containing utterances of mysteries set here and there in the course of a historical narra-
tive or in the substance of a literal context and, as it were, connecting these up into one
object, it binds them together all at once as the wood does which curves under the taut
strings; and, receiving their sound into itself, it reflects it more sweetly to our ears—a
sound which the string alone has not yielded, but which the wood too has formed by
the shape of its body. . . . Often, however, in one and the same literal context, all may
be found together, as when a truth of history both hints at some mystical meaning by
way of allegory, and equally shows by way of tropology how we ought to behave" (*DT*,
p. 121).

16. God's wisdom reveals itself through the beauty of creatures. This is one of the
main themes of *De tribus diebus*, especially its third chapter. *Universus enim mundus
iste sensibilis quasi quidam liber est scriptus digito Dei, hoc est virtute divina creatus,
et singulae creaturae quasi figurae quaedam sunt . . . divino arbitrio institutae ad mani-
festandam invisibilium dei sapientiam. . . . qui autem spiritualis est et omnia dijudicare
potest, in eo quidem quod fors considerat pulchritudinem operis, intus concipit quam
miranda sit sapientia creatoris (De tribus diebus* 3; *PL* 176, 814B, C). "This entire sensible world is like a certain book written by the finger of God, that is, created by divine
power, and individual creatures are like certain figures . . . constituted by the divine will
to manifest the wisdom of the invisible things of God. . . . He who is spiritual and can
judge all things, considering outwardly the beauty of work, inwardly sees how marvelous is the wisdom of the Creator."

17. On the transition from early to late medieval *artes* literature, see Bernhard
Bischoff, "Eine verschollene Einteilung der Wissenschaften," *Archives d'histoire doctrinale et littéraire du moyen âge* 33 (1958): 5–20; Franz H. Bäuml, "Der Übergang mündlicher zur artes-bestimmten Literatur des Mittelalters. Gedanken und Bedenken," in

ture.[18] In the first part, Hugh picks up a concept first formulated by traveling Sophist teachers. They offered instruction in "free or liberal arts"—arts that prepare one for philosophy—which Seneca distinguished from those other arts that require manual skills.[19] The division of these arts by the sacred number of seven appears in late antiquity, and Hugh takes it from Isidore of Seville, via Bede and Alcuin.[20]

Hugh expresses dissatisfaction with the students of his day who, "whether from ignorance or from unwillingness, fail to hold to a fit

---

Fachliteratur des Mittelalters. Festschrift Gerhard Eis (Stuttgart, 1968), pp. 1–10.

All arts lead to wisdom, including the craftsman's. "But the theoretical alone, because it studies the truth of things, do we call wisdom" (*DT* II, 18, p. 73). *Solam autem theoricam, propter speculationem veritatis rerum, sapientiam nominamus* (*DB* p. 37). "But all other pursuits that aim at knowledge can be referred to this search for wisdom: logic, that is concerned with eloquence; ethical and mechanical sciences which are concerned with the place of behavior and works" (*circumspectio morum et operum: DB* II, 18, p. 37). [*Has*] *tres . . . id est ethicam, mechanicam, logicam congrue ad sapientiam referre possumus* (ibid.). "These three, that is, ethics, mechanics, and logic can be fittingly referred to wisdom."

18. Jerome Taylor (*DT*, pp. 3–39) gives the best possible and clear summary of the way Hugh constructs the *Didascalicon*. See also Jean Châtillon, "Le *Didascalicon* de Hugues de Saint-Victor," in *La Pensée encyclopédique au moyen âge* (Neuchâtel: Baconnière, 1966), pp. 63–76. Its influence on the Canons Regular is treated, passim, by Berhard Bischoff, "Aus der Schule Hugos von St. Viktor," in *Aus der Geisteswelt des Mittelalters,* edited by A. Lang, J. Lecher, and M. Schmaus (Beiträge zur Geschichte der Philosophie und Theologie des Mittelalters 3,1; Münster, 1935), pp. 246–50, and by Jean Châtillon, "De Guillaume de Champeaux à Thomas Gallus: Chronique littéraire et doctrinale de l'école de Saint-Victor," *Revue du moyen âge latin* 8 (1952): 139–62, and "Les Écoles de Chartres et de Saint-Victor," in *La scuola nell' Occidente Latino nell' alto medio evo,* 2 vols., Settimane di Studio 19 (Spoleto: Centro Italiano per i studi sull' Alto Medio Evo, 1972), vol. 2, pp. 795–839.

19. For Hugh's place in this tradition see M. Grabmann, *Die Geschichte der scholastischen Methode,* vol. 1, 2d ed. (Freiburg, Br.: Herder, 1957), pp. 28–54 and 235–60; Gillian R. Evans, *Old Arts and New Theology: The Beginnings of Theology as an Academic Discipline* (Oxford: Clarendon, 1980), and "A Change of Mind in Some Scholars of the Eleventh and Early Twelfth Century," in *Religious Motivation: Biographical and Sociological Problems for the Church Historian,* ed. by D. Baker (Oxford: Blackwell, 1978), pp. 27–37; Jean Châtillon, "Les Écoles de Chartres et de St. Victor," in *La scuola nell' Occidente Latino nell' alto medio evo,* 2 vols., Settimana di Studio 19 (Spoleto: Centro Italiano per i studi sull' Alto Medio Evo, 1972), pp. 795–839; Berhard Bischoff, "Eine verschollene Einteilung der Wissenschaften," *Archives d'histoire doctrinale et littéraire du moyen âge* 33 (1958): 5–20.

20. Still the most synthetic and thorough survey of this seven-fold division is Josèphe Marietan, *Le problème de la classification des sciences d'Aristote à St. Thomas* (Paris: Félix Alcan, 1901). My subject is the historical place of Hugh's ethology, implicit phenomenology, and metaphorics of "reading." Bernhard Bischoff, "Eine Verschollene Einteilung der Wissenschaften," *Archives d'histoire doctrinale et litteraire du moyen âge* 33

method of study, and therefore we find many who study but few who are wise." But speaking of the ancients, he says,

> In those days, no one was thought worthy of the name of master who was unable to claim knowledge of these seven. Pythagoras, too, is said to have maintained the following practice as a teacher: for seven years, according to the number of the seven liberal arts, no one of his pupils dared ask the reason behind statements made by him; instead, he was to give credence to the words of the master until he had heard him out and then, having done this, he would be able to grasp the reason of those things himself. We read that some men studied these seven with such zeal that they had them completely in memory, so that whatever writings they subsequently took in hand or whatever questions they proposed for solution or proof, they did not thumb the pages of books to hunt for rules and reasons which the liberal arts might afford for the resolution of a doubtful matter, but at once had the particulars ready by heart.[21]

Hugh looks for students who read so well that without leafing they instantly have details ready in their heart.[22] Memory training, for Hugh, is a precondition for reading, and something which he treats in a manual that readers of the *Didascalicon* are supposed to know.[23]

The treasure chest in the reader's heart

In this particular manual Hugh addresses himself to very young students whom he challenges to expand and refine their memory skills through the construction of an interior treasure chest.[24]

(1958): 5–20 examines his version of the *artes* division. Hugh is unique in conceptualizing the *scientia mechanica* within this framework. See also Peter Sternagel, *Die Artes Mechanicae im Mittelalter: Begriffs- und Bedeutungsgeschichte bis zum Ende des 13. Jh.*, Münchener Historische Studien. Abt. Mittelalterliche Geschichte, ed. by J. Sporl, vol. 2 (Kallmunz: Michel Lassleben, 1966). I have dealt with Hugh's original idea, that *scientia mechanica* studies nature, revealing how man can imitate it, in Ivan Illich, *Shadow Work* (London: Boyars, 1981), pp. 33–36 and 75–95.

21. *DT* III, 3, p. 87.

22. *DB* III, 3, p. 53: *statim singula corde parata haberent.*

23. "Hugh of St. Victor: *De tribus maximis circumstantiis gestorum,*" *Speculum* 18 (1943): 484–93, first edited here by William M. Green. For Hugh's place within the tradition see G. A. Zinn, "Hugh of St. Victor and the Art of Memory," *Viator* 5 (1974): 211–34: "Until now Hugh of St. Victor has not enjoyed recognition as a contributor to the medieval development of the classical art of memory tradition" (p. 211).

24. *Arca*—a place for keeping anything: a chest, box, or coffer; also a coffin or Noah's ark. The monastery's *arca* was kept in the sacristy to store the treasures: chalices and

My child. Wisdom is a treasure and thy heart is the place to store it. When you learn wisdom, you gather valuable treasures; they are immortal treasures that do not fade nor lose their luster. The treasures of wisdom are manyfold, and there are many hiding places in your heart: here for gold, there for silver, elsewhere again for precious stones. . . . You must learn to distinguish these spots, to know which is where, in order to remember where you have placed this thing or that. . . . Just observe the money-changer in the market and do like him. See how his hand darts into the appropriate satchel . . . and instantly draws out the right coin.[25]

To develop this kind of control over one's own memory palace, Hugh asks his pupils to acquire an imaginary inner space, *modum imaginandi domesticum,* and tells them how to proceed in its construction. He asks the pupil to imagine a sequence of whole numbers, to step on the originating point of their run and let the row reach the horizon. Once these highways are well impressed upon the fantasy of the child, the exercise consists in mentally "visiting" these numbers at random. In his imagination the student is to dart back and forth to each of the spots he has marked by a roman numeral. After doing this often enough, these visits will become as habitual as the movements of the moneychanger's hand. When he has been solidly anchored in this "rock bottom," the young student is enabled to place all the events of biblical history within its frame; all are assigned a time and a place within a series: patriarchs, sacrifices, victories.[26]

The seventy tables that follow this introduction contain several thousand items that are mentioned in the Bible. Hugh demands that

---

vestments for the liturgy; relics, mainly the assorted skulls and bones of saints enclosed in precious boxes; and, besides these objects, also books. Only in the eleventh century do books begin to be stored in special, separate arks, the archives; and only at the end of the century do separate libraries become common.

25. Hugh, *De tribus maximis circumstantiis gestorum* (Green, p. 484). Hugh's friend Aelred of Rievaulx writes in *De anima,* bk. 2, c. 3, *Est enim memoria quasi ingens quaedam aula, continens quasi innumerabiles thesauros, diversarum scilicet rerum corporalium imagines per sensus invectas.* "Memory is like an immense hall containing innumerable treasure chests, each holding images of things brought in by the senses." (Aelred of Rivaulx, *Opera omnia,* vol. 1, A. Hoste, O.S.B., and C. H. Talbot, eds., Corpus Christianorum Continuatio Medievalis [Turnhout: Brepols, 1971], p. 707.)

26. *DB* VI, 3, p. 114: *Haec enim quattuor praecipue in historia requirenda sunt, persona, negotium, tempus et locus.* "For these are the four things which are especially to be sought in history—the person, the business done, the time and the place" (*DT,* p. 136). In *De tribus maximis circumstantiis gestorum* (Green, p. 491, lines 16–19): *Tria*

his pupil place each Apostle into the row of Apostles, each Patriarch in the row of Patriarchs, and then trains him to dart back and forth between distinct columns.[27] Certain sentences are used to train the memory, "mnemotechnic phrases." An example is: "In six days the world was perfectly created, and in six epochs man was redeemed." In Paris, one century before the university came into being and in the year before the first preserved rudimentary alphabetic subject index was concocted, this was the training for reference work given to the child monk.

The child's mind was trained to build the memory mazes, and to establish the habit to dart and retrieve in them. Remembrance was not conceived as an act of mapping but of psychomotor, morally charged activity. As a modern youth, from childhood on I was trained to the Baedeker. As a mountain guide I learned to decipher maps and photographs before venturing into the rock. Decades later, when I first arrived in Japan I purchased a map of Tokyo. But I was not allowed to use it. My host's wife simply refused to let me map my way through the city's mazes by looking at them, mentally, from above. Day after day she led me around this, and then that corner, until I could navigate the labyrinth and reach my destinations without ever knowing abstractly where I was. Reference work before the table of contents and the index must have been much more like this kind of mapless orientation for which our modern schools disqualify us.

For more advanced readers, Hugh proposed a much more complex, three-dimensional ark—a space-time matrix built within the mind of the student and modeled on Noah's ark. Only a person who in early youth has been well-trained in darting back and forth through the rather simple-minded columns of *De tribus circumstantiis,* and who has already settled *historia sacra* (which is the "narration of one's salvation") within this two-dimensional frame can follow Hugh in the construction of this advanced three-dimensional multicolored monster memory scheme. The man who has best studied Hugh's writings on

---

sunt in quibus praecipue cognitio pendet rerum gestarum, id est, personae a quibus res gestae sunt . . . loca in quibus gestae sunt, et tempora quando gestae sunt. Haec tria quisquis memoriter animo tenerit, inveniet se fundamentum habere bonum. "The knowledge of things done depends principally on three things, that is, the persons who act, . . . the places, and the times. Whoever holds these things tightly in his memory, will find that he has a good foundation."

27. *De tribus* (Green, p. 488, lines 11–12): *Confusio ignorantiae et oblivionis mater est; discretio autem intelligentiam illuminat et memoriam confirmat.* "Confusion is the mother of ignorance and forgetfulness; but discretion illuminates the intelligence and confirms memory."

the moral and mystical ark has come to the following conclusion: 220 square feet of paper would be needed for a still readable blueprint of Hugh's ark-model of historical interrelationships. Twentieth-century medievalists, who in the great majority have never had any training in mnemotechnics, can perhaps imagine a blueprint of Hugh's ark, but they cannot recapture the experience of having such an ark in their own mind, or "be thoroughly at home with this thought and way of imagining." [28]

The history of memory

Hugh's recovery of the art of memory training, neglected since antiquity, has been recognized. [29] The importance he gives to a trained memory as a prerequisite to reading has been noticed. But the fundamental development by Hugh of the memory matrix from an architectonic-static to a historic-relational model has rarely been commented on. [30] Preliterate Greek speechmaking and epic singing were based not on visual memory but on the recollection of formulas uttered to the rhythm of a lyre. [31] Before practice had demonstrated that the letters of

28. *Hanc autem cogitationem et hunc modum imaginandi domesticum habe usitatum* (*De tribus*, Green, p. 489, lines 24–25).

29. See, for instance, Frances Yates, *The Art of Memory* (Chicago and London: University of Chicago Press, 1966); she recognizes Hugh's existence incidentally, but does not contribute any insight to his historic uniqueness. Gillian R. Evans, "Two Aspects of *Memoria* in the Eleventh- and Twelfth-Century Writings," *Classica et medievalia* 32 (1971–80): 263–78; she notices that from Augustine on, the study of memory as a constitutive faculty must be distinguished from the study of memorization, which is neglected.

30. Joachim Ehlers, in *Hugo von St. Victor: Studien zum Geschichtsdenken und zur Geschichtsschreibung des 12. Jahrhunderts,* Frankfurter historische Abhandlungen 1973 (Wiesbaden: Steiner), does recognize this. The construction of twelfth-century cathedrals can be understood as a public creation of a symbolic universe of *memoria:* the solemnly celebrated reminiscence of *historia.* The renaissance of the individually practiced art of memory in the fourteenth century then appears as a consequence of decline in the Age of Faith. See Martha Heyneman, "Dante's Magical Memory Cathedral," *Parabola* 11 (1986): 36–45. An interesting and much later example for the use of a cathedral as the model for an internalized *memoria* is given by Bernhard Bischoff, "Die Gedächtniskunst im Bamberger Dom," in *Anecdota Novissima* (Stuttgart: Hiersemann, 1984), pp. 204–11.

31. For an initial orientation to the history of research on preliterate recollection see the footnotes to the first chapter of B. Peabody, *The Winged Word: A Study in the Technique of Ancient Greek Oral Composition as Seen Principally through Hesiod's Works and Days* (Albany: State University of New York Press, 1975); and Albert Lord, "Perspectives on Recent Work on Oral Literature," in *Oral Literature: Seven Essays,* ed. by J. Duggan (Edinburgh: Scottish Academic Press, 1975), pp. 1–24.

the alphabet could bind winged words in row after row of script, no one would have conceived of a storage room or wax tablet within the mind. This kind of memory and its artificial enhancement through memory training come into being in the transition from archaic to classical Greece.[32] Some rudiments from the history of memory must be recalled to grasp Hugh's unique place.

What anthropologists distinguish as "cultures" the historian of mental spaces might distinguish as different "memories." The way to recall, to remember, has a history which is, to some degree, distinct from the history of the substance that is remembered.

During the twelfth century the art of disciplined and cultivated recall went through a metamorphosis which can be compared only to that which took place in the transition from preliterate to literate Greece. There is a patent analogy between the discovery of the "word" and "syntax" at the turn of the fifth century B.C., and the discovery of layout and index shortly before the foundation of the University in Europe.

We sometimes forget that words are creatures of the alphabet. The Greek language originally had no word for "a word," singly identified.[33] Greek had only various terms referring to sounds and other signals or expressions: utterances could be articulated by the lips, the tongue, or the mouth, but also by the heart when it spoke to the friend, by the *thymos* (which we might call "gall") which rose in Achilles and drove him into battle, or by the onrush of a wave of blood. Our kind of "words," like the other syntactic parts of speech, acquired meaning only after they had been hatched under the alphabet during the first centuries of its use. This is one first obvious reason why, before the fifth century, a string of "words" could not have been learned or retained. We can fix our mind on such units, and cull them from our mental dictionary, because we can spell them.

In fact, the alphabet is an elegant technology for the visualization of sounds. Its two dozen shapes trigger the memory of utterances that have been articulated by the mouth, the tongue, or the lips, and filter out what is said by gesture, mime, or the guts. Unlike other writing systems, it records sounds, not ideas. And in this it is foolproof: readers can be trained to voice things which they have never heard before.

32. James A. Notopoulos, "Mnemosyne in Oral Literature," *Transactions of the American Philosophical Association* 69 (1938): 465–93.

33. The substance of the next few paragraphs constitutes a pale commentary on Eric A. Havelock, *The Literate Revolution in Greece and Its Cultural Consequences*, Princeton Series of Collected Essays (Princeton: Princeton University Press, 1982).

This much the alphabet has done, and with incomparable efficiency, for the last two millennia.

However, beside these technical and purposeful effects, for which the alphabet can be used as a tool, its mere existence within a society also says something to the members of society, something which rarely if ever has been written down. As the alphabet began to make it obvious that speech can be fixed and sliced into visible units, it became a new means to think of the world as well. Plato already noticed in the *Cratylus* (424d) that letters had come to be considered as the elements of speech. Thus words became the atoms of statements, and the act of speaking could be conceived as the production of language which in turn can be analyzed into its units. Some Greeks turned this symbolic alphabetization of utterance into a paradigm of the metaphysical constitution of the universe. This is how Aristotle puts it:

> Leucippus and his associate Democritus say that the full and the empty are the elements, calling the one being and the other non-being: the full and solid being being, the empty non-being. One substance (for them) generates all things . . . and does so by three modifications, which are these: shape, order and position. They say that the real is differentiated only by "rhythm" and "inter-contact" and "turning". Of these rhythm is shape, inter-contact is order and turning is position. A differs in shape from N. AN differs from NA in order. H differs from ⌶ in position.[34]

Both Plato and Aristotle report here on what they observe among their contemporaries, and not what they subscribe to as their own opinion. But both suggest the analogy between the alphabetic analysis of speech and the philosophical analysis of being which came into existence hand-in-hand. Plato, especially in the *Phaedrus* and *Symposium*, stresses that living recall is superior to memory based on the reference to dry letters which cannot protest when their sense is twisted around by the reader.

The symbol of preliterate memory was the bard, who stitched together the rags of the past. That is the reason why he was called *rhapsode:* stitcher. According to Plato, he was simply inspired to utter that to which the muse impelled him; not by rule of art, but by divine grace he sang (*Ion* 533). The god took away his mind to use him as his minister. The *rhapsode* makes "one man hang down from the other, like the links of the iron chain that hangs from that stone in the dome

---

34. *Metaphysics* 1,4, 985b, 5–18. Richard McKeon, ed., *The Basic Works of Aristotle*, Introduction by R. McKeon (New York: Random House, 1941).

of Heraklea that Empedokles calls 'the magnet'" (*Ion* 535). Like a magnetic force the muse ties the listener to the chain of singers. The bard did not reflect on words, but was driven by the beat of his lyre. Homer was such a singer. But Homer sang in a unique epoch: in a world in which letters already existed, even though most of them were just scratches made by potters as dedications on commemorative vessels. But that was sufficient to let the utterance dawn on Greek eyes. For several generations of preliterate Greeks, the ear was continuously seduced into collaboration with the eye. Reminiscence, which so far had been "managed acoustically on echo principles was met with competition from language managed visually on architectural principles."[35] The result of this still innocent synergy between sound and the awareness of its shape was a distinctive type of creative composition which straight literacy, even in Greece, has never been able to recreate.

The term "rhetoric" was coined for the new, non-oral skill by which a public speaker prepares within his own mind the sentences which he wants to utter in public on some later occasion. Plato clearly distinguished between the esoteric power of creative recall and exoteric script-bound skill of learning a written text by heart.[36] As public speaking became a major art, the rhetor wanted to memorize not only sentences, but also the argumental structure and metaphors he would use to stress his point.

The one most common method used by the Greeks to achieve this purpose was the mental construction of a memory palace.[37] Hugh's rows of numbers that run to the horizon are a flat replica of the same device. To become the student of a reputable teacher, the pupil had to prove that he was at home and at ease in some vast architecture that existed only in his mind, and within which he could move at an instant to the spot of his choice. Each school had its own rules according to which this edifice had to be constructed. It had to contain several visually distinct classes of features such as columns, angles, rafters, rooms, archways, niches, and thresholds.

Early on it was found that the most effective way for locating and retrieving memories was that of randomly affixing to each one a mental label from a large set familiar to the student. For example, to a goat or the sun, a branch or a knife, a sentence was attached for rote memorization. The author who had thus equipped his palace for a

35. Havelock, *Literate Revolution*, p. 9.

36. *Phaidros, Ion.*

37. H. Blum, *Die antike Mnemotechnik,* Spudasmata, Studien zur klassischen Gesetzgebung 15 (Hildesheim: Olms, 1969).

speech or a dispute just moved to the appropriate imaginary room, took in at a glance the object placed on the labels, and had at his fingertips the memorized formulations that—for this particular occasion—he had associated with these emblems.

Hugh's request that young beginners move with ease from one numbered spot to another on the same mental road, and that they jump from the "station" on one to any station on another, thus creating interconnections, introduces them in the simplest way possible to this traditional skill. However, the technique that Hugh adopts to enhance meditative reading had been developed to support something else, public speech.

The lawyer's skill at the service of prayer

The art of memory as a symbolic labeling of memorized speech-acts was created in fourth-century Greece, taught by Sophists and used in politics. In Rome, at least since Quintilian (35–100), its purpose and technique changed. It was mainly used by lawyers. Here memory training stresses the art of internalized reading. The public speaker learned in late Roman antiquity how to "take notes" in his mind and "read them off" on the right occasion.

The rhetorical virtuoso was henceforth the one who could mentally register and label each sentence he intended to use, and promptly recover it from the appropriate architectonic feature in his own inner topology. Today, in an age dazed by the feats of computers, this skill sounds like an impossible undertaking or freakish acrobatics for some academic circus. But such memory training was part of the equipment expected by Hugh from the beginner.

The art of memory is closely intertwined with the art of reading; one cannot be understood without the other. What Hugh does when he "reads" cannot be understood without recognizing the place at which he stands in the history of both arts. He recovers the antique art of the rhetor and teaches it as a reading skill to monastic mumblers.

Greek memory training placed the visual imagination at the service of oral delivery. Romans like Quintilian taught the skill of associating mental emblems with mentally taken notes. But it would be a mistake to assume that these notes fixed to a mental archway or rafter were meant to be silently read. Just as the act of finding was fantasized as a bodily rush to the appropriate part of one's mental architecture, so the act of retrieval engaged the psychomotor innervation of the tongue.

Ut duplici modo iuvetur memoria dicendi et audiendi, "in order doubly to strengthen the memory of speaking and listening," the student is to return again and again to the same spot. Quintilian stresses that the internal reading of notes ought to strengthen memory by mumbling, which trains the tongue, and by strenuous listening to the student's own muttering, which trains the ear: "let the voice be subdued—let it be like a hum" . . . *vox sit modica, et quasi murmur.* In the opinion of Pliny, this active engagement will insure that the learner will be less distracted.[38]

By the second century, exhibitionism by memory freaks had become common in imperial Rome. Following Cicero and Pliny these literary feats were denounced.[39] They constituted exaggerated reliance on a technical skill and could threaten free and creative associative recall when used in the training of young people. The Church Fathers neglected memory training—only in part by falling in with the mood of the time. The main reason for the Christian neglect of artificial memorization must be sought elsewhere. *Memoria* for Christians was primarily a liturgically celebrated ritual at which the major events of the Old and New Testament were re-presented. And, unlike other people—except for the Jews—Christians had one book given them as *the* Good News, or Testament of Revelation. These canonical writings are the new common texture of Christian remembrance.

Lectio, "reading," in this context becomes primarily a ritual commemoration of this one story. The pious reader desires to be possessed by the word, not to manipulate it. He searches the Scriptures to be surprised by redemption and glory. He reads—to himself or listening to others—to nourish the sober drunkenness (*sobria ebrietas*) of his faith. Reading is for the early Christian primarily the interpretation of one book.

Christian sermons were Scripture commentaries; most Church Fathers did not want to deliver speeches on the model of a Roman orator. Among the oratorical skills, mnemotechnics was one which had only limited usefulness for a preaching bishop. The context into which he wanted to place all knowledge and reflection was given to him as "Bible."

Augustine admired his classmate Simplicius who, on demand, could recite any book of Vergil either forward or backward. Reflecting on this friend, however, he examines the way his own live memory works. Precisely when he decides not to forget what touches him most deeply, memory hides it from him, and plays it back at the most inopportune

38. Quintilian is the author of the two quotes. They, and the Pliny opinion, are found in Helga Hajdu, *Das mnemotechnische Schrifttum des Mittelalters* (Amsterdam: E. J. Bonset, 1967), p. 27. Original edition, Leipzig, 1936.
39. Hajdu, *Das Mnemotechnische Schrifttum.*

time. What he wants to develop in himself is not memory but consciousness which makes him express his loving understanding when he comments on Scripture: he wants to avoid any show of knowledge. In the Christian usage, *memoria* refers to the purpose for which the community assembles; and then to "consciousness" of being part of a new people. For more than half a millennium, memory training was neglected.

Alcuin, Charlemagne's teacher and confidant, puts himself, under the name of Albinus, into an imaginary dialogue with the emperor, intent on restoring antique learning.

> Charles: And what can you tell us about that worthy part of rhetoric, which is memory?
>
> Albinus: What else should I tell you than that which Cicero already said: Memory is a treasure that holds all things. Unless these things are used as a guardian of all we thought and found, be this words or things, these come to nothing, no matter how important they might be.
>
> Charles: Now, tell me if there are rules by which it [memory] can be acquired or enlarged.
>
> Albinus: We have no rules except these: practice in speaking, the habit of writing, application to reflection and the avoidance of liquor which threatens both health and the integrity of the mind.[40]

The dialogue is written as the teacher's answer to the royal ruler. Charlemagne wants to revive mnemotechnics for a worldly reason: he thinks it useful for the training of classical lawyers who would restore the splendor of Roman courts. Alcuin, the greatest scholar of the time, insists that he has little to offer.

Memory training as prelude to wisdom

Early twelfth-century scholarship is characterized by the effort to gather, organize, and harmonize the legacy of the Christian past as it pertains to jurisprudence, theological doctrine, and Scripture.[41] The *Decretum Gratiani,* the *Sententiae* of Peter Lombard, and the *Glossa ordinaria* are the outstanding results of this effort. They are all written

---

40. Alcuin, *Dialogus de rhetorica et virtutibus,* opusculum tertium, n. 328; *PL* 101, 941A–B. See also, Harry Caplan, *Rhetorica ad Herrenium. De ratione dicendi,* with an English translation (Cambridge, Mass.: Harvard University Press, 1954).

41. R. L. Benson and G. Constable, eds., *Renaissance and Renewal in the Twelfth Century* (Cambridge, Mass.: Harvard University Press, 1982).

by 1150, and remain the major textbooks used in the basic training of clerics in these three fields until well into the Reformation. Hugh seems to be the first one to seriously revive classical memory training, and was then the last major figure to propose memory as the sole or principal means of retrieving information. But memory does not cease to be trained.[42] From 1150 on, new artificial finding devices provide some of the key metaphors according to which the mechanics of memory and the methods for its training are devised. Then, in the early fifteenth century, the earlier discipline of memory training makes an unusual comeback. All this gives to Hugh's two mnemotechnic treatises, the elementary *De tribus* and the almost monstrous, two-part *De arca Noe,* such exceptional importance. As in archaic Greece the eye had been seduced into collaboration with the ear to hold fast to the inspiration of the Muse, and preserve the "once-and-for-all *Iliad,*" then attributed to Homer, so before scholasticism Hugh taught the practice of monastic, commemorative mumbling in a carefully constructed inner space—a *claustrum animae* (the soul's cloister)—whose layout, however, was not an arbitrarily invented memory palace, but the revealed structure of space-time which he calls *historia.*

By reviving ancient architectural memory training, Hugh hopes to prepare boys born around 1120 to read their way toward wisdom in an age in which the new collections could only too easily have scattered their brains and overwhelmed them. He offers them a radically intimate technique of ordering this huge heritage in a personally created, inner spime.[43]

Historia as foundation

Hugh not only revives the old art of memorization but radically transforms it by placing it at the service of *historia.*[44] Reading is for him equivalent to the re-creation of the texture of *historia* in the ark of

42. A good collection of twelfth-century references to memory is C. Meier, "Vergessen, erinnern. Gedächtnis im Gott-Mensch-Bezug. Zu einem Grenzbereich der Allegorese bei Hildegard von Bingen und anderen Autoren des Mittelalters," in *Verbum et Signum,* ed. M. Fromm et al. (Munich: Fink, 1975), pp. 143–94.

43. The term *spime,* i.e., space-time, is taken from Einstein.
On the "Church" as an ordering scheme for history in the school of St. Victor, see Jean Châtillon, "Une Ecclésiologie médiévale: L'idée de l'Église dans la théologie de l'école de Saint-Victor au XIIᵉ siècle," *Irénikon* 22 (1949): 395–411. Even mythical events could be fitted into this "history:" Marie-Dominique Chenu, "*Involucrum:* le Mythe selon les théologiens médiévaux," *Archives d'histoire doctrinale et littéraire du moyen âge* 30 (1955): 75–79.

44. G. A. Zinn, Jr., "*Historia fundamentum est:* The Role of History in the Contemplative Life According to Hugh of St. Victor," in *Contemporary Reflections on the Medi-*

the reader's heart.[45] His concept of science is "based explicitly on the assumption that time is subject to an order that can be investigated through the literal study of Scripture."[46] Everything can make sense when it is related to this *ordo* of time; and nothing is meaningful that is not placed by the reader into this *ordo*. Hugh's moral and spiritual Ark of Noah is more than a mnemotechnic palace with biblical features. The Ark stands for a social entity, a process that begins with creation and continues to the end of time, what Hugh calls "the

---

eval Christian Tradition: Essays in Honour of Ray C. Petry, ed. G. H. Shriver (Durham, N.C.: Duke University Press, 1974), pp. 135–58.

45. *DB* VI, 3, p. 116: *Habes in historia quo Dei facta mireris, in allegoria quo eius sacramenta credas, in moralitate quo perfectionem ipsius imiteris.* "You have in history the means through which to admire God's deeds, in allegory the means through which to believe his mysteries, in morality the means through which to imitate his perfection" (*DT,* p. 138). The only facts that Hugh admits as a starting point and foundation of theological reflection are historical events that are literally described in Holy Scripture and cyclically celebrated throughout the liturgical year. *DB* VI, 3, p. 117: *Vide quia, ex eo quo mundus coepit usque in finem saeculorum, non deficiunt miserationes Domini.* "See how, from the time when the world began until the end of the ages, the mercies of God do not slacken" (*DT,* p. 139). Putting his thoughts in the form of a dialogue between *ratio,* reason (R.), and *anima,* the soul (A.), Hugh writes in *De vanitate mundi,* III; *PL* 176, 724D–725A: A. *Valde admiror, et stupeo in memetipsa cum dispositionem divinam in rebus transactis considero, quoniam ex ipsa rerum praetereuntium ordine nescio quo pacto fixam quamdam providentiam attendo.* R. *Quid mirum? Quia enim Deus nobis per opera sua loquitur, quid aliud quam vocem loquentis ad nos percipimus, cum oculos mentis nostrae ad consideranda mirabilia ejus aperimus?* A. "I really wonder, and am even stupified, when I look for a divine disposition in events which have occurred, because from the way itself that these things have happened I cannot figure out what rule to use to see the inherent working of providence. R. Why the wonder? Since God speaks to us through his works, what else is there to perceive, except the voice of him who speaks to us, if we have the eyes of our mind open to consider his marvelous deeds?"

46. Gillian R. Evans, "Hugh of St. Victor on History and the Meaning of Things," *Studia Monastica* 25 (1983): 223–34: "In writing Genesis, Hugh explains that Moses is a writer of history (*historiographus*). He sets out the history (*texens historiam*), from the beginning of the world up to the death of Jacob. Two things are accordingly to be looked for in reading Genesis, the *veritas rerum gestarum* or truth of the events, and the *forma verborum;* 'for just as we know the truth of things through the truth of words so, conversely, when the truth of things is known we may more easily know the truth of words. For through that historical narration we are carried on to the higher understanding of things.' (*PL* 175, 32–33: *Quia per istam historicam narrationem ad altiorum rerum intelligentiam provehimur.*) It appears that the distinction which was nascent between 'historical' strictly speaking and 'literal' lies close to the heart of the distinction between the significance of words and the significance of things in Scripture" (p. 232). See also Herbert Grundmann, "Die Grundlagen der mittelalterlichen Geschichtsanschauung," *Archiv für Kulturgeschichte* 24 (1934), reprinted in Grundmann, *Geschichtsschreibung im Mittelalter* (Göttingen: Vandenhoeck, 1978).

Church."[47] The activity which Hugh calls "reading" mediates between this macrocosmic Church and the microcosmos of the reader's personal intimacy.[48] Each person, each place, each thing within this spatiotemporal cosmos must first be literally understood. It then reveals itself as also something else: as sign for something to come in the future, and as accomplishment of some other thing that, by analogy, has pointed towards its coming.[49]

47. Ehlers, *Arca significat ecclesiam*, pp. 121–87.

48. *Arca Noe morali*, IV, 2; PL 176, 666B–C: *Deinde consideremus deorsum in mundo isto magnam quamdam, et horribilem omnium rerum confusionem, et infinitam humanarum mentium distractionem; sursum autem apud Deum perpetuam et inconcussam stabilitatem. Post haec imaginemur quasi humanum animum de hoc mundo sursum ad Deum ascendentem, et in ascendendo magis semper ac magis in unum sese colligentem, et tunc spiritaliter videre poterimus formam arcae nostrae, quae in imo lata fuit, et sursum in angustum surrexit . . . Similiter enim nos de hoc profundo, de hac convalle lacrymarum per quaedam incrementa virtutum, quasi per quosdam gradus in corde nostro dispositos, ascendentes paulatim in unum colligimur, quousque ad illam simplicem unitatem, et veram simplicitatem, aeternamque stabilitatem, quae apud Deum est, pertingamus.* "Then let us consider the really great and horrible confusion among all phenomena here below in this world, and the infinity of distraction in peoples' minds; above, however, with God, there is a perpetual and immovable stability. Then imagine the human spirit rising from this world to God, continually becoming more and more recollected and simple through its ascent, and thus we shall be able to see spiritually the shape of our ark—it was broad far below in the depths, and then surged up high and narrow . . . Similarly, as we ascend out of these depths—this valley of tears—through a sure growth in the virtues accompanied by an ever greater strengthening of the heart, bit by bit we become more collected into ourselves and unified, until finally we reach that simple unity and true simplicity, the eternal stability found in God."

49. The replacement of a palace by the image of the ark floating on the chaos generated by the deluge of sin also transforms the very concept of *memoria*. The ark stands for a web of events foreshadowed in the Old Testament, made into a worldly reality through the coming of Christ, and floating on towards the Apocalypse. Hugh seeks refuge within this ship of salvation. *Arca Noe morali*, IV, 7; PL 176, 672D–673A: *Et sicut in diebus Noe aquae diluvii universam terram operuerunt, sola autem arca aquis superferebatur, et non solum mergi non poterat, verum etiam quanto amplius aquae intumescebant, tanto altius in sublime elevabatur, ita et nunc intelligamus in corde hominis concupiscentiam hujus mundi esse, quasi quasdam aquas diluvii arcam vero, quae desuper ferebatur, fidem Christi, quae transitoriam delectationem calcat, et ad ea quae sursum sunt, aeterna bona anhelat.* "And as in the days of Noah when the waters of the flood covered the whole earth, the ark alone was borne upon the waters, and was not only unsinkable but actually rose higher as the waters rose, so now let us see that the desire of this world in the heart of man is as it were the waters of the flood, while the ark which is borne up upon them is the faith of Christ, which treads down transitory pleasure and aspires to those everlasting benefits that are above" (*Hugh of Saint-Victor, Selected Spiritual Writings*, trans. by a Religious of C.S.M.V. [New York: Harper and Row, 1962], pp. 138–39). The lusting for this world within the heart of people is, so to speak, the deluge; the embodiment of the ark of *historia* in the heart of the reader creates a place of refuge for him within the history of salvation. *Arca Noe morali*, IV, 8; PL

All Creation is pregnant

Exegesis implies three steps: first, literal reading by which the first, material sense of Holy Scripture is properly embedded in the soul's ark;[50] second, allegorical interpretation; and, third, personal recognition on the part of the reader that he too has his place within this order,[51] and that this "order" is temporal. "First of all, the student of Sacred Scripture ought to look among history, allegory and tropology

---

176, 675B–C: *Sola ergo navis fidei mare transit, sola arca diluvium evadit, et nos si salvari cupimus non solum ipsa in nobis sit, sed nos in ipsa oportet maneamus. . . . In omni enim homine, hoc diluvium est; vel potius omnis homo in hoc diluvio est, sed boni in eo sunt sicut ii, qui in mari portantur a navibus, mali vero in eo sunt sicut naufragi, qui volvuntur in fluctibus.* "For only the ship of faith crosses this sea, only the ark transcends the flood, and if we want to be saved it is not sufficient for the ark to be in us; we must also remain in it. . . . For this is the flood in every man, or, rather, everyone is in the flood, the good in it like those carried across the sea in ships, the evil like the shipwrecked, pulled under by the waves."

Up to Hugh's time, pictorial arts represented the Ark of Noah as a typological scheme and not as a seaworthy boat. This changes during the twelfth century. For this iconographical transformation see Don Cameron Allen, "The Legend of Noah: Renaissance Rationalism in Art, Science, and Letters," *Illinois Studies in Language and Literature* 23, 2–3 (1949): 155ff. See also Joachim Ehlers, *"Arca significat ecclesiam:* ein theologisches Weltmodel aus der ersten Hälfte des 12. Jahrhunderts," in *Jahrbuch des Institutes für Frühmittelalterforschung der Universität Münster,* vol. 6 (1972), pp. 121–87.

50. G. A. Zinn, "Hugh of St. Victor and the Ark of Noah: A New Look," *Church History* 40 (1971): 261–72. Hugh attempts to make the "letter itself" a proper subject for study. He searches a literal understanding of the lines of Scripture to extract and visualize the *order* of those events that, alone, can be the bearer of deeper meanings. "Before drawing out the honey of this deeper meaning," Hugh insisted upon a thorough understanding of the literal sense, "the wax of the comb enclosing the honey" (p. 272). The Ark of Noah, reconstructed in the reader's heart, thus reminds him of such a honeycomb of delicious reminiscences.

51. Hugh's originality lies in his request that the reader mentally construct this ark in his mind, and then live in it, as in his mental home. The idea that the cosmos could be represented around Sacred History as its time axis is quite common in the first half of the twelfth century.

Friedrich Ohly ("Die Kathedrale als Zeitraum: zum Dom von Siena," in Friedrich Ohly, *Schriften zur mittelalterlichen Bedeutungsforschung* [Darmstadt: Wissenschaftliche Buchgesellschaft, 1972], pp. 171–273) examines in great detail how this same concept is represented in the architecture and ornamentation in the Cathedral of Siena. The interior architecture of the cathedral, the graphic representation of the world and the iconographic program of the church portal were all constructed with the intent to make the time axis of sacred history tangible.

Medieval geographic maps are used for a similar purpose. Anna Dorothea von den Brincken ("*Mappa Mundi* und Chronographie. Studien zur *imago mundi* des Mittelalters," *Deutsches Archiv für Erforschung des Mittelalters* 24 (1968): 118–86, esp. pp. 125–61) demonstrates that the purpose of maps was that of representing simultaneously the course of universal history and the totality of historical space *(den Ablauf der Welt-*

for that [appropriate] order. . . . He should ask which of these three precedes the other in the order of study."[52] Hugh here refers to Pope Gregory the Great, for whom reading is a three-step construction program, "where first the [literal] foundation is laid, then the [analogic] structure is raised upon it and, finally, when the work is finished, the building is dressed in colors."[53]

From his earliest writings, he shows irritation at people who "press the breasts of Holy Scripture" to extract its allegorical sense before they have solidly embedded all historical detail into their memory.[54]

> Since no doubt mystical grasp of Scriptural sense can be gained only if first its literal sense has been well established, I cannot but wonder at the impudence of those who pretend to teach allegorical meanings when they are still ignorant of the literal sense.[55]

In the *Didascalicon* he angrily says of such mythomaniacs: "The knowledge of these fellows is like that of an ass. Don't imitate persons of this kind."[56] He speaks directly to his reader:

> You learn history and diligently commit to memory the truth of the deeds that have been performed, reviewing from beginning to end what has been done, when it has been done, where it has been done, and by whom it has been done. . . . Nor do I think that you will be able to become perfectly sensitive to allegory, unless you have been first grounded in history.[57]

---

geschichte in Verbindung mit einer Beschreibung des ganzen historischen Raumes darzustellen).

During the twelfth century in a large number of churches the tympanum (the sculpted ornamental panel between the arch and the lintel) of the main entrance had the same purpose. See, e.g., Joseph Anton Endres, *Das Jakobsportal in Regensburg und Honorius Augustodunensis. Ein Beitrag zur Ikonographie und Liturgiegeschichte des 12. Jahrhunderts* (Kempten: Kösel, 1903). This portal translates into stone the *imago mundi* of Honorius Augustodunensis, the author of the most explicit treatise on the correspondence of macro/micro cosmos in the very early twelfth century.

52. *DT* VI, 2, p. 135.

53. *DB* VI, 2, p. 113. See *DT,* pp. 222–23, nn. 3 and 9.

54. Henri de Lubac, "Hugues de Saint-Victor: les mamelles trop pressées," in Henri de Lubac, *Exégèse médiévale: les quatre sens de l'écriture,* Vol. 1 (Paris: Aubier, 1961), pp. 301–17.

55. *DT* VI, 10, pp. 148–49. Hugh takes this sentence directly out of Cicero, *De oratore* 2.9.38.

56. *DT* VI, 3, p. 136. *Quorum scientia formae asini similis est. noli huismodi imitari (DB,* p. 114).

57. *DT* VI, 3, pp. 135–36. *Ut videlicet prius historiam discas et rerum gestarum veritatem, a principio repetens usque ad finem quid gestum sit, quando gestum sit, ubi ges-*

Hugh elaborates the doctrine about the triple sense of the Bible in such a way that the act of reading becomes an act of worship at whose center stands the incarnation of wisdom:

> Unless God's wisdom is first known bodily [*corporaliter*] you . . . cannot be enlightened for its spiritual contemplation. For this reason you must never look down upon the humility in which God's word reaches you. It is precisely this humility which will enlighten you.[58]

Hugh knows that *corporaliter* implies: "taken from the clay of the earth in the act of creation." This is the reason why, in the next sentence, the book appears to him as a humble clay tablet, like Adam's body before the Creator breathed spirit into its face. God's word might appear to you to be but clay, telling you things in a visible and corporal way. Do not forget that this clay on which you step is the same with which Jesus (in John 9) has opened the eyes of the blind man. Just read Scripture and learn what it says bodily (*corporaliter*). The hard morsels can be swallowed only if they have been well chewed.[59]

> *History* is the story of things done, which we find in the literal sense; *allegory* is when through what is done, something else in the past, present, or future is signified; *tropology* is when through what is done, something which should be done is signified.[60]

At the marriage of Cana the flowing waters of the literal sense will then be transformed into inebriating wine.

---

tum sit, et a quibus gestum sit, diligenter memoriae commendes. . . . *neque ego te perfecte subtilem posse fieri puto in allegoria, nisi prius fundatus fueris in historia* (DB, pp. 113–14).

Marie-Dominique Chenu, "La Décadence de l'allégorisation. Un témoin, Garnier de Rochefort," in *L'Homme devant Dieu. Mélanges de Lubac*, Vol. 2 (Paris, 1964), pp. 129–36. This insistence on the literal reading of Biblical history contravenes the tendency toward wild moral analogies which were quite characteristic for many authors in the second generation of Cistercians.

58. *De scripturis*, cap. 5; PL 175, 14–15A.

59. DB VI, 4, p. 118: *Solidus est cibus iste, et, nisi masticetur, transglutiri non potest.* "Such food is solid stuff and, unless it be well chewed, it cannot be swallowed" (DT, p. 139).

60. *De sacramentis*, I, prol., cap. 4; PL 176, 185: *Historia est rerum gestarum narratio, quae in prima significatione litterae continetur; allegoria est cum per id, quod factum dicitur, aliquid aliud factum sive in praeterito, sive in praesentia, sive in futuro significatur. Tropologia est, cum per id quod factum dicitur, aliquid faciendum esse significatur.*

✥ THREE

Monastic Reading

Meditation

The "reading" Hugh teaches is a monastic activity. For those who engage in it,

> Three things are necessary . . . natural endowment, practice and discipline.[1] By natural endowment [*natura*] is meant that they must be able to grasp easily what they hear, and retain firmly what they grasp; by practice is meant that they must cultivate by assiduous effort the natural endowment they have; and by discipline is meant that by leading a praiseworthy life [*laudabiliter viventes*] they must combine moral behavior[2] with their knowledge.[3]

1. *Natura, exercitium,* and *disciplina* are the three terms whose relative importance is discussed in the Latin didascalic tradition by, among others, Cicero, *De oratore,* 1.4.14; Quintilian, *Institutio oratoria,* III, v. 1; Augustine, *De civitate Dei,* 11.25; Boethius, *In topica Ciceronis commentaria,* VI, *PL* 64, 1168C. Within this triad, *natura* refers to the native quality of the mind, *ingenium.* On Hugh's way of using the term *natura,* see Hugh's own chapter on this: *DB* I, 10, and the commentary in *DT,* pp. 193–95. The word *disciplina* used by Hugh instead of the more common "art," *ars,* stresses a shift of emphasis in *didascalica* from the art of reading needed by the future orator to the moral excellence pursued by the monk.

2. *Mores cum scientia componant,* "they must combine the right life style with their studies." The Latin *mores* is much closer to that which we would call "habits" or "way of life" than to our "morality."

3. *DT* III, 6, p. 90. *Tria sunt . . . necessaria: natura, exercitium, disciplina. in natura consideratur ut facile audita percipiat et percepta firmiter retineat; in exercitio, ut labore et sedulitate naturalem sensum excolat; in disciplina, ut laudabiliter vivens mores cum scientia componat (DB, 57).*

See also Hugh's *De meditando seu meditandi artificio; PL* 176, 993A–998A, which provides a pithy sequence of comments on meditation.

The *studium legendi* challenges the reader to invest everything in the ascent of the steep road toward wisdom: starting with the child's play of memory training, on to *historia,* then interpretation by *analogia* between the events of *historia,* and further on to *anagogia,* the incorporation of the reader in the *historia* that he has come to know.

On the transition from *cogitatio,* which is conceptual analysis, to *meditatio,* incorporation, Hugh says in book III, chapter 10,

> Meditation is sustained thought along planned lines.[4] . . . Meditation takes its start from reading, but is bound by none of the rules or precepts of reading. Meditation delights to range along open ground, where it fixes its free gaze upon the contemplation of truth, drawing together now these, now those causes of things, or now penetrating into profundities, leaving nothing doubtful, nothing obscure. The beginning of learning [*principium doctrinae*] thus lies in reading but its consummation lies in meditation.[5]

Doctrina here stands for neither dogma nor policy. It stands for a personal realization that consists in becoming learned. *Principium doctrinae* is the start on the road to learning, not the first day of instruction on the way to "an education." Hugh speaks of apprentice-

---

4. *Cogitatio frequens cum consilio* (*DT,* p. 92; *DB,* p. 59). I would prefer to translate: "Meditation is deliberate and sustained thought." "Deliberateness" is closer than modern "planning" to the sense of inner guidance, which *consilium* implies. Hugh deals with *consilium* as the flowering of a virtue in his writings about the gifts of the Holy Spirit. A. Gardeil, in "Dons du Saint Esprit" (*Dictionnaire de théologie catholique,* vol. 4, cols 1728–81 [Paris: Letouzey, 1939]), traces the history of this doctrine and Hugh's contribution to its evolution. These seven gifts are conceived of as the "flowering" of the natural virtues that Aristotle had defined, and that come to the saintly as a gratuitous gift from God. Hugh discusses the gifts in *De quinque septenis seu septenariis* (*PL* 175, 405A–414A); *Summa sententiarum,* ch. 17 (*PL* 176, 114D–116D); *De sacramentis,* bk. II, pt. 13, chs. 1–6 (*PL* 176, 525A–531C). Roger Baron argues that an opusculum, *De septem donis spiritus sancti,* is an independent work and publishes it, along with a French translation, in *Hugues de Saint-Victor. Six opuscules spirituels* (Paris: Les Éditions du Cerf, 1969), pp. 120–33. Migne simply places it as the last chapter of *De quinque* (410C–414A). See also Marie-Thérèse d'Alverny, "La Sagesse et ses sept filles. Recherches sur les allégories de la philosophie et des arts libéraux du IXᵉ siècle," in *Mélanges F. Grat,* vol. 1 (Paris, 1946), pp. 245–78.

5. *DT* III, 10, pp. 92–93. *Meditatio principium sumit a lectione, nullis tamen stringitur regulis aut praeceptis lectionis. delectatur enim quodam aperto decurrere spatio, ubi liberam contemplandae veritati aciem affigat, et nunc has, nunc illas rerum causas perstringere, nunc autem profunda quaeque penetrare, nihil anceps, nihil obscurum relinquere. principium ergo doctrinae est in lectione, consummatio in meditatione* (*DB,* p. 59).

ship which starts when one acquires familiarity with the tools of the trade and then leads to their mastery by meditative reading.

> If any man will learn to love it [meditation] very intimately and will desire to be engaged very frequently in it, [it] renders his life pleasant indeed, and provides the greatest consolation to him in his trials.[6]

Meditative reading can sometimes be difficult, a chore which must be faced with courage, *fortitudo*. But the reader, sustained by the "zeal to inquire," will derive joy from his application. Eagerness comes with practice.[7] To foster his zeal, the student needs encouraging example rather than instruction.[8] Wisdom is of great beauty, like the maiden in the "Song of Songs." To be as close to the Sunamite woman as was King David is a delight. And wisdom will not relinquish her lover. Did not the Sunamite creep into David's bed to warm his old and decaying body?[9]

Hugh encourages his readers to seek pleasure in everything they can learn. "Later you will realize that nothing has been superfluous. Stifling knowledge gives no joy." [10] He encourages an attitude in which the reader advances because he yearns for that mastery which puts the

---

6. *DT* III, 10, p. 93. *Quam si quis familiarius amare didicerit eique saepius vacare voluerit, iucundam valde reddit vitam, et maximam in tribulatione praestat consolationem (DB, p. 59).*

7. *DB* III, 14, p. 64: *Studium quaerendi ad exercitium pertinet.*

8. Ibid: *In quo [studio] exhortatione magis quam doctrina lector indiget.*

9. Ibid., p. 65: *Sola Abisac Sunamitis senem David calefecit quia amor sapientiae etiam marcescente corpore dilectorem suum non deserit.*

10. *DB* VI, 3, p. 115: *Omnia disce, videbis postea nihil esse superfluum. coarctata scientia iucunda non est.* The whole passage is as follows (with Taylor's translation): *Sicut in virtutibus, ita in scientiis quidam gradus sunt. sed dicis: 'multa invenio in historiis, quae nullius videntur esse utilitatis, quare in huiusmodi occupabor?' bene dicis. multa siquidem sunt in scripturis, quae in se considerata nihil expetendum habere videntur, quae tamen si aliis quibus cohaerent comparaveris, et in toto suo trutinare coeperis, necessaria pariter et competentia esse videbis. alia propter se scienda sunt, alia autem, quamvis propter se non videantur nostro labore digna, quia tamen sine ipsis illa enucleate sciri non possunt, nullatenus debent negligenter praeteriri. omnia disce, videbis postea nihil esse superfluum. coartata scientia iucunda non est.* "As in the virtues, so in the sciences, there are certain steps. But, you say, I find many things in the histories which seem to be of no utility: why should I be kept busy with this sort of thing? Well said. There are indeed many things in the Scriptures which, considered in themselves, seem to have nothing worth looking for, but if you look at them in the light of the other things to which they are joined, and if you begin to weigh them in their whole context, you will see that they are as necessary as they are fitting. Some things are to be known for their own sakes, but others, although for their own sakes they do not seem worthy of our labor, nevertheless, because without them the former class of things cannot be

mind to rest. "Reading" is an iconogram for the foretaste of wisdom. To set the tone for the reader, Hugh quotes Psalm 54.7 from the Vulgate: *Quis dabit mihi pennas columbae, ut volem et requiescam?*[11]

Communities of mumblers

Hugh's meditation is an intensive reading activity and not some passive quietist plunge into feelings. This activity is described by analogy to body movements: striding from line to line, or flapping one's wings while surveying the already well-known page. Reading is experienced by Hugh as a bodily motor activity.

In a tradition of one and a half millennia, the sounding pages[12] are echoed by the resonance of the moving lips and tongue. The reader's ears pay attention, and strain to catch what the reader's mouth gives forth. In this manner the sequence of letters translates directly into body movements and patterns nerve impulses. The lines are a sound track picked up by the mouth and voiced by the reader for his own ear. By reading, the page is literally embodied, incorporated.

The modern reader conceives of the page as a plate that inks the mind, and of the mind as a screen onto which the page is projected and from which, at a flip, it can fade.[13] For the monastic reader, whom Hugh addresses, reading is a much less phantasmagoric and much more carnal activity: the reader understands the lines by moving to their beat, remembers them by recapturing their rhythm, and thinks of them in terms of putting them into his mouth and chewing. No wonder that pre-university monasteries are described to us in various sources as the dwelling places of mumblers and munchers.[14]

- Peter the Venerable (1092/94–1156), the learned abbot who rules Cluny, usually sits at night on his bed indefati-

---

known with complete clarity, must by no means be carelessly skipped. Learn everything; you will see afterwards that nothing is superfluous. A skimpy knowledge is not a pleasing thing" (*DT*, p. 137).

11. "Oh that I had wings like a dove! For then I would fly away, and be at rest" (King James Version).

12. For quotations see Joseph Balogh, "Voces Paginarum," *Philologus* 82 (1926–27): 84–109, 202–40.

13. Or even conceives his brain as a state "that ink may character," as is maintained by W. McCulloch, *Embodiments of Mind* (Cambridge: MIT Press, 1965), pp. 387–98.

14. Giles Constable, "Monachisme et pèlerinage du moyen âge" *Revue historique* 101 (1977): 3–27.

gably chewing the Scriptures by turning them over in his mouth.[15]

- During the dark hours between midnight prayers and dawn, John of Gorze (died 976) "like a bee quietly hums the Psalms without interruption."[16]

- For Gregory the Great, "Sacred Scripture is sometimes food, sometimes drink for us."[17] Reading it, "One finds honey indeed when one tastes the sweetness of holy under-standing."[18]

- In a letter to a monk, Bernard of Clairvaux says, "if you prepare your interior ear . . . and keep your inner senses open, this voice of your God will be sweeter than honey and the honeycomb."[19] On another occasion he says that "my heart was burning in me all night, and a fire lighted up my meditation," as he read the Scripture in prepara-tion for his homily.[20]

15. *Ore sine requie sacra verba ruminans* (Peter the Venerable, *De Miraculis* I, 20; *PL* 189, 887A).

16. *In morem apis psalmos tacito murmure continuo revolvens* (*Vita Joannis abbatis Gorziensis; PL* 137, 280D).

17. He goes on to say, "In the more obscure places, it is food, broken up through study, made nourishing through chewing. It is drink in the clearer places, and is ab-sorbed as soon as it is read." *Scriptura enim sacra aliquando nobis est cibus, aliquando potus. Cibus est in locis obscurioribus, quia quasi exponendo frangitur, et mandendo glutitur. Potus vero est in locis apertioribus, quia ita sorbetur sicut invenitur.* Book 1, no. 29, Gregory the Great, *Morales sur Job,* First part, bks. 1 and 2. Intro. by Robert Gillet, O.S.B. (Paris: Éditions du Cerf, 1975), p. 208.

18. *Mel quippe invenire est sancti intellectus dulcedinem degustare.* Ch. 5, bk. 16, *In expositionem beati Job moralia; PL* 75, 1124C.

19. *Huic voci Dei tui, dulciori super mel et favum, si praeparas aurem interiorem . . . vacante interno sensu. . . .* "Epistola 107 ad Thomam Praepositum de Beverla," *PL* 182, 248C. C. Gindele ("Bienen-, Waben- und Honigvergleiche in der frühen monastischen Literatur," *Review of Benedictine Studies* 6–7 (1977–78): 1–26 [ed. 1981]) notices that since Christian antiquity, metaphors for spiritual experiences taken from the language of bee-keeping appear whenever new communities of monks grow out of old hermi-tages.

Honey, in antiquity, was thought to be a kind of heavenly dew which is collected by the bees. Sugar was practically unknown, and honey provided the most intense degree of sweetness, with the apple next. The contrary of sweetness is the bitter taste of hell and gall. W. Armknecht, *Geschichte des Wortes 'süß'; bis zum Ausgang des Mittelalters,* Germanische Studien 171 (Berlin: Ebering, 1936).

20. *Tota hac nocte concaluit cor meum intra me, et in meditatione mea exarsit ignis.* "Sermo in festo omnium sanctorum," *Sermones; PL,* 183, 454C.

56   *Monastic Reading*

- Augustine encourages his monks, "Read it [Scripture], because it is sweeter than all honey, more pleasing than any bread, and you will find it gives more joy than any wine."[21]

During this period the reading-meditating monk is often compared with a cow chewing its cud. For example, St. Bernard exhorts his brothers: "You must be pure, ruminating animals, that what is written might come to be: 'A desirable treasure rests in the mouth of the wise' [Prov. 21.20]."[22] Speaking about the words of the Canticle of Canticles, Bernard also says, "Enjoying their sweetness, I chew them over

21. *Legite eam, quia omni melle dulcior, omni pane suavior, omni vino hilarior invenitur.* "Sermo 38," *Sermones ad fratres in eremo commorantes; PL* 40, 1304. Compare also *Chronicon Centulense* IV 10 (*PL* 174, 1319B) and IV 26: *Divini verbi favos sibi congerebat* "He gathered together the honeycombs of the Divine Word for himself" (ibid., 1346).

"Sweet" refers primarily to an agreeable experience on the tongue, in the ear or even to the touch. In the first millennium, among Christian authors, it is used for the taste of the Word. Only during the later Middle Ages does the meaning shift to an intrinsic quality of certain foods: No longer is honey as sweet as God's Word, but almost as sweet as sugar. Friedrich Ohly, "Geistige Süße bei Otfried," in Friedrich Ohly, *Schriften zur mittelalterlichen Bedeutungsforschung* (Darmstadt: Wissenschaftliche Buchgesellschaft, 1977), pp. 93–127, esp. pp. 98–99; J. Ziegler, *Dulcedo Dei. Ein Beitrage zur Theologie der griechischen und lateinischen Bibel*, Alttestamentliche Abhandlungen 13,2 (Münster: Aschendorfsche Verlagsbuchhandlung, 1937); W. Armknecht, *Geschichte des Wortes* "süß."

22. *Vos estote animalia munda et ruminantia, ut fiat sicut scriptum est: Thesaurus desiderabilis requiescit in ore sapientis.* "Sermo in festo omnium sanctorum," *Sermones; PL* 183, 455C. It was believed that animals such as ruminants were "clean" animals. The comparison of the meditating monk with the grazing cow, sheep, or goat remains an uninterrupted motif. Jean Leclercq (*L'Amour des lettres et le désir de Dieu: initiation aux auteurs monastiques du moyen âge* [Paris: Cerf, 1957]; translated as *The Love of Learning and the Desire for God* [New York: Fordham Univ. Press, 1982]) quotes from an anonymous *Mariale* of the twelfth-century manuscript Paris B.N. lat. 2594 f. 58v: *Monachus in claustro iumentum est Samaritani in stabulo: huic foenum apponitur in praesepie dum assidue ruminando imitatur memoria Jesu Christi.* "A monk in his monastery is like the Samaritan's beast in the stable. Hay is given to one in his stall; the other assiduously chews, nourishing himself on the memory of Jesus Christ." In a similar vein, Irénée Hausherr quotes a Greek monk: "An old man said, The shepherd gives his sheep good forage to eat, but they also consume many of the weeds they come upon. If they swallow burning nettles they will seek out grass to ruminate on (*anamerychatai*) until the bitterness of the nettles disappears. In the same way meditation on the Scriptures is a good remedy for men against the attack of demons" (*The Name of Jesus* [Kalamazoo: Cistercian Publications, 1978], p. 176).

and over, my internal organs are replenished, my insides are fattened up, and all my bones break out in praise."[23]

For an ocular reader, this testimony of the past can be shocking: such a reader cannot share the experience created by the reverberation of oral reading in all the senses.[24] In addition, the vocabulary for flavors and odors has withered and shrunk.[25]

The page as a vineyard and garden

When Hugh reads, he harvests; he picks the berries from the lines. He knows that Pliny had already noted that the word *pagina,* page, can refer to rows of vines joined together.[26] The lines on the page were the thread of a trellis which supports the vines. As he picks the fruit from the leaves of parchment, the *voces paginarum* drop from his mouth; as a subdued murmur, if they are meant for his own ears, or *recto tono,* if he addresses the community of monks. There is an expression which allows us to distinguish the two kinds of activity: *sibi legere,* which means "reading to oneself," in contrast to *clara lectio,* meant for the ears of others. No wonder that reading throughout antiquity was considered a strenuous exercise. Hellenistic physicians prescribed reading as an alternative to ball playing or a walk. Reading presupposed that you be in good physical form; the frail or infirm were not supposed to read with their own tongue. At one solstice, Nicholas of Clairvaux had submitted with all the other monks to the customary quarterly purging

23. *Suaviter rumino ista, et replentur viscera mea, et interiora mea saginantur, et omnia ossa mea germinant laudem.* "Sermo 16," *Sermones in Cantica Canticorum; PL* 183, 849C.

24. During the twelfth century increasing attention was paid to the physical reflection of spiritual experiences which accompanied reading. Karl Rahner's "La Début d'une doctrine des cinq sens spirituels, chez Origéne," *Revue d'ascétique et de mystique* 13 (1932): 113–45, deals with the roots of this doctrine in Origen; and his "La doctrine des sens spirituels au moyen âge, en particulier chez Saint Bonaventure," *Revue d'ascétique et de mystique* 13 (1932): 263–99, reviews later perception and elaboration.

25. Taste and smell were not clearly distinguished, but were much more vividly expressed, to describe emotions felt while thinking with affection or during meditative reading. The vocabulary available for odors, fragrances, and smells was much richer in the vernacular language of the Middle Ages than it is in modern European tongues. Artur Kutzelnigg, "Die Verarmung des Geruchswortschatzes seit dem Mittelalter," *Muttersprache* 94 (1983–84): 328–46.

26. Pliny 17.169. See A. Ernout and A. Meillet, *Dictionnaire étymologique de la langue latine: histoire des mots* (Paris: Librarie C. Klincksieck, 1932), *pagina* and *pagus;* and Pliny, *Natural History,* vol. 5, trans. by H. Rackham (Cambridge: Harvard University Press, 1971), p. 116. Rackham explains that *pagina* is used here as a term for four rows of vines joined together in a square by their trellis.

and bleeding, but this time the fast in combination with the cupping had left him too weak for a while to continue his reading. When Peter the Venerable had a cold which made him cough when he opened his mouth, he could not read, neither in the choir nor in his cell "to himself." [27]

Not only did oral activities predominate in the act of reading, they also determined the task of the eyes. The root of the English word "to read" connotes "to give advice," "to make out," "to peruse and interpret." The Latin *legere* comes from a physical activity.[28] *Legere* connotes "picking," "bundling," "harvesting" or "collecting."[29] The Latin word for the branches and twigs that are collected is derived from *legere*. These sticks are called *lignum*, which contrasts with *materia*[30] somewhat as firewood can be distinguished from timber. The German "to read" (*lesen*) still clearly conveys the idea of gathering beech sticks (the word for "letter" is equivalent to sticks of beechwood, reminding us of the runes used in magical incantations).[31]

For Hugh, who uses Latin, the act of reading with the eyes implies an activity not unlike a search for firewood: his eyes must pick up the letters of the alphabet and bundle these into syllables. The eyes are at the service of the lungs, the throat, the tongue, and the lips that do not usually utter single letters but words.

Lectio as a way of life

Both for the classical rhetor or sophist and for the monk, reading engages the whole body. However, for the monk, reading is not one activ-

---

27. The most readable and dense description of monastic reading is still Jean Leclerq, *Love of Learning*, especially "*Lectio* and *Meditatio*," pp. 15–17, where these two anecdotes and their sources are given.

28. *Dictionnaire étymologique*, s.v. *lego, legere*. "To love," *di-ligere*, comes from the same root: A "*di*" et "*lego*," quasi sit eligere aliquem e multis . . . "From 'di' and 'lego,' as if to pick someone out from among many" (Aegidio Forcellini, *Lexicon totius latinitatis*, orig publ. 1864–1926; repr. Bologna, 1965). Isidore of Seville: "Some have said that 'to love' comes to us naturally, while 'to be affectionate' [*diligere*] is only from choice." *Alii dixerunt amare nobis naturaliter insitum, diligere vero electione (Differentiarum sive de proprietate sermonum, 1.17; PL 83, 12A–B).

29. Vergil and Cicero stress this connection. *Dictionnaire étymologique*.

30. From *mater*, mother-part of the tree, meant for construction materials.

31. F. Kluge, *Etymologisches Wörterbuch der deutschen Sprache*. 18th ed. (Berlin: De Gruyter, 1960). The German equivalent for letter is *Buchstab(e)*. *Stab* = rod, twig: the vertical trace of the rune. As the runes came to be written on parchment instead of wooden tablets or stone slabs, the composible word came into being. The German word "*lesen*," to read, comes from "*lesan*," collect, gather, select, lift. "*Buchstaben lesen*" connoted the gathering of rods covered with runes, an activity connected with divination.

ity but a way of life.[32] Reading goes on whatever the monk does following his particular rule. This rule was established by St. Benedict and divides the day into two activities that are deemed equally important: *ora et labora,* pray and toil.[33] Seven times a day the members of the small community of the ideal monastery meet in church. They listen to recitations done on one tone (*recto tono*), with rigidly defined inflections to mark questions, direct speech, or the end of a pericope, and they sing from the book of Psalms. In between, when the monk milks or plows, makes butter or chisels, the recitation in common turns into a subdued drone in which each picks his own lines. These lines are the road of his pilgrimage toward heaven, both when he prays and when he works.[34] Reading impregnates his days and nights.[35]

This commitment to uninterrupted reading is of Jewish, rabbinical origin, like the plainchant which anchors the lines in the heart. Gregorian chant takes its inspiration from that of the synagogue. The desire to live with the book is also a part of Jewish mysticism.[36]

After the pious Jew has attended service in the synagogue and listened to passages from the Torah and the Prophets, he humbly continues to mouth passages from these readings while he watches his wares in the market or sits on the steps of his house. A rabbi does this until these "readings taste to him as sweet as a mother's milk to a babe."[37] He remembers Ezekiel 3 where God's messenger holds out a scroll to his servant and this scroll "was written all over on both sides." Ezekiel is bidden to "eat this roll," to "ingest it." Indeed, "as he swallows the roll . . . it tastes as sweet as honey." God does not pre-dict but prescribe the fate of the Jewish people—and the fate of each Jew is experienced by discovering his own destiny as a postscript. More often than

32. B. Calati, "La *lectio divina* nella tradizione monastica benedettina," *Benedictina* 28 (1981): 407–38, is a good guide. See also A. Wathen, "Monastic Lectio: Some Clues from Terminology." *Monastic Studies* 12 (1976): 207–16; P. C. Spahr, "Die *lectio divina* bei den alten Cicterciensern. Eine Grundlage des cisterciensischen Geisteslebens," *Analecta Cisterciensia* 34 (1978): 27–39; M. Van Aasche, "Divinae vacari lectioni," *Sacris Erudiri* 1 (1948): 13–14.

33. *Ora et labora:* On the difficulty for a modern reader to seize the meaning given to terms like work, labor, toil, see Ivan Illich, *Shadow Work* (London: Boyars, 1981), Bibliographic Note, pp. 122–52.

34. In the Greek and Russian Churches, the joining of word and breath is mumbling prayer and to this day remains a recognized and esteemed way of "the pilgrimage through life." See Hausherr, *The Name of Jesus,* esp. p. 174 on murmuring in the tradition of Greek monks.

35. The story of this lifestyle and of its evolution is told and richly embroidered by texts in Leclercq, *Love of Learning.*

36. George Steiner, "Our Homeland the Text," *Salmagundi* 66 (1985): 4–25.

37. B. Gerhardson, *Memory and Manuscript: Oral Tradition and Written Transmission in Rabbinic Judaism and Early Christianity* (Uppsala: Gleerup, 1961).

not the postscript has a bitter taste. "The Jew would seem to have been intent to certify the road mapped for him by the Prophet."[38]

Hugh wants his student, by searching the three senses of scripture, to embody the sacred past of the whole world in his own present. He wants him to interpret the exodus of the Jews out of Egypt as a prefiguring of the way from Jerusalem to Golgotha, of the way Christians follow Jesus, applying the stories to himself: abandon his family for the monastery, which appears under the image of the desert. Unhoused, he finds his temporary home in the pages of the book.

Thus, the meaning which is given to the *studium legendi* by Hugh and his age was shaped by Old Testament ideas. Further, the Benedictine Rule creates a framework in which, symbolically, the whole body is involved in lifelong reading. The individual monk might be a *rudis*— an unlettered servant or uncouth dullard. Even so, he attends the seven daily assemblies in the choir and, in front of the book, sings the Psalms. They have become part of his being, and like the most learned brother, he can mouth them while he watches goats.

The process by which the written text of Scripture becomes part of each monk's biography is typically Jewish rather than Greek. Antiquity had no one book that could be swallowed. Neither Greeks nor Romans were people of a book. No one book was—or could be—at the center of the classical way of life, as it is for Jews, Christians, and Muslims. For the first Christian millennium, memorization of this one book was performed by a process which stands in stark contrast to the building of memory palaces. The book was swallowed and digested through the careful attention paid to the psychomotor nerve impulses which accompany the sentences being learned. Even today, pupils in Koranic and Jewish schools sit on the floor with the book open on their knees. Each one chants his lines in a singsong, often a dozen pupils simultaneously, each a different line. While they read, their bodies sway from the hips up or their trunks gently rock back and forth. The swinging and the recitation continue as if the student is in a trance, even when he closes his eyes or looks down the aisle of the mosque. The body movements re-evoke those of the speech organs that have been associated with them. In a ritual manner these students use their whole bodies to embody the lines.

Marcel Jousse has studied these psychomotor techniques of fixing a spoken sequence in the flesh.[39] He has shown that for many people,

---

38. Steiner, "Homeland," p. 12.
39. "Corporage," is the term he uses: *La Manducation de la parole* (Paris: Gallimard, 1975).

remembrance means the triggering of a well-established sequence of muscular patterns to which the utterances are tied. When the child is rocked during a cradle song, when the reapers bow to the rhythm of a harvest song, when the rabbi shakes his head while he prays or searches for the right answer, or when the proverb comes to mind only upon tapping for a while—according to Jousse, these are just a few examples of a widespread linkage of utterance and gesture.[40] Each culture has given its own form to this bilateral, dissymmetric complementarity by which sayings are graven right and left, forward and backward into trunk and limbs, rather than just into the ear and eye. Monastic existence can be viewed as a carefully patterned framework for the practice of such techniques.

Otia monastica

It is, however, not a social technique incorporated in the rule which makes the monk, but rather the attitude with which he approaches the book as the center of his life. In the short chapter on meditation (III, 10), Hugh refers to the spirit in which this life of reading ought to be lived. He uses the word *vacare,* which says all but just cannot be translated into English. The word occurs in the sentence which speaks of meditation as a skill and urges the reader to enjoy it. "If any man will learn to love it [meditation] very intimately (*familiarius amare*), and will desire to be engaged (*vacare voluerit*) very frequently upon it, [it] renders his life pleasant indeed.[41] Jerome Taylor elegantly renders *vacare voluerit* as "will desire to be engaged." But this misleads a modern student. One does not then see that the word *vacare* is a crucially important technical term used for the definition of the Christian monk.[42] Rufinus (ca. 435–510) was the first to define the monk as someone "who in solitude makes himself free for God alone," *solus soli Deo vacans.*[43]

40. Marcel Jousse, *L'Anthropologie du geste* (Paris: Gallimard, 1974). Jousse was a French Jesuit stationed in Beirut, who spent his entire life in the study of the embodiment of Semitic sayings. He first explored the connection between movement and memory ("Le Style oral rythmique et mnémotechnique chez les verbo-moteurs," *Archives de Philosophie* 2 (1924): 1–240) and then the dissymmetric, bilateral nature of these movements corresponding to voice rhythms ("Le Bilatéralisme humain et l'anthropologie du langage," *Revue anthropologique,* Aug.–Sept. 1940, pp. 1–30). His influence on the young Millman Parry during the late 1920s led Parry to develop his theory on orality.

41. *DT* III, 10, p. 93. See note 6, above.

42. Like modern English, classical Latin has the noun, *vacatio,* with the meaning "freedom, exemption, immunity" (*Oxford Latin Dictionary*). It is not this noun, but the corresponding verb that is used by Hugh.

43. Rufinus, *Historia Monachorum* 1; *PL* 21, 391B.

Vacare means "to have been set or become free." When Christian authors use the term the stress is not on the release a person gets, but on the freedom he takes of his own volition. The term stresses "the desire to be engaged" in a new way of life rather than the release or flight from one's old habits of bondage and lifestyle. The verb is also used in classical Latin. Seneca, the Stoic tutor of Nero and contemporary of Peter and Paul, distinguishes three ways of life in which a person might choose to "engage" himself: lust, contemplation, or (political) action.[44] With generosity, he urges, one should choose what to be free for. True leisure can be found only by those who give themselves to wisdom (*sapientiae vacant*). In this classical sense, the verb was still used in Hugh's time. It meant being "absorbed" by wine, "immersed" in a life of carnal pleasure, "engrossed" in studies. However, no author of the twelfth century could have used the term to designate these "deviations" without connoting that they were disorders, in contrast to the true freedom which the Christian ought to take. This last sense was first given to the term by St. Augustine. Shortly after his baptism in 387 he went to Africa, feeling God's calling to practice *otium* (leisure),[45] and founded a small community in the town of Thagaste. He declares the purpose of the group's common life is "to be deified by leisure."[46] He strongly urges his dear friends "love leisure, that you might refrain from all earthly pleasure, but remember that there is no place free from snares."[47] He says elsewhere, "My leisure is not spent in nurturing idleness, but in exploring wisdom. . . . I draw back from distracting activities, and my spirit devotes itself to heavenly desires."[48]

44. Seneca, *Ad Serenum de otio* (*Dialogi* 8), 7.1: *Praeterea tria genera sunt vitae . . . unum voluptati vacat, alterum contemplationi, tertium actioni.*

45. *Postremo . . . de otio meo modo gaudeo; quod a superfluarum cupiditatum vinculis evolavi . . . quod quaero intentissimus veritatem.* "Finally . . . I now enjoy my leisure; I have escaped from the bonds of superfluous desires. . . . I most intently seek the truth. . . ." *Contra academicos*, Bk. 2, ch. 2; *Oeuvres de Saint Augustin*, vol. 4, R. Jolivet, ed. and trans. (Paris: Desclée de Brouwer, 1948), p. 66.

46. *Deificari . . . in otio.* St. Augustine, "Letter 10." See Georges Folliet, "*Deificari in otio.* Augustin, Epistola X, 2," in *Recherches augustiniennes*, vol. 2, ed. Georges Folliet (Paris: Études augustiniennes, 1962), pp. 225–36. St. Augustine, *Letters*, vol. 1, trans. by Sister Wilfred Parsons, S.N.D. (Washington: Catholic University of America Press, 1951), pp. 23–25.

47. *Sic ergo, dilectissimi, diligite otium, ut vos ab omni terrena delectatione refrenetis et memineritis nullum locum esse, ubi non possit laqueos tendere.* Letter 48, to Eudoxius, *Epistolae Sancti Augustini*, Al. Goldbacher, ed., vol. 34 (Prague: Bibliopola academiae litterarum caesareae vindobonensis, 1895), pp. 137–40.

48. *Otium meum non impenditur nutriendae desidiae, sed percipiendae sapientiae . . . ego requiesco a negotiosis actibus, et animus meus divinis se intendit affectibus.* "Tractus 57," *Tractatus in Johannis evangelium; PL* 35, 1791.

Hugh thus demands that the reader who desires to reach perfection engage himself in leisure (*otium*). "This especially is that which takes the soul away from the noise of earthly business and makes it have, even in this life, a kind of foretaste of the sweetness of eternal quiet."[49] Meditative reading brings the soul to rest.

Hugh here distinguishes between the pilgrimage and the stroll, the strenuous *lectio* and the leisurely *meditatio*. He distinguishes the two styles of movement but stresses their similarity. In the monastic tradition, the two ways of reading are but two moments in the same *lectio divina*. Hugh does not perceive a break between philosophy and theology, a distinction on which the Scholastics would soon afterward build their method. Only during the thirteenth century would the distinction between the "light of reason" and the "light of faith" lead to two kinds of reading: philosophy, in which reason throws its light on things (*lumen rationis*) and then gropes for the reasons that brought them into being, and theology, in which the reader submits to the authority of God's word and its light (*lumen fidei*) when he interprets the sensible and rational world.[50]

In Hugh, these two distinct engagements of the reader are still aspects of the same *otium*. The two kinds of "light" that can be thrown onto the page are still only two moments of one and same *studium*. *Lectio* is forever a beginning, *meditatio* a *consummatio*, and both integral to *studium*. The study of creatures teaches us to search for their creator; then this creator will furnish the soul with knowledge, and drench it in joy, making meditation a supreme delight.[51] For Hugh

---

49. *DT* III, 10, p. 93. *Ea enim maxime est, quae animam terrenorum actuum strepitu segregat, et in hac vita etiam aeternae quietis dulcedinem quodammodo praegustare facit (DB, p. 59).*

50. Which is always, first of all, the world of *historia*: "The sense of history which Hugh shows in his writings was characteristic of a particular segment of twelfth-century society: monks and canons regular. History had no place in the liberal arts and consequently in the later university curriculum. . . . The masters in the schools tended to move away from the practice of integral biblical reading in *lectio divina* with its historical frame to a program oriented around collections of *quaestiones* covering theological topics in a systematic, objective manner. . . . Abelard . . . broke decisively with any notion of an historical economy for *divinitas*. . . . To be logically consistent, statements of faith must be constant through the ages, a position counter to that embraced by Hugh. . . . For the dialecticians the tense of the verb was incidental, not essential" (G. A. Zinn, Jr., "*Historia fundamentum est:* The Role of History in the Contemplative Life According to Hugh of St. Victor," in *Contemporary Reflections on the Medieval Christian Tradition. Essays in Honor of Ray C. Petry,* ed. by G. H. Shriver [Durham, N.C.: Duke University Press, 1974]), pp. 135–58.

51. *DT* III, 10, p. 93. *Cumque iam per ea quae facta sunt eum qui fecit omnia quaerere didicerit et intelligere, tunc animum pariter et scientia erudit et laetitia perfundit, unde fit ut maximum in meditatione sit oblectamentum (DB, pp. 59–60).*

there is only one kind of reading that is worthwhile, *lectio divina*. This places him at the end of one thousand years during which *lectio* and *otio vacare* had defined each other.

The demise of the *lectio divina*

At the beginning of the thirteenth century, even the term *lectio divina* becomes less frequent and disappears entirely from some contexts.[52] For the friars, Franciscans and Dominicans, pious reading which nourishes by contemplation is only one of the basic ways of using the book. The term *lectio spiritualis* is used to distinguish this from academic pursuits, which now monopolize the word *studium*.

When Hugh refers to reading that is done for any ulterior purpose, distinct from personal progress toward wisdom, he refers to it with harsh warnings.[53] One of his contemporaries, William of St. Thierry, who died six years after Hugh, already holds a different opinion on this point. He discriminates between one kind of reading which is done with affection (*affectus*), in which the reader assimilates his experience to that of the author, and another which has the purpose of increasing factual knowledge.[54] The new way of reading the newly laid-out page calls for a new setting within the city: colleges that engender the university, with its academic rather than monastic rituals. The *studium*

---

52. Jean Leclercq, "Les Caractères traditioneles de la *lectio divina*," in *La Liturgie et les paradoxes chrétiens* (Paris, 1963), pp. 243–57. See also Jaques Rousse and Herman Joseph Sieben, "*Lectio divina* et lecture spirituelle" in *Dictionnaire de spiritualité*, vol. 9, cols. 470–84 (Paris: Beauchesne, 1975). The first part of this article deals explicitly with the transformation I am describing here. For introduction of the Benedictine tradition in the high-medieval Cistercian monasteries, see P. C. Spahr, "Die *lectio divina* bei den alten Cisterciensern. Eine Grundlage des cisterciensischen Geisteslebens," *Analecta Cisterciensia* 34 (1978): 27–39. For the earlier history, U. Berlière, "Lectio divina," in *L'Ascèse bénédictine des origines à la fin du 12ᵉ siècle*, Collection Pax (Maredsous, 1927).

53. For example, *De arca Noe moralia*, IV, 6; *PL* 176, 672C: *Reprobi dum temporalibus inhiant, cognitionem aeternorum perdunt. Electi autem, dum temporalia Dei beneficia recolunt, ad agnitionem aeternorum proficiunt.* "The reprobate, while panting after temporary things, lose their perception of the things eternal; but the elect, while pondering God's temporal benefits, advance to knowledge of the everlasting ones" (*Hugh of St. Victor, Selected Spiritual Writings* trans. by a Religious of C.S.M.V. [New York: Harper and Row, 1962], p. 138).

54. In this latter case, the page becomes an "object"—in German, *Gegen-stand*—and its content a subject-matter. L. Dewan, "*Obiectum*. Notes on the Invention of a Word," *Archives d'histoire doctrinale et littéraire de moyen âge* 48 (1981): 37–96, examines the steps by which the term *obiectum* came into use around 1220.

legendi ceases to be a way of life for the great majority of disciplined readers, and is viewed as one particular ascetical practice now called "spiritual reading." On the other hand, "study" increasingly refers to the acquisition of knowledge. *Lectio* divides into prayer and study.

❦ FOUR

Lectio in Latin

Hugh's pupils were the last of their kind, the last medieval Latinists for whom reading, writing, and Latin were all part of the same thing. Within their own lifetime Latin became one among other languages. The next generation of students composed vernacular poetry alongside Latin verses. It discovered that Roman lettershapes could register vernacular speech. For Hugh's pupils the shape of Roman letters still had a Latin voice. By its Roman letters Latin was visibly one of the three holy languages, next to Hebrew and Greek. What people spoke was *sermo*, experienced as something as different from the use of language, *lingua*, as with us singing or dancing is something different in kind from speech. Latin was sound and letters in one; and it kept not only letters but theory captive. The speculative grammarians of the mid-twelfth century remain prisoners of Latin. What they call modal logic is an ontological interpretation of grammatical categories defined by Cicero's contemporaries.[1]

Latin monasticism

Hugh's pupils did not learn Latin as a second, dead, or learned language. They entered into Latin as an integral part of the monastic way of life. Religious *conversio*, as the commitment to monastery life was then called, led into Latin, letters, lifelong rootedness, and the complex

---

1. Jan Pinborg, *Die Entwicklung der Sprachtheorie im Mittelalter,* Beiträge zur Geschichte der Philosphie und Theologie des Mittelalters vol. 42, fasc. 2 (Münster:

ritual of prayer as just different facets of monastic obedience. The dialects spoken in the novice's home were almost never written. Nor were they conceived yet as a mother tongue.[2] This was as true for the peasant as for the knight. The alphabet did not yet throw a shadow on everyday speech. There was no way of analyzing the vernacular in syllables or words. Stories told in Romance or Germanic tongues still followed the rules of oral societies, flowed by like water, even though the age of epic poetry had long past, and chroniclers sometimes recorded these tales—usually in Latin. The time for the concept of language as a generic term, allowing a comparison of two kinds—vernacular and Latin—had not yet arrived.[3]

This does not mean that Latin was unheard outside the walls of the cloister. Its sounds were in the atmosphere of Hugh's youth. When a father offered his child at the porter's lodge to receive instruction, the little one was already acquainted with Latin sounds.[4] He had certainly picked them up in the responses made by the laity at Mass and Vespers in the parish church. But once the child had entered the silence of the cloister, Latin became the main outlet for his voice.[5] Monastic silence at work, in the kitchen, in the fields and stable, created the background against which Latin would loom large.

Aschendorfsche Verlagsbuchhandlung, 1979), pp. 58–59. See also Jan Pinborg, *Medieval Semantics. Selected Studies on Medieval Logic and Grammar,* Collected Studies Series 195, ed. Sten Ebbesen (London: Variorum Reprints, 1984).

2. Karl Heisig, "Muttersprache: Ein romanistischer Beitrag zur Genesis eines deutschen Wortes und zur Entstehung der deutsch-französichen Sprachgrenze," *Muttersprache* 22 (1954): 144–74. Romans knew the *patrius sermo,* the father's accent which betrayed a man's origin. The tie between motherhood and tongue was first established along the upper Rhine in the late ninth century, in territorial disputes between the Abbey of Gorz and neighboring monasteries. The term "mother tongue" is rarely used in documents of the twelfth century, and always denotes a speech form, *sermo,* as distinct from *lingua,* the Latin language.

3. Franz H. Bäuml, "Der Übergang mündlicher zur artesbestimmten Literatur des Mittelalters. Gedanken und Bedenken," in *Fachliteratur des Mittelalters. Festschrift Gerhard Eis* (Stuttgart, 1968), pp. 1–10; Franz H. Bäuml and Edda Spielmann, "From Illiteracy to Literacy: Prologomena to a Study of the Nibelungenlied," in *Oral Literature. Seven Essays,* ed. Joseph J. Duggan (London: Scottish Academic Press, 1975), pp. 62–73.

4. The history of popular participation in the Mass during the Middle Ages is compendiously treated by A. Franz, *Die Messe im deutschen Mittelalter. Beiträge zur Geschichte der Liturgie und des religiösen Volkslebens* (Freiburg, Br.: Herder, 1902).

5. Among Cistercians silence was so strictly enforced that a complex sign language was created; see Robert Z. Barakat, *The Cistercian Sign Language: A Study in Non-Verbal Communications,* Cistercian Studies Series No. 11 (Kalamazoo, Michigan: Cistercian Publications, 1975).

Gregorian chant

From the day of his entry the child sat with the other novices at the feet of the monks. Seven times each day the community gathered for prayer, the *opus Dei*—God's work.[6] Each week all the 150 Psalms of David had to be recited at least once. Soon the young man would know them by heart. The recitation of the Psalms was interrupted by antiphons and responsories, but these could be easily learned. Within a few weeks the child would associate the rustling of cloaks at the end of each prayer with the rising of the monks and the *gloria Patri*. The rhythmic repetition of the gesture of rising and bowing and its coincidence with a small canon of short formulas was easily associated with pious feelings and habits even before the novice was able to spell out the literal meaning of the Latin words. *Deo gratias*—thanks be to God—is felt as a response of relief at the end of a long Bible reading which takes place in the middle of the night. So also, in the refectory at noontime, it is the anxiously awaited sign that mealtime prayers are over and dinner may begin.[7]

Most of the Latin the pupil heard in the cloister was not conversationally modulated speech. Rather, it was a series of stylized invitations and responses, intoned according to the strict rules of plainsong.[8] Recitation differs from speech as much as the sound of dictation differs from that of an ordinary conversation. Prayers and lessons, lectures and calendar information were recited, not told. Latin was the articulation of song as much as of letters. There are many theories on the origins of plainsong, and its roots in the synagogue. On one point, however, all authorities are agreed: it exhibits peculiarities which can be detected in no other kind of music whatever, peculiarities so marked that they can scarcely fail to attract the attention of the most superficial hearer, and so constant that we find no difficulty in tracing them

6. For Introduction to the history of monastic hours, see Josef A. Jungmann, *Christian Prayer through the Centuries* (New York: Paulist Press, 1978). For orientation on the rich older literature, Henry Leclercq, "Bréviaire," in *Dictionnaire d'archéologie chrétienne et de Liturgie*, vol. 2, cols. 1262–1316 (Paris: Letouzey, 1925).

7. P. Riché, "La Vie quotidiènne dans les écoles monastiques d'après les colloques scolaires," in *Sous la règle de Saint Benoit,* Hautes études médiévales et modernes 47 (Geneva, 1981), pp. 417–26.

8. For general orientation to the history of Latin church singing, see Willi Apel, *Gregorian Chant* (Champaign: University of Illinois Press, 1958); for orientation to its musicological archaeology, see Henry Leclercq, "Chant romaine et grégorien," in *Dictionnaire d'archéologie chrétienne et de Liturgie*, vol. 3, cols. 256–311 (Paris: Letouzey, 1913); completed by A. Gatard, "Chant Grégorien du 9ᵉ au 12ᵉ siècle," in *Dictionnaire d'archéologie chrétienne et de liturgie*, vol. 2, col. 311–21 (Paris: Letouzey, 1913).

through every successive stage of development through which plainsong has passed from the third to the nineteenth century.[9] One of its characteristics is its tie to Church Latin, which remained to this day as tight as the tie of Roman letters to Latin in Hugh's youth. The simplest portion of plainsong were the so-called *accents* to be used in reading. They may be regarded as "the reduction under musical laws of the ordinary accents of spoken language, for the avoidance of confusion and cacophony in the union of many voices . . . as the impersonal utterance of the language of corporate authority, as distinguished from the oratorical emphasis of individual elocution."[10] Public reading of the twelfth century strikes the twentieth-century ear as a strange kind of song. Strict rules were given for the distinctive accent to be used for different kinds of books: the literally mono-tonous *cantus lectionis* for the glosses; the *tonus prophetiae, epistolae, evangelii* by which anyone, without understanding a word, would know that the Old Testament, St. Paul, or the Gospel, respectively, was being read. The more solemn parts of the liturgy had and still have their distinguishing musical characteristics corresponding to the season in which they are read. The Latin of the time was the product of the choir as much as of the scriptorium.

By the time of Hugh, western monasticism had been guided for over five hundred years by the Rule of St. Benedict. This Rule, still followed today, demands that the monks get up after midnight for more than a full hour of common prayer.[11] The rules of St. Victor in their twenty-eighth chapter assign to the book, *in persona*, the task of awakening the monks.[12] Even small details of the ceremony are spelled out in this chapter. At the appointed hour, preceded by two candles, the book is carried through the dormitories. He who carries it must not lazily push against the heavy volume with his head, nor cradle it negligently in his outstretched arms; he should proceed with great dignity, letting the book's upper edge rest on his chest. At each turn the monks in the small procession sing, "*Benedicamus domino,*" and the sleeping novices, at the very moment of waking, will stumble or step into the world of Latin with the answer, "*Deo gratias.*" Even brothers who are sick,

9. Consult on terminology George Grove, *A Dictionary of Music and Musicians* (New York: Macmillan, 1880), esp. vol. 2, pp. 760–69.

10. Ibid., vol. 1, p. 17.

11. C. Gindele, "Die Strukturen der Nokturnen in den lateinischen Mönchsregeln vor und um St. Benedikt," *Revue bénédictine* 64 (1954): 9–27.

12. Lucas Jocqué, and Ludovicus Milis, eds., *Liber ordinis Sancti Victoris Parisiensis,* Corpus Christianorum: Continuatio Medievalis 41 (Turnhout: Brepols, 1984), pp. 136–38.

and are not compelled to rise, should be gently nudged to acknowledge the nocturnal visit by the book.[13]

After fastening their belts, the monks will assemble in the darkness of the choir. The book is placed on the lectern in the middle of the nave. One candle is lighted in front of it, certainly not just to facilitate the recognition of the letters, but to remind us that Christ is the light which shines from these pages into the dark. The ceremonial celebration of the book, Latin, chant, and recitation thus form an acoustic phenomenon embedded in a complex architecture of rhythm, spaces, and gestures. All this could not but stick to the bones of the pupils when, after a short sleep before dawn and two more morning assemblies for Mass and the "little" hours, they finally sit cross-legged in front of a drill master for their *dictatus,* to give shape with their hands—inscribing the words on their wax tablets—to the Latin in whose melodic use they were already steeped.

The Latin monopoly over letters

The student used to Latin learned his words from the traces that the stylus left in the beeswax he had smoothed on his writing tablet before class. The teacher pronounced each syllable separately, and the pupils repeated in a chorus of syllables and words. As the teacher dictates to the pupil the pupil dictates to his own hand.[14] The *deogratias* which was a familiar utterance now takes on the shape of two successive words. The single words of Latin impress themselves as a sequence of syllables on the ear of the pupil. They become part of his sense of touch, which remembers how the hand moved to cut them in the wax. They appear as visible traces which impress themselves on the sense of sight. Lips and ears, hands and eyes conspire in shaping the pupil's memory for the Latin words. No modern language is taught through such an intense use of psychomotor memory traces left in the hand and eye as a result of writing.[15]

When we think of the alphabet, we see in it a tool for recording

13. *Potest tamen frater, quo circuit, facto modesto signo, infirmos, si dormierint, excitare* (ibid., pp. 138–40).

14. F. Gasparri, ed., "L'Enseignement de l'écriture à la fin du moyen âge: à propos du *Tractus in omnem modum scribendi,* ms 76 de l'abbaye de Kremsmünster," *Scrinium* 3 (1979): 243–65, table 3.

15. The student who applies himself to calligraphy in the Chinese tradition memorizes ideograms but does not intend to learn a language. The student who applies himself to the rudiments of Devanagari, the syllabic system created to record Sanskrit, traditionally is asked to concentrate his attention on the way his speech organs produce the different sounds and *sandhis* (ligatures). The student of the Semitic languages, Hebrew and Ara-

speech sounds. For one and a half thousand years this simply was not so. The letters, which without any change in form and number have proven their capacity to encode hundreds of different languages, were for this long time used for one exclusive purpose: writing Latin. But not Latin as it was spoken; rather, as it was alphabetized during the last centuries B.C. During the 650 years when Rome governed the Mediterranean world, not one of the tongues of the conquered and governed peoples was ever recorded in Roman letters. The monopoly of Latin over the Roman alphabet was so absolute that it has never been viewed as the result of a "taboo," and has never been considered as a surprising historical anomaly. This neglect of an available technology seems as impressive as the neglect of the wheel in pre-Columbian cultures, where only gods and playthings were ever put on a carriage.

The monopoly of Latin over the Roman letters, and equally of Greek over the Greek alphabet, was anchored in deep assumptions about the relation of shape and sound. When Cyril and Methodius, around 850, created "glagolic" as the appropriate language into which they could translate the Greek Bible for the Bulgarians, they also devised a new alphabet. They never thought of enlarging the Greek alphabet with a few signs needed to record Slavonic sounds.

This neglect of available tools in the face of unaccustomed tasks is even more startling if one considers that the Roman alphabet was not even used to write the Latin which people actually spoke. Starting with the first century A.D., the dialects spoken by Roman legionaries settled in Gallia and Hispania had ceased to sound like that spoken in their homes in Latium or Campania.[16] And even here, in the native regions of Latin, the orthographic conventions of 300 B.C. no longer reflected the cadences and sounds which people actually used when they spoke. During this entire period—from antiquity to Hugh's lifetime—and in the vast and politically differentiated area from the Black Sea to Spain, the Roman alphabet was not used to write down what people said in ordinary speech. Until the thirteenth century, it remained essentially a tool at the service of formal dictation.

---

bic, approaches the experience of the monastic pupil; but of course, he neither traces nor contemplates signs that stand for the intonation, the vowel sounds.

16. Carlo Battisti, "Secoli illetterati. Appunti sulla crisi del latino prima della riforma carolingia," *Studi Medievali* (1960): 369–96. According to E. Pulgram, "Spoken and Written Latin," *Language* 26 (1950): 458–66, after the year 1000 the way Latin was pronounced had ceased to have any influence on Latin orthography. See also Roger Wright, "Speaking, Reading and Writing Late Latin and Early Romance," *Neophilologus* 60 (1976): 178–89.

There were exceptions: for example, the cursive hand was used by Roman notaries to authenticate documents and by Roman rhetors to prepare notes for their speeches; it was occasionally used by people such as St. Jerome to pen a letter by his own hand in candlelight, rather than to dictate when his scribe was available. Even after the loss of cursive skills, many an early and high medieval cleric penned his own notes. There was nothing intrinsic to the Carolingian minuscule alphabet which made the scribe a necessity for the author.

There are also some instances where the Roman alphabet was used before Hugh's time to record non-Latin speech forms. Anglo-saxon before the Norman conquest is the outstanding example. Furthermore, the alphabet was occasionally used in the attempt to create translations. Under Charlemagne the Benedictine monasteries around Lake Constance worked on Germanic-Latin glossaries from which they then produced vernacular versions of the Rule of St. Benedict and parts of the Gospel. But the more such evidence is examined, the more the use of the alphabet in recording non-Latin documents appears as a set of exceptions confirming the identification of Roman letters with Latin.

Only after Hugh's death—and then quite suddenly—does the alphabet begin to be used by chroniclers and notaries to record actual speech. A recording device available for so long, and known by people born into languages distinct from Latin, was only now routinely used to fix these in written form. From the point of view of the historian of technology, this is a privileged instance to test fundamental hypotheses. Instead of confirming the theory that tasks become possible when the tools to perform them become available, or the other which says that tools are created when tasks come to be socially desirable, this use of the ABC suggests that an eminently suitable and complex artificial device already available within a society will be turned into a tool for the performance of a task only at that historic moment when this task acquires symbolic significance. The page had to give birth to the visible text, the "faithful" had to give birth to the moral self and the legal person before the dialect spoken by that person could be visualized as "a" language.

The alphabetic recording of Germanic or Provençal dialects did not immediately lead to the recognition that the alphabetization of speech had brought about the creation of other languages comparable to Latin. One of the best proofs for this comes from Uwe Pörksen:[17] For the first two generations in which there was a heavy demand for Provençal texts in Germany, and vice versa, not one of the great songs

17. In conversation with the author.

was translated directly from one vernacular language into the other. In every instance, a Latin version of the song was made first, and only then a translation from the Latin language into recorded vernacular speech. Then, by the end of the twelfth century, it seemed natural to use Roman letters for Germanic, Romance, Italian. The phonography of a kind of Latin which had already ceased to be spoken when Vesuvius buried Pompeii, only after a full millennium became a phonetic recording device for the registration of actual speech. Whatever is said, whatever is sung and, soon, whatever is thought, can end up on the surface of a leaf. As the text is now detached from the concrete object, from this rather than that specific parchment, so the signs of the ABC have acquired their independence from Latin.

But Latin does not overnight lose its immemorial claim to be the only true language. Slowly but inexorably the idea takes hold that not only scribes but all speakers use language when they speak, and this language can be written, analyzed, taught, and translated.[18] This reified abstraction of speech, called language, can start on its career to define reality in a new way. To speak can now be conceived as spelling out one's thought.

The lines of the *Didascalicon* are still written to be mouthed. The native sound of the alphabetic signs is still Latin. Greek or Hebrew morsels are carried along by the flow of Latin, over which a few dozen genial contemporaries born between 1060 and 1110 have acquired an exceptional hold.

A century later, St. Francis writes the first poem in the Italian tongue. Quite unlike the Flemish Hugh, born at the dawn of the twelfth century, who could not dictate, author, or formulate the deepest movements of his heart unless he gave them a Latin expression, the merchant's son of Umbria, at the dawn of the thirteenth century, was able to write his praise of sun and moon as a vernacular love song conceived on the model of a Provençal lay. As a matter of course, he uses Roman letters to record, word for word, what he has to say to the poor. While Hugh's pilgrimage to Wisdom leads up the rungs of Latin lines, Francis of Assisi exposes his naked self on Italian street corners.

18. Ivan Illich, *Shadow Work* (London: Boyars, 1981). See especially the second and third chapters on the first grammar of a spoken European tongue, the *Gramática Castellana,* by E. A. de Nebrija, published 1492.

❦ FIVE

Scholastic Reading

Hugh adds a preface

Shortly after Hugh died in the cloister of St. Victor on the left bank of
the Seine in Paris in 1142, Abbot Guilduin had a list of Hugh's works
prepared, which came to rest in Merton College in Oxford. According
to this list, the *Didascalicon* had no introduction.[1] Hugh is one of the
few early authors for whom an inventory has been preserved, and for
this reason one is inclined to trust it. However, there is also contrary
evidence. In some manuscripts going back to the time when Hugh was
still alive, a preface precedes the first chapter.[2] In Buttimer's critical
edition of the *Didascalicon*, this introduction takes up sixty-two lines.
It is, therefore, a major text, since only a few of the chapters in the
whole *Didascalicon* exceed it in length.

This preface is written in Hugh's style; in tone and structure it is so
characteristic of Hugh's work that it is generally accepted as authentic.
But historians are not in agreement on why it is missing in some manuscripts. According to one opinion, Hugh wrote it for the first version
and later tried to suppress it. Others think that only years after the
Didascalicon had been passing from hand to hand did Hugh feel the
need of an introduction, and the copies that lack it are made from

1. Joseph de Ghellinck, "La Table des matières de la première édition des oeuvres de
Hughes de St.-Victor," *Recherches des sciences religieuse* 1 (1910): 270–96. The first
reference to the *Didascalicon* by incipit.
2. R. Goy, *Die Überlieferung der Werke Hugos von Sankt Viktor. Ein Beitrag zur
Kommunikationsgeschichte des Mittelalters*, Monographien zur Geschichte des Mittelalters 14 (Stuttgart, 1976). A major study of all manuscripts by Hugh.

earlier manuscripts. Be this as it may, the introduction tells a lot about the social ambience in which Hugh wrote.[3]

The duty to read

There are many persons whose nature has left them so poor in ability[4] that they can hardly grasp with their intellect even easy things and of these persons I believe there are two sorts. There are those who, while they are not unaware of their own dullness,[5] nonetheless struggle after knowledge with all the effort they can put forth and who, by tirelessly keeping up their pursuit,[6] deserve to obtain as a result of their will power what they by no means could possess as a result of their work. Others, however, because they know that they are in no way able to encompass the highest things neglect even the least and, as it were, carelessly at home in their own sluggishness, they all the more lose the light of truth in the greatest matters by their refusal to learn those smallest of which they are capable.[7]

Hugh opens the preface with a double distinction. There are some who are much less gifted than others, and among the dull, there are two kinds. For the first, the humble, Hugh opens the prospect that their discipline will lead them to insights beyond the reach of their intelligence.[8] The second, the complacent, he sees going from bad to worse: "not knowing stems from weakness; but contempt of knowledge springs from a wicked will."[9]

Reading, for Hugh, is a moral rather than a technical activity. It is at the service of personal fulfillment. Hugh is as much concerned with how to support the well-intentioned blockhead as to prevent the vain from rotting.

3. Still delightful to read: Charles H. Haskins, "The Life of Medieval Students Illustrated by Their Letters," *The American Historical Review* 3 (1897–98): 203–29.

4. *Multi sunt quos ipsa adeo natura ingenio destitutos reliquit* (DB, p. 1).

5. *Licet suam hebetudinem non ignorent* (DB, p. 1).

6. *Studio insistentes* (DB, p. 1).

7. *DT*, preface, p. 43.

8. The opening sentence of the preface sounds to me like a defence of his book by the author, called forth by a strange—and little known—academic sect, called Cornificians. They maintained that study-discipline was futile for those lacking in ability, and superfluous for those possessing it. See Daniel McGarry, *The Metalogicon of John of Salisbury* (Berkeley: University of California Press, 1955), pp. 9–33.

9. *DT*, preface, p. 43. *DB*, praefatio, p. 1: *nescire siquidem infirmitatis est, scientiam vero detestari, pravae voluntatis.*

However, there is still another sort of man whom nature has enriched with the full measure of ability and to whom she shows an easy way to come to truth. Among these, even granting inequality in the strength of their ability, there is nevertheless not the same virtue or will in all for the cultivation of their natural sense through practice and learning.[10]

After having divided the dull into two moral classes, Hugh ranges the gifted by endowment, virtue, and will. He then turns to two special classes among those who are well endowed: the irresponsible and those who are socially handicapped. Of the able,

> many . . . are caught up in the affairs[11] and cares of this world beyond what is needful; or they are given over to the vices and sensual indulgences of the body; they bury the talent of God in the earth[12] seeking from it neither the fruit of wisdom nor the profit of good work.[13]

These he holds to be *valde detestabiles*, "utterly detestable."[14] If this statement were made by Hugh only about monks (many of whom never became technically literate) it would be surprising by its harshness. But, as I shall argue, Hugh here addresses, indirectly, the common man, whom he blames if and when the latter allows *negotia* (affairs, negotiations—distractions from leisure) to interfere with the search for *studium*, which is *otium*.

In spite of slender income

For others, lack of family wealth and a slender income[15] decrease the opportunity for learning. [Hugh is aware of the fact that the leisure he advocates is based on material conditions.] Yet, we decidedly do not believe that these [persons] can be altogether excused by these circumstances, since we see many laboring in hunger, thirst, and nakedness to attain the fruit of knowledge.[16]

---

10. *DB*, praefatio, p. 1: *non eadem tamen omnibus virtus aut voluntas est per exercitia et doctrinam naturalem sensum excolendi. DT*, preface, p. 43. For the meaning of *exercitium, exercitia*, see Jean Leclercq, "Exercices spirituels; antiquité et haut moyen âge," in *Dictionnaire de spiritualité*, vol. 4, cols. 1903–8 (Paris: Beauchesne, 1960).

11. *Negotia*: neg-*otium* is the negation of leisure, *otium*. It is, in this context, the choice of a lifestyle opposite to that of the monk who engages (*vacat*) in leisure (*otium*).

12. Mt. 25.18.

13. *DT*, preface, p. 43.

14. *DB*, praefatio, p. 1.

15. *Census*, sustenance.

16. *DT*, preface, pp. 43–44.

The *studium legendi,* according to Hugh, is a vocation addressed to all which translates into a duty to learn. "All," be they dull or bright, more or less able, be their will powerful or weak, become blameworthy if they refuse to advance in learning. No one before Hugh had formulated in such terms the doctrine of a universal duty to learn.

By raising the issue of economic inequality Hugh makes it clear that he does not address a closed monastic community. In a twelfth-century monastery, descent would count for the social status of a monk in the abbey; but independent economic resources would not affect the daily living conditions of individuals. If the novice was gifted, he was free to advance his literate skills, regardless of family background. Many novices would enter the convent at the age of seven, acquire these skills as children, and then vow themselves to lifelong residence (*stabilitas*) within the monastery they had entered. "Lack of family wealth and slender income" and, as a consequence, "laboring in hunger, thirst, and nakedness," was not the lot of a novice. Hugh here addresses not monks but the general population, the inhabitants of a budding and bustling medieval town. For townsmen, economic conditions obviously determine the student's leisure for studies.

> It is one thing when a person is not able, or to speak more truly, not easily able to learn [*discere*], and another when one is able but unwilling to learn [*scire*]. Just as it is more glorious to lay hold upon wisdom by sheer exertion, even though no resources support one, so, to be sure, it is more loathsome to enjoy natural ability and to have plenty of wealth, yet to grow dull in idleness [*torpere otio*].[17]

Quite obviously it would be wrong to understand Hugh as an advocate of universal education, schooling, or what we understand today by "literacy." Yet, in this treatise, *De studio legendi,* Hugh speaks of a universal call to learning.

No doubt, the idea that "all men" are called to learn some specific thing is implicit in the doctrine of the Church. All are called to the faith and to its profession. And Islam, in a formal sense, has given a specific expression of the duty to learn: Muslims have to know the prayers which they recite five times each day, be they in community or utterly alone. Hugh, in twelfth-century Paris, defines the duty to learn as a duty to read.

That Hugh thinks of townspeople, and not only of novices who become canons or of other children boarded with them, is also made plausible by something else: the entirely different manner in which he

17. *DT,* preface, p. 44.

addresses young boys who have left their families to become members of the community at St. Victor.

The Canon Regular edifies by his *lectio*

Hugh's treatise *De institutione novitiorum* is addressed to such new-comers "from the world." [18] On almost every page it stresses or implies the special, uncommon calling these children have accepted. While the introduction to the *Didascalicon* urges all those who come in contact with Hugh to accept *studium* as a duty, *De institutione* stresses the obligation of a select group. It emphasizes the assumptions current in the cloister of St. Victor in Hugh's generation about the purpose of the life of the community and its members.[19] *Studium,* as part and parcel of the way of life chosen by the aspiring canon, is for him a means to recover the image of God in himself, a likeness that had been obscured by sin.[20] But in his *studium* the novice is responsible not only for the state of his soul; by the example he gives through the manner in which he studies, it is his special task to "edify" the town community.[21]

When Hugh addresses novices, he wants them to study *coram Deo et coram hominibus. Coram*—"before the eyes of" or "in the face of"—both God and men. To the universal duty of all men to learn or study there corresponds the duty of the canon regular to teach: by his

18. This short but detailed work of about twenty pages (*PL* 176, 925A–952B) covers what the novices should do in various places, how they should dress, behave, speak, study, and eat.

19. See *PL* 176, 928A. On the history of the cloister of St. Victor, see Fourier Bonnard, *Histoire de l'Abbaye royale et de l'ordre des Chanoines Réguliers de St. Victor de Paris. Première période 1013–1500* (Paris: Savaète, 1907). On Hugh's *Didascalicon* within the new approach to teaching, see Jean Châtillon, "Le *Didascalicon* de Hugues de Saint-Victor," in *La Pensée encyclopédique au moyen âge* (Neuchâtel: Baconnière, 1966), pp. 63–76.

20. *De institutione,* prologue; *PL* 176, 925–26. Aelred of Rievaulx, *Speculum charitatis,* bk. 1, chs. 3–5; *PL* 195, 507C–510B. See also, Aelred of Rievaulx, *Opera omnia,* vol. 1, *Opera ascetica,* A. Hoste, O.S.B., and C. H. Talbot, eds. (Turnhout: Brepols, 1971): *De speculo caritatis,* bk. 1, ch. 1 (pp. 13–14); *De anima,* bk. 3, nos. 28–29, (p. 743); no. 44 (p. 751); nos. 50–51 (p. 754).

On the road that leads from the "region of dissemblance" to the restoration of God's image and likeness in the reader, see, for the school of St. Victor, Robert Javelet, *Image et ressemblance au 12e siècle de St. Anselm à Allain de Lille* (2 vols.; Paris: Letouzay, 1967), vol. 1, pp. 266–69, and notes, vol. 2, pp. 288ff.

21. *Docere,* which translates as "teach," had come in Church Latin to mean above all "to preach." *Instruere* (to instruct) and occasionally also *instituere* (to order) were used for the activity by which a teacher instructs someone who is in the role of a pupil. Though Hugh does use both terms, he stresses the task of the cleric as *edificare* (to edify).

way of life (*vita*) and his wisdom (*doctrina*), by his words (*verbo*) and his example (*exemplo*).[22] The study of Hugh's pupils is conceived by him as an activity that is social because it is exemplary. In his introduction Hugh says that with the first three books of the *Didascalicon* he *instructs* the reader in the rules to be observed in choosing and perusing secular books, and in the following sections he teaches how sacred books "ought to be read by the man who seeks in them the correction of his morals and a form of living."[23] With his novices Hugh has in mind their vocation, namely, what they will one day teach others by the example of their *forma vivendi*.[24]

Hugh here redefines the purpose of life in the cloister in the spirit of a new kind of ecclesial community to which he belongs, the Augustinian canons. He uses traditional language, but with a radically innovative stress. By emphasizing *exemplum* as the task of the teacher, and *aedificatio* as its result in the town community at large, Hugh recognizes that the new Canons Regular, and not just he as a person, stand on a watershed between monastic and scholastic reading.

The Rule of St. Benedict makes no explicit suggestion that one monk should be an example to the other.[25] Much less is monastic life presented as a moral example for people who "live in the world." Deference toward the fellow monk, tolerance of his weakness, love of each other, and obedience toward the abbot characterize the ideal monk as Benedict defines him in his Rule. Within the old Benedictine tradition it would be a loss of independence and freedom if the monk who prac-

22. Caroline Walker Bynum, *Docere verbo et exemplo: An Aspect of Twelfth-Century Spirituality*, Harvard Theological Studies 31 (Missoula: Scholar Press, 1979). See also, Caroline Walker Bynum, "The Spirituality of Regular Canons in the Twelfth Century: A New Approach," *Medievalia et Humanistica*, n.s. 11 (1973): 3–24. The crucial difference between canons and monks is not that canons claim the right or duty to preach, nor that they discuss preaching more frequently in their treatises *de institutione noviciorum*, but that they claim that *educare verbo et exemplo* is a crucial component of their life. See also, Marie-Dominique Chenu, "Moines, clercs et laïcs au carrefour de la vie évangélique," *Revue d'histoire ecclésiastique* 49 (1954): 59–80; E. W. McDonnell, "The Vita Apostolica: Diversity or Dissent," *Church History* 24 (1955): 15–31; Zoltan Alszegy, "Die Theologie des Wortes bei den mittelalterlichen Theologen," *Theologie und Predigt*, 1958: 233–57.

23. *DT*, preface, p. 45. *Deinde docet qualiter legere debeat sacram scripturam is qui in ea correctionem morum suorum et formam vivendi querit* (*DB*, p. 3).

24. See Marie-Dominique Chenu, "Civilisation urbaine et théologie. L'École de Saint-Victor au XIIᵉ siècle," *Annales: économies, sociétés, civilisations* 29 (1974): 1253–63.

25. A terminological study of the Benedictine Rule shows that *educare* is not the task of the teacher, but *regere* (to guide), *servire* (to serve), or *instruere* (to instruct). See B. Jaspert, "La tradizione litteraria dei termini *audire, aedificare, memorare, vacare*," *Review of Benedictine Studies* 6–7 (1977–78).

tices virtue were to look over his shoulder to worry about the example he might give outside the cloister. St. Bernard, who is Hugh's contemporary, carries this old tradition into the twelfth century. He, too, wrote a treatise on the formation of novices. The title itself indicates the different stress: *De gradibus humilitatis* talks to the aspiring Benedictine about "the degrees of humility" and never suggests that the monk should worry about edifying his community or people beyond the cloister wall. Hugh's *De institutione* is saturated with concern for the public influence of the canon, exercised by means of edification.

Hugh's community does not live according to the Rule of St. Benedict, but according to the one attributed to St. Augustine, which is two hundred years older. Benedict wrote his Rule after the decline of the Roman Empire, after the practical disappearance of Roman city life in western Europe. He wrote it for communities of a dozen monks each, who often lived in depopulated areas and provided for their own sustenance, thereby restoring wasteland to agriculture. There were few people around to give an example to in the dark period between the fall of Rome and the arrival of Arabic and Mongol invaders. Augustine's was written before this civilization cave-in.[26] He and his companions are still brought up in the spirit of citizenship. Mutual aid and the importance of mutual influence among brethren are mentioned in the Rule.[27] For Augustine, "two things are conscience and reputation. Conscience is for you, reputation for your neighbor. He who would trust his conscience and neglect his reputation is cruel. . . . Before all, show yourself an example of works."[28]

The Canons Regular, who come into being with the reformation of later medieval towns, choose the rule of Augustine over the rule of St. Benedict. They are concerned with the example they give those to whom they preach.[29] Hugh is one of the major figures in this renewal. He lives with the new concern for the example given by engaging in *lectio divina,* just before the *lectio divina* splits up into *lectio spiritualis,* which is prayer, and *studium,* which comes to be the acquisition

26. Henri-Irénée Marrou, *Saint Augustin et la fin de la culture antique,* 4th ed. (Paris: Boccard, 1958).

27. Melchoire Verheijen, ed., *Praeceptum,* 2 vols. (Paris: 1967), I, 115–19, 423, 426–28.

28. As quoted in Walker Bynum, "The Spirituality of Regular Canons in the Twelfth Century," p. 15.

29. Anselm of Havelberg, "Epistola Apologetica" (*PL* 188, 1229A): the Regular Canon "being generally sought out by rude people is chosen and accepted, and like a lantern lighting a dark place, teaching by word and example, is loved and honoured." See also G. Severino, "La discussione degli *ordines* di Anselmo de Havelberg," *Bolletino dell' Istituto Storico Italiano per il Medioevo e Archivo Muratoriano* 78 (1967): 75–122.

of knowledge. This position at a divide makes it possible for Hugh to speak of the canon-as-a-student as an individual who through his example contributes to the edification of an early twelfth-century town.[30] Two generations later the *studium legendi* can no longer articulate or mediate such a relationship between the learned and the unlettered. Reading in the thirteenth century loses its analogy to the bell which is heard and remembered by all the townsfolk, though it principally regulates the hours of canonical prayer for the cloister. Scholastic reading then becomes a professional task for scholars—and scholars who, by their definition as clerical professionals, are not an edifying example for the man in the street. They define themselves as people who do something special that excludes the layman.

The flipping of the page

M.-D. Chenu speaks of the watershed of certainties and perceptions that was crossed during the twelfth century, and that brought with it a transformation at least as deep as that which occurred in the age of the Reformation.[31] Southern speaks of it as a hinge time.[32] Another metaphor for it might be that of a page which is turned. Western culture, with its science and literature and philosophy, comes into existence with alphabetic writing, and cannot be understood without it. This western historical chronotope[33] has a history; the epochs of this history correspond to major mutations in the use of the ABC.[34] Around 1140 a page is turned. In the civilization of the book the monastic page is closed and the scholastic page opens. The cloister of St. Victor institutionalizes the precarious moment at which the page is being turned.

30. Benedictine monasteries occasionally accepted pupils who were not meant to become monks. Canons first open schools for such pupils in their cloister. R. Grégoire, "Scuola e educazione giovanile nei monasteri dal sec. IV al XII," in *Esperienze di pedagogia cristiana nella storia*, I (1983), pp. 9–44; Richard W. Southern, "The Schools of Paris and the School of Chartres," in *Renaissance and Renewal in the Twelfth Century*, ed. R. L. Benson and Giles Constable (Cambridge, Mass.: Harvard University Press, 1982), pp. 113–37.

31. Marie-Dominique Chenu, "L'Éveil de la conscience dans la civilisation médiévale," in *Conférence Albert le Grand 1968* (Montréal: Institut d'Études Médiévales, 1969), pp. 1off. and pp. 36ff.

32. Richard W. Southern, *The Making of the Middle Ages* (16th printing, New Haven: Yale University Press, 1976).

33. Or, to use Einstein's term, "spime," i.e., space-time.

34. Eric Havelock, *The Literate Revolution in Greece and Its Cultural Consequences*, Princeton Series of Collected Essays (Princeton: Princeton University Press, 1982), is a collection of papers that argue this point.

In Hugh's generation, St. Victor is peopled by a number of very sensitive men. They constitute a community, an urban college that established itself in a suburb of Paris. They share the life and many of the aspirations of a rising citizenry that challenges the predominance of feudalism. In contrast to Clairvaux, where Bernard reforms Benedictine life in a highly feudal style, St. Victor recovers the civic spirit of late antiquity, expressed in the rule of St. Augustine, and "defeudalises" monastic tradition.[35] The cloister becomes a metaphor for the recollection of the reader in his own interiority,[36] while the social demarcation and physical distance between townspeople and canons fades.

A new meaning can now be given to the relationship between the lay population and the cloistered ("regulated") cleric: he does eminently and visibly what all are called to pursue because they both live in the same world where, as Hugh insists, nothing is meaningless. "All of nature speaks of God, all of nature teaches man, all of nature reproduces its essential form—nothing in the universe is sterile." [37] The book of creation comprises both sides of the cloister walls, the arts of this world and Scripture both tell of God's work. As the leaf in the book of civilization is turned from the monastic to the scholastic page, a radical change takes place also in the reader: his social status before and after the turn is not the same.

The monastic reader—chanter or mumbler—picks the words from the lines and creates a public social auditory ambience. All those who, with the reader, are immersed in this hearing milieu are equals before the sound. It makes no difference who reads, as it makes no difference who rings the bell. *Lectio divina* is always a liturgical act, *coram*, in the face of, someone—God, angels, or anyone within earshot. There was no need, in the time between Benedict and Bernard, to insist on the social responsibility of the reader. It was obvious that his readings would reappear in the comments he would weave into his homily or letters.

Fifty years after Hugh, typically, this was no longer true. The technical activity of deciphering no longer creates an auditory and, therefore, a social space. The reader then flips through the pages. His eyes mirror the two-dimensional page. Soon he will conceive of his own mind in analogy with a manuscript. Reading will become an individualistic activity, intercourse between a self and a page.

35. Chenu, "L'Éveil de la conscience," p. 37.
36. *Claustrum animae.*
37. *DT* VI, 5, p. 145. *Omnis natura Deum loquitur, omnis natura hominem docet, omnis natura rationem parit, et nihil in universitate infecundum est (DB, p. 123).*

Hugh writes his *De institutione* as well as the *Didascalicon* at a moment when this transition is being prepared but has not yet happened. His reflections on the act and meaning of "reading" crown a tradition which grew during centuries. Yet in many subtle ways he also helps bring about the imminent landslide. He urges the student to devote himself to gratuitous *studium* and, simultaneously, to be a conscious individual example on this road.

Hugh "discovers" a universal duty to engage in study. He rediscovers the exemplary function which is assumed by the individual person who dedicates his life to learning. By doing so he draws the last consequences from the medieval praxis, in which the *lectio divina* is not just a clerical task.

The new cleric monopolizes letters

Clergy is derived from the Greek word for "lot" or "selection." Since the second century there has always been some clear distinction between laity and clergy in the Church. As much as the clergy's position might have changed, as much as its function might have evolved, the word has always connoted hierarchy and elite. Further, in both the eastern and western Church, from the third to the eleventh century, clergy was an elite made up exclusively of men.[38] It was seen as a group of men at the special service of the bishop, helping him to mediate revelation and grace to the people. That people, the laity, comprised men and women, monks and nuns.[39] During this whole period, the clergy were seen and treated as special representatives of the people as a whole. They defined themselves as those Christians who are charged to intercede with God for the whole of the Church, including the members of the clergy themselves.[40]

38. Elizabeth Schüssler-Fiorenza (*In Memory of Her: A Feminist Theological Reconstruction of Christian Origins* [New York: Crossroad, 1986]) uses feminist hermeneutics to argue the disappearance of coequal discipleship of women in the first and second century.

39. Toward the end of this period, especially in the struggles about investitures, in church law, and only for some purposes, monks and even nuns came to be defined as clerics.

40. Étienne Gilson, *Heloise and Abaelard* (Ann Arbor: University of Michigan Press, 1960). See the first chapter for a detailed discussion of the meaning given to the term "cleric" in the exchange of letters between the two. Yves Congar, "Modèle monastique et modèle sacerdotal en Occident de Grégoire VII (1073–1085) à Innocent III (1198)," in: *Études de civilisation médiévale (IXᵉ–XIIᵉ). Mélanges offerts à Edmond-René Labande* (Poitiers, 1973), explains that the clerical state in the eleventh century was an amorphous concept; it could mean as much as "ordained" or as "literate" and increasingly was defined as a right and a duty to the care of souls.

Against this background, monastic reading done during the early Middle Ages and well into the eleventh century is a service performed by a special community which represents the whole Church—and it is always done "for all" (*pro omnibus*). The monastic *lectio divina* continues the liturgical celebration of Mass performed by a priest (who himself might be a monk). Thus, when Hugh urges the *studium legendi* on "all," he urges those who live within the walls of the city not to behave like clergy, but to take their lives as seriously as monks. Reading for its own sake rather than for the management of laws and the recitation of clerical formulas was, traditionally, associated with the monk rather than with the clergy.

Chenu suggests a landslide; I like to think of it as a book-quake whose rumblings Hugh perceived. At the last moment of the old regime of the book, he proposes the *studium legendi* as a new ideal, a civic duty, and universal learning as a gratuitous, celebrative, leisurely intercourse with the book.

Of course this is not the constellation under which the universal duty to read and write became a fundamental ideal of modern societies. Gradually, over time, reading became a must for apologetical catechism, political pamphleteering, and then technological competence. When, much later, the ideal of universal literacy was formulated, reading skills for "all" were advocated in order to incorporate everyone into the new clerical culture, which was by then the opposite of a monastic style of life. Still, the redefinition of the reader which is already under way in Hugh's time was one step toward "reading" as the presupposition for citizenship, which our century accepts.

As a page in the history of the alphabet turns, the cleric comes to be seen as the one who can manage the new layout and consult the indices that give access to it. His scholastic skills make him into a cleric, be he priest ordained as helper to the bishop, lawyer at the service of a prince, scribe in a town hall, Benedictine monk, mendicant friar, or university teacher. The social duality opposing the bishop's pastoral and liturgical crew (clergy) to all the people (including their specialized contemplative readers, monks) gives way to a new duality. This novel late medieval social duality opposes those who are scribes and those who are not. The new technology of reading and writing put into place during the later twelfth century is immediately claimed as a scribal monopoly. The scribes define themselves as the literate, as opposed to those who are only hearers of the written word, simple lay people.[41]

41. The new clerics are the ones who need reference tools: W. Goetz, "Die Enzyklopädien des 13. Jahrhunderts," *Zeitschrift für die deutsche Rechtsgeschichte* 2 (1936): 227–50.

The new *scholastic* clergy veils the discontinuity. It claims continuity with the liturgical-pastoral clergy of old, and thereby inherits ecclesiastical status along with its traditional privileges. For instance, the rogue or vagabond who in the thirteenth or fourteenth century is arrested for a capital crime may claim clerical immunity from cruel punishment if he proves himself capable of deciphering or writing some simple sentences. This person is handed over to an ecclesiastic court, and thereby exempted from torture or, at least, from defaming death on the wheel.

Hugh's *Didascalicon* was written under the assumption that the new world then emerging, together with city freedoms and new peasant rights, would continue to "read" the old page. In fact, a new kind of book was read by people who came to read in a new frame of mind.[42] I like to imagine that Hugh, some years after dictating the *Didascalicon*, came to suspect that this might happen and prefaced the *Didascalicon* when he noticed how it could be misread.[43] I further like to fancy that this preface was embarrassing to the new clergy and that its disappearance from some early manuscripts may be due to purposeful suppression by a new cleric.

Reading, as it is culturally defined since the thirteenth century, is a competence reserved to the clergy and those taught by them.[44] Reading is not to be what Hugh envisioned: a way of life for those who are edified by nonfunctional, gratuitous exemplary readers, and who then freely emulate them.

42. For orientation on the state of research on later medieval literacy and illiteracy, consult Franz H. Bäuml, "Varieties and Consequences of Medieval Literacy and Illiteracy," *Speculum* 55 (1980): 237–65.

43. See Goy, *Die Überlieferung der Werke Hugos von Sankt Viktor.* One hundred twenty-five manuscripts of the *Didascalicon* have been preserved; more than of any other of Hugh's sixty works. Further, substantial parts of the *Didascalicon* are preserved in thirty-one manuscripts by other authors. Of the complete manuscripts, thirty-four are from the twelfth century, thirty-one from the thirteenth, and forty from the fifteenth. Since, as a rule of thumb, many more manuscripts of this kind are lost from the thirteenth than from the fifteenth century, and the number of copies preserved remains substantially the same, we may assume that Hugh was read by more people in the fifteenth century than in the thirteenth. Hugh was read throughout France, Germany, and eastern Europe, mostly by Benedictines, Cistercians, Augustinians, and Carthusians. Giles Constable, "The Popularity of Twelfth-Century Spiritual Writers in the Late Middle Ages," in *Religious Life and Thought* (London: Variorum, 1979); Jean Châtillon, "De Guillaume de Champeaux à Thomas Gallus: Chronique littéraire et doctrinale de l'école de Saint-Victor," *Revue du moyen âge latin* 8 (1952): 139–62; Bernhard Bischoff, "Aus der Schule Hugos von St. Viktor," in *Aus der Geisteswelt des Mittelalters,* ed. A. Lang; J. Lecher; and M. Schmaus; Beiträge zur Geschichte der Philosophie und Theologie des Mittelalters Band 3, Heft 1 (Münster, 1935), pp. 246–50.

44. There is a strong association between the new literacy and the celibacy of the secular clergy in the early twelfth century. In the tradition of Roman law, concubinage

Only in the twenties of the twelfth century could Hugh's utopia be formulated. Only at that point could the project be conceived that the renewal of society[45] be rooted in the universal acceptance of the call to the *studium legendi*. The way of life of monks in their prayerful search for wisdom did not become the model for universal literacy; rather, the way of life of scholastic clerks did. The *vita clericorum* became the ideal *forma laicorum,* the model to which laymen had to aspire, and by which they were inevitably degraded into the "illiterate," to be instructed and controlled by their betters.[46]

Silent reading

When historians observe the phenomenological break in twelfth-century reading they tend to reduce what happened to a transition from loud to silent intercourse with the page. Though this approach can easily veil the main issue pursued here—namely, the impact of alphabetic technique on the interpretation of human action—the "discovery" of silent reading is a good place to start.[47]

---

was an institution independent from both prostitution and marriage. Later imperial law accentuated the difference between concubinage and marriage, insisting on a choice between the freedom of the former and the security of the latter. The emperors from Constantine to Theodosius left this tradition intact. The Church was much less interested in the form of this relationship than in its indissolubility. Clerical concubinage of the first millennium must be seen in this context.

Only during the Gregorian reform of the late eleventh century were priests presented with a choice: to turn out their concubine or to lose benefice and livelihood. Both options put a new distance between priest and faithful, and fostered the formation of clerical communities which were not monastic in the old, Benedictine style.

The greater distance between the bishop's helpers and the laity had both financial and literary consequences. The Church became a *beneficium* (a benefice), perceived as a *corporatio* (a clerical corporation), and the clergy attempted to monopolize a new notarial power, which increased as charters prevailed over given words.

45. Gerhart H. Ladner, "Terms and Ideas of Renewal," in *Renaissance and Renewal in the Twelfth Century,* ed. R. L. Benson and Giles Constable (Cambridge, Mass.: Harvard University Press, 1982), pp. 1–33. See also Gerhart H. Ladner, *The Idea of Reform: Its Impact on Christian Thought and Action in the Age of the Fathers,* Part 1 (Cambridge, Mass.: Harvard University Press, 1961).

46. Herbert Grundmann, *"Literatus-illiteratus.* Der Wandel einer Bildungsnorm vom Altertum zum Mittelalter," *Archiv für Kulturgeschichte* 40 (1958): 1–65.

47. An encyclopaedic introduction to research on silent reading during the Middle Ages: P. Saenger, "Silent Reading: Its Impact on Late Medieval Script and Society," *Viator* 113 (1982): 367–414.

The first formal, explicit statement about the existence of a specifically silent way of reading is one more of Hugh's contributions.[48] "Reading consists of forming our minds upon rules and precepts taken from books."[49] And reading "is of three kinds: the reading of him who teaches, and reading of him who learns, and the reading of him who contemplates the book by himself."[50] Hugh distinguishes three situations: that of the person who listens to the voice of the pages as he reads aloud for the sake of others; that of the person who is read to, who reads through or "under" a teacher or lector; and that of the person who reads by inspecting the book.[51]

True, silent reading was occasionally practiced in antiquity, but it was considered a feat.[52] Quintilian speaks with admiration of one scribe who can visualize a whole sentence before reading it out, aloud. Augustine was puzzled by his teacher Ambrose, who occasionally read a book without moving his lips. Scribes usually copied books as they were dictated by another. When they were alone, in front of the original, they read it out loud, transcribing as much as they could keep in their auditive memory. Early monastic scriptoria were noisy places. Then, during the seventh century, a new technique, pioneered in Ireland, reached the continent. It consisted in placing spaces between single words. As this technique became common, monastic scriptoria

48. Occasional attempts to engage in muted, if not silent, reading within the *lectio divina* were made at earlier times. Joseph Balogh, "Voces Paginarum," *Philologus* 82 (1926–27): 84–109 and 202–40, gathers evidence from monastic authors since the seventh century.

49. *DT*, III, 7, p. 91. *Lectio est, cum ex his quae scripta sunt, regulis et praeceptis informamur (DB, p. 57).*

50. *DB*, III, 7, pp. 57–58: *Trimodum est lectionis genus: docentis, discentis, vel per se inspicientis.* Taylor (*DT*, III, 7, p. 91) translates the last three words in a different way: "and the independent reader's."

A parallel passage in Hugh's *De modo dicendi et meditandi: trimodum est genus lectionis, docentis, discentis vel per se inspicientis. Dicimus enim, lego librum illi et lego librum ab illo et lego librum (PL, 176, 877).*

For the purposes of exploring what Hugh did and meant to do when he read, a commentary on this very short work could be as fruitful as a commentary on the *Didascalicon.*

For interpretation of this work, see Saenger, "Silent Reading."

51. See also John of Salisbury, *Metalogicon,* 1.24 (ed. Daniel McGarry [Berkeley: University of California Press, 1955], p. 36). The word "reading" is equivocal. It may refer either to the activity of teaching and being taught, or the activity of studying things by oneself.

52. F. di Capua, "Osservazioni sulla lettura e sulla preghiera ad alta voce presso gli antichi," *Rendiconti dell'Accademia di Archeologia, Lettere e Belle Arti di Napoli,* n.s. 28 (1953–54): 59–62.

became silent.[53] Copyists could grasp single words with their eye as if they were ideograms and transfer them to the page on which they were working. However, this budding ability to read by sight alone is not yet the meditative silent return to the pages that followed reading, the exercise to which meditation and the "third mode of reading" pertain.[54]

We must look at the history of medieval writing techniques in order to understand this stage in the history of reading. Our attempt at a historical ethology of reading demands that we be able to observe how the dividing line between activities classed as "reading" and other activities classed as "writing" shifts over the decades.

Today it seems obvious that these two verbs refer to easily distinguishable acts. Historically this is not so. Bonaventure a century later still gropes to differentiate between the scribe, the compiler, the commentator, and the author. We must now distinguish more carefully between the author as dictator and his secretary as scribe.

The *scriptor* holds the pen and the *dictator* directs it. Only in exceptional circumstances would the 12th-century author of a page take the stylus into his own hands to put a draft onto a wax tablet. The idea of taking the reed or of penning it on expensive parchment would not occur to an author. This was the task of another person, called *amanuensis*, the scrivener or penman who lends his hand to the *dictator*.

We have good descriptions of some authors at work. Origen dictates to a major staff.[55] His rich friend Ambrose of Nicomedias provided him with the necessary funds. His huge productivity in a short time can be explained only if one attends to the fact that Roman stenography had just then reached its highest point.[56] At fixed intervals *tachy-*

53. Karl Christ, *The Handbook of Medieval Library History*, trans. and ed. by Theophil M. Otto (Metuchen, N.J.: Scarecrow Press, 1984), p. 30. The original: *Handbuch der Bibliothekzwissenshcaft*, vol. 3, *Geschichte der Bibliotheken*, chap. 5, "Das Mittelalter" (2d ed., Wiesbaden: Verlag Otto Harrassowitz, 1950–65).

54. The evolution of two iconographic types can be used to reconstruct the history of reading in the early and high Middle Ages: the representation of Evangelists and that of the *dictator* surrounded by scribes. Evangelists write under dictation from God, often represented by a bird twitting into their ear—until 700. Then a new type appears: the Evangelist who copies from a narrow scroll occasionally borne in its beak by a bird. See E. Kirschbaum. "'Evangelien' and 'Autorenbildnis,'" in *Lexikon für christliche Ikonographie*, vol. 1, cols. 301–2, and vol. 2, cols. 696–98 (Freiburg: Herder, 1968).

55. For a detailed description of Origen's working method, see Joseph de Ghellinck, *Patristique et moyen âge: études d'histoire littéraire et doctrinale*, 2 vols. (Paris: Desclée de Brouwer, 1947). See also Theodore C. Skeat, *The Use of Dictation in Ancient Book Production*, Proceedings of the British Academy 42 (London, 1956). See pp. 179–208.

56. A. Mentz, "Die tironischen Noten. Eine Geschichte der römischen Kurzschrift," *Archiv für Urkundenforschung* 17 (1942): 222–35.

graphers, speed writers, replaced each other. After taking several wax tablets in shorthand, they then dictated from them to an intermediary, who put them into fully extended longhand. Only from this draft a small army of women, *calligraphers*, penned the master from which copies for the reader would be made. Ambrose counted on a similar establishment. However, of Ambrose we know that he was an exception to the rule. Occasionally he was seen reading without even a murmur, and he himself tells us that, sometimes at night, next to a lighted candle, he would pen a letter to a friend. He even invented a term for such an autograph: *"hic lucubratiunculam dedi,"* "here I am addressing you a little candle bottom!"

Among the authors of the twelfth century there is one about whose habits we are particularly well informed: Bernard, the abbot who could draw on the monks of a large community to staff his writing room, the scriptorium.[57] We know the names of five of his secretaries. This enables us to reconstruct the classification of activities as they were divided among his assistants.[58] Bernard talks (*loquitur*) or says (*dicit*) something. These utterances (*dicta*) are put down by another hand (*a-manu-ensis*, "handy-man"). This scribe draws them on a waxed board with his *stylus*, a pointed instrument made out of wood or horn. He scratches the letters into the wax-covered surface. What he does reminds the onlooker of plowing (*exarare*). Not infrequently this first-stage scribe is called a plowman and the lines are perceived as furrows from which the seed of words will flower.[59] The metaphor which compares the *dictator* with the sower, and the scribe with the plowman, comes from Isidore of Seville and by Hugh's time has been well established.

In fact, the image of the plowman nicely renders the toil imposed on a medieval amanuensis, if he is compared to his analogue in antiquity. The technique of shorthand had been lost in the interval. Cicero and

---

57. On the praxis in the scriptorium of the twelfth century, see J. Vezin, "L'Organisation matérielle du travail dans les scriptoria du haut moyen âge," in *Sous la Règle de saint Benoît* (Geneva, 1982), pp. 427–31; J. Vezin, "La Fabrication du manuscrit," in *Histoire de l'édition française*, ed. H. J. Martin and R. Chatier (Paris: Promodis, 1982), pp. 25–48; J. Vezin, *Les 'scriptoria' d'Angers au 11° siècle* (Paris: H. Champian, 1974).

58. This reconstruction was attempted by Jean Leclercq, "Saint Bernard et ses secrétaires," *Revue bénédictine* 61 (1951): 208–29.

59. Peter the Venerable (d. 1156) *Libri epistolarum*, Bk. I, letter 20; *PL* 189, 97D: Monks cannot work in the fields, "but—what is better—their pen in hand is converted into a plow for cultivating fields of holy letters on the page." *sed (quod est utilius) pro aratro convertatur manus ad pennam, pro exarandis agris divinis litteris paginae exarentur.* Quoted in L. Gougaud, "Muta praedicatio," *Revue bénédictine*, 42 (1930), p. 171.

Origen spoke at any speed they wanted; their secretaries could follow them word for word. Bernard had to switch from speaking (*dicere*) to a different deliberate diction (*dictare*) if he wanted his sentences taken down *verbatim*.[60] His time had not only lost the Roman signs for tachygraphy, but the monks in Clairvaux also did not know cursive writing. Sometimes a *dictator* had to repeat a word several times until his novice got it right. But most texts from medieval authors are not that carefully dictated and are not their author's words in the modern sense.

Scriptura (scripture) or *littera* (the literal line) come into being when, in the *dictator*'s absence, the rough letters on the tablet are carefully penned on parchment. In Bernard's case we have two clean copies prepared from the same dictation which resulted in two distinct texts. We may assume that they were taken down and elaborated by two different monks. No doubt, sometimes Bernard follows the example of Cicero and asks that his letter be re-read to him, to hear how it sounds, perhaps to make a change for the better, a *correctio*. Much more often his dictation is put into circulation without his review.[61] The habit of signing a text—unless it is a charter—has not yet been established.[62]

Even on those rare occasions when Bernard engages in the *correctio* of a dictation, this in no way resembles the proofreading we know. Proofreading is the correction of an ideal copy that will then be printed, producing many exact copies. Bernard just took it for granted that his dictation would change each time it was copied. Besides this, proofreading presupposes that one person read aloud while another silently scans, a skill which was neither practiced nor in demand at the time. We know that when Bernard spoke, told, or dictated a passage, his amanuensis listened and mumbled. He picked up Bernard's dictation, and—in the conception of his time—then dictated it by mumbling to his own hand: The scribe's mouth guided the hand that held the stylus.[63] Writing—like reading—remained a mumbling activity.

60. For the etymological shift from *dicere* (say), to *dictare* (say with emphasis), toward "compose," see A. Ernout, "Dictare, dicter, allem dichten," *Revue des études latines* 29 (1951): 155–61.

61. Pascale Bourgain. "L'Édition des manuscrits," in *L'Histoire de l'édition française*, ed. H. J. Martin and R. Chartier (Paris: Promodis, 1982), pp. 48–75.

62. W. Schlögl, *Die Unterfertigung deutscher Könige von der Karolingerzeit bis zum Interregnum durch Kreuz und Unterschrift. Beiträge zur Geschichte und zur Technik der Unterfertigung in Mittelalter,* Münchener Historische Studien, Abt. Geschichtliche Hilfswissenschaften 16 (Kallmünz: Michael Lassleben, 1978).

63. P. Rassow, "Die Kanzlei St. Bernhards von Clairvaux," *Studien und Mitteilungen zur Geschichte des Benediktinerordens und seiner Zweige* 34 (1913): 63–103 and 243–93.

This is the reason why a monk, who for punishment was banned to his cell with the order to observe strict silence, was also forbidden to write; he could not have guided his own pen without breaking the silence the abbot had imposed on him.

The scholastic *dictatio*

Hugh spoke to his students. A century later, Thomas Aquinas lectured to them. If Hugh spoke in front of any open book the page was of parchment and he commented on its lines. Thomas came to class with his own lecture notes. Unlike Hugh, Thomas wrote in cursive style, fit for jotting down key words. And he wrote on paper which was flat, cheap, and did not have to be nailed down like rambunctious leather. Hugh's novices read his speeches or utterances (*loquela, dicta*), while university students followed Thomas's composition (*compositio*).

By the late thirteenth century, students had gotten used to taking dictation from their teachers.[64] The teacher's spoken words were grasped by the student as he read back to himself the dictation he had just taken. Early twelfth-century students in miniatures are shown listening to their teacher. Late fourteenth-century students either take dictation or sit in front of an outline of the teacher's lecture that they have picked up from a public copyist before class. The scholastic argument has become so articulate and complex that it can be followed only if assisted by a visual aid.

In the fourteenth century, disputes arose among teachers at the Sorbonne concerning the appropriate way of imparting a lecture.[65] There was discontent among students, shared by some faculty, because several teachers used their students as copyists to whom they dictated books written by others, with the intent of peddling the product resulting from their class.

This form of exploitation was certainly an extreme. But we know from the disputes that by the late fourteenth century most university teaching consisted of dictation and the taking of notes. What the teacher did was called *nominare* (spell out) or *pronunciare ad pennam* (articulate for the pen). It was also called *legere ad calamum:* reading right into the reed with which the student inks the page. The students

---

64. In Spanish universities, it is still common that a student asks me, "Maestro, ¿donde dicta?" (Where do you dictate your class?).

65. The Senate of the Sorbonne repeatedly requested that teachers limit dictation to summaries. However, the frequency with which these ordinances had to be repeated makes it probable that they were not observed.

came to be seen as readers.[66] From the texts of concerned teachers we can see that it was usual for the lecturer to repeat one and the same phrase several times until he was certain that every student had gotten it down. The auditor of antiquity and the crowd of Hugh's novices had turned into an army of scribes, understanding the teacher's argument only by looking at its text.

In Hugh's time, *philosophari* still meant "to live the life of a monk" (*monachum agere*). By the thirteenth century the identification of *lectio, philosophari,* and *conversio morum* had retired into a few cloisters, and Hugh's incipit had ceased to be understood.[67]

66. Istvan Hajnal, *L'Enseignement de l'écriture aux universités médiévales* (Budapest, 1954). See also B. Michael, *Johannes Buridan: Studien zu seinem Leben, seinen Werken und zur Rezeption seiner Theorien im Europa des späten Mittelalters* (Phil. Diss., Berlin, 1985), pp. 239 ff.

67. Jean Leclercq, *Études sur le vocabulaire monastique du moyen âge*, Studia Anselmiana Fasciculum 48 (Rome: St. Anselmo, 1961); see pp. 39–79. Du Cange, *Glossarium mediae infimae latinitatis*, vol. 6, pp. 237 and 305.

 # SIX

From Recorded Speech to the
Record of Thought

The alphabet as a technology

Hugh's *Didascalicon* is, among other things, a crucial witness about a turning point in the history of that technology which has shaped western reality in a most profound way. The technology to which I refer is, of course, the alphabet.[1] The twelfth century inherited twenty-odd Roman letters.[2] The basic sequence of these letters went back via the Etruscans and seventh-century Greeks to the Phoenicians, and from there to some north Semitic tribe in Palestine. Further, the Middle Ages inherited a set of tools for writing: wax tablets, parchment, stylus, reed, pen, and brush.[3] From the late imperial epoch, the Middle Ages inherited the book: the techniques of cutting a scroll into sheets, of

1. For an introduction to the study of the alphabet as a technology, and its history as such, see Walter J. Ong, *Orality and Literacy: The Technologization of the Word* (London: Methuen, 1982), and also the annotated bibliography of Ivan Illich and Barry Sanders in *ABC: The Alphabetization of the Popular Mind* (San Francisco: North Point Press), 1988.

2. "The only permanent additions of the Middle Ages were the signs U, W, and J; actually they were not additions, but differentiations from existing letters: U (for the vowel sound U to distinguish it from the consonantal V) and the consonantal W were both easy differentiations of V—while J, the consonantal 'i' is only a slight alteration" (David Diringer, *The Alphabet: A Key to the History of Mankind*, vol. 1, 3d ed. [New York: Funk and Wagnalls, 1968; orig. 1848]).

3. The stylus was used to scratch letters on tablets of wax. The writing brush was made from a reed, cut to a point and frayed so as to absorb ink more easily than a clean-cut and sliced edge. Since the sixth century A.D., the pen was made from a quill. It was sometimes a feather (Latin, *penna*) whose point was stuffed with absorbent material.

stitching these sheets together, and binding them between covers into a book.

These technical elements were left substantially unchanged during the twelfth century. But, during the middle of the century they were integrated into a set of new techniques, conventions, and materials. Some of these innovations were rediscoveries of skills known in antiquity—cursive handwriting is an example.[4] Other techniques were imported: the technique to fabricate a new plastic, paper, was imported from China via Toledo. Other, more subtle techniques were outright inventions made in western scriptoria: alphabetic arrangement of key words, subject indexing, and a kind of page layout suited for silent scanning. Finally, the time of the great Gothic cathedrals was also the time in which the truly portable book was constructed. As a result, the inherited two dozen letters and their ABC sequence became part of a qualitatively new technology and the basis for a set of unprecedented personal and social patterns of behavior.[5]

I want to discover how these old and new technologies were integrated shortly after 1128 (the year when the first copies of Hugh's manuscript began to circulate), to grasp in which ways this integration led to a form of reading different from that practiced a century earlier and a century later. I read the *Didascalicon* out of my general interest in the symbolic interaction of "technology and culture"—more precisely, tradition and purpose, materials, tools, and formal rules for their use.[6]

4. The transition from a script in which single letters, lower case *minuscules* or upper case *majuscules,* are neatly placed next to each other to one in which all the letters of a word or expression are flowing as one single line from the writer's tool, is both technically and symbolically an important change which happens during the late twelfth and early thirteenth century. In this transition several factors are mirrored: the increasing use of the pen (rather than of dictation) by the author; a new status of the literate segment of the population; and a new set of instruments—mainly the introduction of paper. On this consult O. Hörm, *Schriftform und Schreibwerkzeug. Die Handhabung der Schreibwerkzeuge und ihr formbildender Einfluß auf die Antiqua bis zum Einsetzen der Gothik* (Vienna, 1918).

5. Michel Rouche, "Des origines à la Renaissance," in *Histoire générale de l'enseignement et de l'éducation en France,* ed. L. -H Parias, vol. 1 (Paris: Nouvelle Libraire de France, 1983). The first four carefully edited and illustrated volumes deal with successive stages of written culture in France. Both the techniques of writing and reading and their relevance to reading are examined by the contributors.

6. It would be tempting at this point to speak of a transformation of media and communication in the twelfth century. To speak of newly created hardware, such as paper and vellum and felt-tipped feathers, and new software, such as footnoting, highlighting, indexing, letter-style changes, etc. I carefully abstain from this use of recently shaped concepts to explain long past events. This commentary of the *Didascalicon* ought to

I want to understand what Hugh did when he read the book of his time, what habits and meanings were shaped by the interplay of the social skill of reading and the recording technique called "book" or *litterae* at that time. I want to interpret what Hugh intended to do by reading, to understand what significance he gave to the use of alphabetic technology and reading habits within the context of a Canon Regular's life. I want to understand the symbolic effects of an age-specific technology on the habits of a particular historical time.[7]

From the trace of utterance to the mirror of concept

Before Hugh's generation, the book is a record of the author's speech or dictation. After Hugh, increasingly it becomes a repertory of the author's thought, a screen onto which one projects still unvoiced intentions.

As a young man, Hugh was introduced to monastic reading. He mainly *listened* to the book. He listened when he read it to himself, when he chanted the responses in choir, when he attended a lecture in the chapter room. Hugh wrote a treatise on the art of reading for people who would listen to the sound of the lines. But he composed his book at the end of an epoch; those who actually used the *Didascalicon* during the next four centuries no longer read with tongue and ear. They were trained in new ways: the shapes on the pages for them became less triggers for sound patterns than visual symbols of concepts. They were literate in a "scholastic" rather than "monastic" way. They no longer approached the book as a vineyard, a garden, or the landscape for an adventuresome pilgrimage. The book connoted for them much more the treasury, the mine, the storage room—the scrutable text.

In Hugh's generation the book is like a corridor with the *incipit* as its main entrance. If anyone thumbs through it hoping to find a certain passage, there exists little more chance of happening upon it than if the book had been opened randomly. But after Hugh the book can be entered randomly, with a good chance of finding what one looks for. It is still a manuscript, not a printed book, but technically it is already

provide distance to twentieth-century concepts, and stress the reasons for which their application to medieval scriptoria around 1150 veils more than it reveals of the historical meanings of events for the people who experienced them.

7. Ludolf Kuchenbuch, *Schriftlichkeitsgeschichte als methodischer Zugang: das Prümer Urbar 893–1983*, Einführung in die Ältere Geschichte, Kurseinheit 2 (Hagen: Fernuniversität, 1987).

a substantially different object. The flow of narration has been sliced up into paragraphs whose sum total now makes up the new book.

What this meant can be illustrated by an experience known to most of us today. Until the late 1970s, musical records could be replayed, but there was no sure and easy way of access to a specific passage. By the late 1980s not only elapsed-time counters, but also index numbers to identify movements, operatic scenes, and so on, had become standard features on audio players, enabling random access. In a similar way, the book for the monastic reader was a discourse which you could follow, but into which you could not easily dip at a point of your choosing. Only after Hugh does easy access to a specific place become a standard procedure.[8]

Before Hugh, old books grew by mere accretion. During Hugh's lifetime, editing starts; legal decrees are ordered and collected; all known commentaries of Church Fathers on the Bible, verse by verse, are assembled; Abaelard gathers contrasting opinions on the same theological issue. Tradition is cannibalized and compiled according to the new editors' whim. But Hugh is not one of them.

After Hugh's death, students begin to use these compilations. A new kind of reader comes into existence, one who wants to acquire in a few years of study a new kind of acquaintance with a larger number of authors than a meditating monk could have perused in a lifetime. These new demands are both stimulated and met by new reference tools. Their existence and use is profoundly new. And once these tools are invented they remain fundamentally unchanged until the text composer program of the 1980s. A mutation of comparable depth begins only then.

These shifts from the recording of speech to the recording of thought, from the record of wisdom to the record of knowledge, from the transmission of authorities inherited out of the past to the storage of promptly usable, well-coined "knowledge" can of course be understood as a reflection of a new mentality and economy during the twelfth century. The changes in literate technique can be viewed as a response of the clerical trades to the demands of princes, lawyers, and merchants. But I want to look at this interaction between society and the page from the particular perspective of the impact of the recording technology. How did the use of new techniques foster new ways of conceiving reality?

8. Edwin A. Quain, "The Medieval *Accessus ad Auctores*," *Traditio* 3 (1945): 215–64. See also Nigel F. Palmer, "Kapitel und Buch: zu den Gliederungsprinzipien mittelalterlicher Bücher," *Frühmittelalterliche Studien* 23 (1989): 43–88.

In the hundred years after Hugh's death, the estimated number of written accounts and legal charters in England multiplied by a factor of 50 to 100.[9] This alphabetical technologization of the word had enormous consequences both on a practical and symbolic level.[10] Described reality became legally more powerful than the witness's word; charters got the last word at court. In my interpretation of the *Didascalicon*, I have explored how these changes affected the axioms by which social reality emerges, how they affected the mind-set of future generations.

From the comment on a story to the story about a subject

In Hugh's youth, learned books were either venerable "scriptures" (Bible, Church Fathers, philosophers) or commentaries upon them. The teacher let the text of a scripture determine the sequence of his own exposition. *Ordo glossarum sequitur ordinem narrationis.* Sometimes the *glossa* was visually incorporated into the *narratio* upon which it commented. But glosses were also written on the margin or between the lines. This way of glossing is a visual consequence of the mental process of monastic reading. For example, an *auctoritas* says that "all forms of science are at the service of Holy Scripture." Nothing which went through the mind of the reader was deemed inappropriate as a commentary to such a text. Texts then grew out of tangents appended to older texts, which were slowly absorbed by them.

During the first quarter of the twelfth century a new kind of order appears on the manuscript page.[11] Interlinear glossing becomes less frequent. By design, gloss and text enter into a new kind of marriage.

9. M. T. Clanchy, *From Memory to Written Record, England 1066–1307* (Cambridge, Mass.: Harvard University Press, 1979), reviews what is known about the increasing use of written records, and the manner in which this increase both reflects and enhances the perception of the relationship between individuals and society. Clanchy stresses the effect of literate documents on everyday life, purposely leaving aside parallel developments in literature, science, and philosophy. See also Alexander Murray, *Reason and Society in the Middle Ages* (New York: Oxford University Press, 1978), a social history of literate competence and of the powers it confers on the literate from 1050 to about 1300.

10. Ivan Illich, *Schule ins Museum: Phaidros und die Folgen,* introduction by Ruth Kriss-Rettenbeck and Ludolf Kuchenbuch (Bad Heilbrunn: Klinkhardt, 1984), esp. pp. 53–64.

11. Nikolaus M. Haering, "Commentary and Hermeneutics," in *Renaissance and Renewal in the Twelfth Century,* ed. R. L. Benson and Giles Constable (Cambridge, Mass.: Harvard University Press, 1982), pp. 173–200, summarizes the state of our

In this order, each is given its due: the gloss is subordinated to the dominant main text. It is written in smaller letters. The way in which the unequal partners are wedded betrays careful planning. The author himself becomes aware that the layout is part of a visual whole which helps to determine the understanding of the reader.

Around 1150 Peter the Lombard[12] personally supervises the calligrapher who copies the dictation taken by his secretary. The book on which they work together is a verse-by-verse commentary on the Psalms. Before writing each page the calligrapher had to figure out the proportion of verse and matching commentary that would fit together on that page.

A new aesthetic sense expresses itself in the allocation. This textual patterning of the book page had such a strong hold on the imagination that Gutenberg and his pupils did what they could to make its essentials survive into the age of print. This is not to say that earlier manuscripts are not, quite frequently, marvels of a harmonious spatial interplay of lines, glosses, and miniatures with botanical creepers. But the new abstract beauty obtained primarily by means of the layout of script is the result of a mid-twelfth-century calculating approach to the use of letter sizes. It reflects the new pleasure of projecting mentally organized and quantified patterns of "knowledge" onto the empty space of the page.

In the Lombard's commentaries, key words are underlined with bright red, mercury-based lines. He does not leave it up to the reader to recognize quotes; he introduces primitive quotation marks to indicate where they start and end. In the margin, references to the source from which he quotes are given.

These ordering devices enable the Lombard to make a text of Aristotle subservient to his own mental picture of its structure. But he is a man of his age. He does not dare to manipulate Holy Scripture in the same way.[13] His commentary follows it line by line. In graphic contrast, his *Sententiae* on Aristotle are not a collection of comments, tan-

---

knowledge about the use of the gloss towards the end of the twelfth century. Gerhard Powitz, "Textus cum commento in codices manuscripti," *Zeitschrift für Handschriften-kunde* 5, 3 (1979): 80–89, deals with the transformation of layout.

12. Jean Châtillon, "Les Écoles de Chartres et de Saint-Victor," in *La scuola nell' Occidente Latino nell' alto medio evo*, 2 vols., Settimana di Studio 19 (Spoleto: Centro Italiano per i studi sull' Alto Medio Evo, 1972), pp. 795–839. On the recommendation of St. Bernard, Peter had come to St. Victor in 1139 to follow Hugh's commentaries on Holy Scripture.

13. P. C. Spicq, *Esquisse d'une histoire de l'exégèse au moyen âge* (Paris, 1946), is still a masterly introduction to the history of exegesis.

gents, and excursions following one verse after another. This commentary evolves visually as Peter's own line of thought is nourished by frequent references to a work of Aristotle. Here the gloss has the purpose of bringing out an *ordo* which Peter has read into a text. The learned book has ceased to be a sequence of commentaries that are strung like beads on the thread of somebody else's narration. The author now takes it upon himself to provide the *ordinatio*. He himself chooses a subject and puts *his* order into the sequence in which he will deal with its parts. The visible page is no longer the record of speech but the visual representation of a thought-through argument.[14]

Ordinatio: visible patterns

The patterns created by this new graphic technique enhance the written language which comes into being. By the early thirteenth century a terse sequence of glosses at the beginning of each chapter gathers the argument which will be treated. These arguments are put into a numerical sequence, *prima causa, secunda . . . quinta.* Standard rhetorical questions, like punctuation, precede the conclusion of each argument. These questions are "marked" by a formula which frequently begins with *obicitur,* which means "one might object." An *auctoritas,* a quote or "straw man" expresses doubt about the author's just-treated *argumentum,* and gives the author a chance to clarify his point of view with a *responsio,* his answer. These signs are highlighted on the page by special colors. The reader immediately recognizes where the tempter or *adversarius* has been given his say. The visual marker shifts the task of perceiving the author's *ordinatio* from the inner ear to the eye, and from the rhythm of sound to a new factitious space. Reliance on this visual architecture of the *ordinatio* makes it increasingly necessary, when reading, to have the book under one's eyes.[15]

---

14. W. Goetz, "Die Enzyklopädien des 13. Jahrhunderts," *Zeitschrift für die deutsche Rechtsgeschichte* 2 (1936): 227–50. Encyclopedias of the new kind first appear around 1225 (that of Bartholomaeus Anglicus), followed in 1240 by *De rerum natura* by Thomas Chantimpré and Vincent of Beauvais, who digest 2,000 books by 450 authors.

15. Malcolm B. Parkes, "The Influence of the Concepts of *Ordinatio* and *Compilatio* on the Development of the Book," in *Medieval Learning and Literature. Essays presented to Richard William Hunt,* ed. Jonathan James Graham Alexander and M. T. Gibson (Oxford: Clarendon, 1976), pp. 115–41. "Thirteenth-century scholars paid close attention to the development of good working tools based on scientific principles. The drive to make inherited material available in a condensed or more convenient form led them to recognize the desirability of imposing a new *ordinatio* on the material for this purpose. In the thirteenth century this led to the development of the notion of *compilatio*

Statim inveniri: instant access

Beyond his concern with layout, the Lombard is also aware of a new time frame to which the act of reading has been moved. He wants to lighten the burden of the student and speed up reading. He wants to decrease the need for extended leafing through the pages, and insists on chapter titles which allow the reader to find immediately what he is looking for. He arranges his *Sententiae* in such a way that "for him who searches it be not necessary to turn the leaves of many volumes, but that he may encounter quickly without toil what he is after."[16]

---

both as a form of writing and as a means of making material easily accessible. Compilation was not new (it is implicit in the work of Gratian and Peter Lombard); what was new was the amount of thought and industry that was put into it, and the refinement that this thought and industry produced. The transmission of these refinements on to the page led to greater sophistication in the presentation of the text" (p. 127).

Vincent of Beauvais elevated *compilatio* into a literary form: "In working out his scheme, with commendable humility he followed the example of the Almighty '[. . .] *ut iuxta ordinem sacrae scripturae, primo de creatore, postea de creaturis, postea quoque de lapsu et reparatione hominis, deinde vero de rebus gestis iuxta seriem temporum suorum, et tandem etiam de iis quae in fine temporum futura sunt, ordinate disserem*' [As with the order of Sacred Scripture, I shall carefully proceed, first dealing with the Creator, then creatures, and after that the fall and redemption of man, and then past events according to when they occurred, and finally even those things which will take place at the end of time]. In the *Speculum naturale*, he follows the chronological order of the six days of creation given in the Book of Genesis. At the lower end of *ordinatio*, his procedure was influenced by the *modus definitivus* of his own age. Since, according to Alexander of Hales, '[. . .] *apprehensio veritatis secundum humanam rationem explicatur per divisiones, definitiones, et ratiocinationes*' [the apprehension of truth by human reason is achieved through divisions, definitions, and arguments], Vincent achieves the subordination of his material by dissecting his *auctoritates* and redeploying the diverse materials into discrete, self-contained chapters. In the *Speculum naturale*, the third, fourth, and fifth days of creation give him the opportunity to review all that was then thought about minerals, vegetables, and animals. By dividing his work into books and chapters he is able to include as many as 171 chapters on herbs, 134 chapters on seeds and grains, 161 chapters on birds, and 46 chapters on fish. In the *Speculum historiale* by the same process of redeployment into discrete units he includes such material as the account of the ancient gods, and the 'biographies of leading authors' of antiquity accompanied by extracts from their works, all subordinated within the framework of universal history. In all, the *Speculum maius* is divided into 80 books, and 9,885 chapters. It is the classic example of the principle of *compilatio* which emerged in the thirteenth century, 'divide and subordinate'" (p. 128).

16. Peter the Lombard compiled his *Sentences: ut non sit necesse quaerenti, librorum numerositatem evolvere, cui brevitas, quod queritur, offert sine labore . . . ut autem, quod quaeritur, facilius occurat, titulos quibus singulorum librorum capitula distinguuntur, praemisimus (PL 192, 522).*

Hugh insists on patience[17] and leisurely tasting[18] of what can be found on the page.[19] Peter wants to give his pupils all the help he can to locate with ease and speed what they want to read in the book.[20] The scholastic reading which Peter's generation invents stands in clear contrast with the monastic approach of a Bernard of Clairvaux, who insists that his monks engage in the hard labor necessary to "discover at great pains the hidden delights of Scripture," and warns them "not to tire from the foreseeable difficulties they will encounter in this search."[21]

Alphabetic indexing

As already mentioned, the huge twelfth-century compilations are not yet reference tools in the modern sense.[22] For example, the *Glossa or-*

17. *DB* V, 2, p. 96: *Sic et mel in favo gratius, et quidquid maiori exercitio quaeritur, maiori etiam desiderio invenitur.* "Thus also is honey more pleasing because enclosed in the comb, and whatever is sought with greater effort is also found with greater desire" (*DT*, p. 121). *DB*, IV, 1, p. 70: *Contra, divina eloquia aptissime favo comparantur, quae et propter simplicitatem sermonis arida apparent, et intus dulcedine plena sunt.* "The Sacred Scriptures, on the other hand, are most fittingly likened to a honeycomb, for while in the simplicity of their language they seem dry, within they are filled with sweetness" (*DT*, p. 102).

18. *Sapientia* for the Latin speaker evokes *sapere*, "to taste." The search for wisdom connotes the aspiration towards something of ultimate, exceptional taste: *hoc ergo omnes artes agunt, hoc intendunt ut divina similitudo in nobis reparetur, quae nobis forma est, Deo natura, cui quanto magis conformamur, tanto magis sapimus* (*DB*, II, 1, p. 23). "All the arts are designed to work toward this end, namely, that the divine likeness might be restored in us; what to us is an ideal, to God is nature; the more we are assimilated to this image, the more we taste." However, the expression "in good taste," to which we are accustomed, appears only during the last decade of the fifteenth century, in Spain, and was probably coined by Queen Isabella.

19. *DB* III, 13, pp. 62–63: *Considera potius quid vires tuae ferre valeant. aptissime incedit, qui incedit ordinate. quidam, dum magnum saltum facere volunt, praecipitium incidunt. noli ergo nimis festinare. hoc modo citius ad sapientiam pertinges.* "Consider rather what your strength will bear. He proceeds best who goes forward prudently. Some, wishing to make a great leap of progress, sprawl headlong. Therefore, do not hurry too much. In this way you will come more quickly to wisdom."

20. R. H. Rouse and M. A. Rouse, "*Statim inveniri*. Schools, Preachers, and New Attitudes to the Page," in *Renaissance and Renewal in the Twelfth Century,* ed. R. L. Benson and Giles Constable (Cambridge, Mass.: Harvard University Press, 1982), pp. 201–25.

21. Cited in Parkes, "The Influence of the Concepts of *Ordinatio* and *Compilatio*." Mangenot, "Concordances," in F. G. Vigroux and Louis Pirot, *Dictionnaire de la Bible* (Paris: Letouzey, 1907–); Anna Dorothea von den Brincken, "*Mappa Mundi* und Chronographie. Studien zur *imago mundi* des Mittelalters," *Deutsches Archiv für Erforschung des Mittelalters* 24 (1968): 118–86.

22. R. H. Rouse, "L'évolution des attitudes envers l'autorité écrite: le développement des instruments de travail au XIIIᵉ siècle," in *Culture et travail intellectuel dans l'Occi-*

dinaria[23] is a collection of commentaries by the Church on the entire Latin Bible. Several monasteries collaborated over three to four generations.[24] Long sections surround the Biblical text, and short comments are interlinear. But there is no other cohesion in these many, partly overlapping, compilations than the text of the sacred book. The *glossatores* just do not think of any more obvious way to edit, anthologize, and order the material than arranging the passages as on-going commentaries to the Bible. Since all things that can be written about derive their meaning from their reference to an event related in the Bible, the most logical place to look up an opinion by Chrysostom is not by "subject" but within this book. But techniques for "searching" the Scriptures become common only toward the end of the twelfth century.[25]

Perhaps the most revolutionary of the new searching devices are those based on what we call alphabetization.[26] We are by now so accustomed to encyclopedias and telephone directories that the use of the a–b–c–d . . . z sequence to create subject lists seems as natural as the use of letters to spell a word. Scholars increasingly recognize that

---

dent médiéval. *Bilan des Colloques d'humanisme médiéval* (Paris: Centre National de la Recherche Scientifique, 1981), pp. 115–44.

23. *Ordinaria* is a designation used only since the fourteenth century.

24. B. Smalley, "La Glossa Ordinaria," *Recherches de théologie ancienne et médiévale* 9 (1937): 365–400.

25. R. H. Rouse and M. A. Rouse, "The Verbal Concordance of the Scriptures," *Archivum Fratrum Praedicatorum* 44 (1974): 5–30. The concordance to the Bible "did not evolve over generations, but was invented and perfected through careful tinkering and adjustment in less than 50 years" (p. 5). Anna Dorothea von den Brincken, "*Tabula Alphabetica*. Von den Anfängen alphabetischer Registerarbeiten zu Geschichtswerken," in *Festschrift für Herman Heimpel*, Veröffentlichungen des Max Planck Institut für Geschichte (Göttingen: Vandenhoek, 1972), pp. 900–923. See also E. Mangenot, "Concordances," in F. G. Vigroux and Louis Pirot, *Dictionnaire de la Bible* (Paris: Letouzey, 1907–); Quain, "The Medieval *Accessus ad Auctores*"; and Richard H. Rouse, "La naissance des index," in *Histoire de l'édition française*, ed. Henri-Jean Martin (Paris: Promodis, 1983), pp. 77–85, and "Concordances et index," in *Mise en page et mise en texte du livre manuscrit*, ed. Henri-Jean Martin and Jean Vézin (Paris: Éditions de la Librairie-Promodis, 1990), pp. 219–28.

26. Horst Kunze, *Über das Registermachen*, 2d ed. (Leipzig: 1966; M. A. Rouse and R. H. Rouse, "Alphabetization, History of," in *Dictionary of the Middle Ages*, vol. 1 (New York: Macmillan, 1982), pp. 204–7; and Homer G. Pfander, "The Medieval Friars and Some Alphabetical Reference-Books for Sermons," *Medium Aevum*, Oxford, 3 (1934): 19–29, on fifteen reference books of friars from the thirteenth through the fifteenth century that provide alphabetical lists of Biblical allusions, patristic quotations, stories, analogies, and references to other sources for literally thousands of sermon topics.

truly phonetic writing was a one-time invention, made in Greece around 770 B.C. The use of signs for both consonants (which are obstacles to breath) and for vowels (which indicate the color given to the column of air that is "spirited" out of the lungs) constitutes a technique of immense social significance. It disembeds those societies which use it from the community of all other cultures. But few scholars have yet realized that the arrangement of names or subjects in the order of these letters is a comparable technical breakthrough, something done in the course of a generation. In analogy to the watershed which divides pre-alphabetic Greek oral culture from Greek culture under the aegis of letters and science, so it seems reasonable to speak of the pre- and post-index Middle Ages.[27]

Without any application to indexing purposes, the a–b–c sequence maintained an intense resistance to change for centuries. Since the dawn of history it remained, fundamentally, as fixed as the shapes of the Greco-Roman letters. The non-use of this sequence for subject listing is therefore a quite remarkable and significant fact. It no more occurred to eighty-five generations of alphabet users to order things according to an a–b–c than it has occurred to the makers of the *Encyclopedia Britannica* to arrange articles by their references to the chapters and verses of the Bible. The Greeks inherited the sequence from the Phoenicians. They revolutionized it by distinguishing consonants and vowels. Later, the Romans dropped some signs which were not needed in the Italic language and added a couple, expanding and contracting the a–b–g–d of the Greeks into the Roman ABC. The appearance of the letters changed over the millennia. Hugh's reading was done mainly on letters reshaped in the ninth century.[28] But for 2,700 years the sequence of the letters remained substantially unchanged. The ABC was, and remained until quite recently, a magical incantation automatic even to people who did not recognize the shapes which they spoke of as A or C. In Hugh's childhood, every schoolboy learned to

27. Obviously the reference from an index to the text could not be made by "page-number" until printing—250 years later—insured that in every copy of a given edition the first word on the first line would be, e.g., "Rome." Reference had to be made by "book, chapter, and verse." See H. J. Koppitz, "Buch," in *Lexikon des Mittelalters*, vol. 2, p. 802. Sets of leaves had been numbered occasionally in antiquity. In order to insure correct sequencing in the bindery, they were commonly marked in the lower righthand corner of a new set with numerals called *custodes*, watchmen, in the Middle Ages. Then, so-called *reclamantes* were written on the following first page of the set.

28. David Ganz, "The Preconditions of Caroline Minuscle," *Viator* 18 (1987): 23–43. The production of normative script required a "grammar of legibility" which facilitated the understanding of these texts by clerics whose native speech was Germanic and whose Latinity was seldom Augustinian.

recite the alphabet and knew it as well as the Our Father. But up to Hugh's time, this sequence of shapes was never used as an ordering device for the purpose of listing concepts or things.[29]

Then, during the middle of the twelfth century, an avalanche of previously unthought-of devices appeared: indices, library inventories, and concordances. These are all devices engineered to search and find in books a passage or a subject that is already in the mind. The stuff from which these instruments are made, namely, the two dozen letters and their millennial order, remains unchanged. But the technical use to which the rote order memory of the ABC is now being put is an essential ingredient in a conceptual revolution.[30] This revolutionary use of a trivial sequence rather than concrete events to order subject categories is but one expression of the twelfth-century desire to recognize and create a new kind of order. This will has been well studied. It finds its aesthetic expression in architecture, law, economics, and new cities, but nowhere as clearly as on the page. The new page layout, chapter division, distinctions, the consistent numbering of chapter and verse, the new table of contents for the book as a whole, the summaries at the beginning of the chapter referring to its subtitles, the introductions in which the author explains how he will build up his argument, are so many expressions of a new will to order.[31]

In each of them a cultural impulse, a mental purpose, and a graphic device combine to achieve something unprecedented. However, in no instance can we study the influence of the technology on the mind-set as clearly as in their creation of alphabetic indexes. The mental topol-

29. Alphabetic Psalms or poems could be witty games, or mnemonic triggers: they did not order things but lines in the sequence of the aleph-beth. Glossaries were not unknown: lists of alphabetically arranged Greek words with their Latin equivalent written next to them. But what they order are words, not reference to things or pages on which these things appear as subjects. Some very first attempts at indexing in this latter sense were made by a monk in the generation previous to Hugh. But he did not get very far, because his alphabetic ordering did not penetrate beyond the second letter of the words he listed. These premonitions only underline the surprising speed with which the modern index later imposed itself in the course of a couple of generations.

30. Albertus Magnus, in *De Animalibus* (*Opera Omnia*, ed. Auguste Borgnet, 38 vols. in 90 [Paris, 1890–99], vol. 12, p. 433), excuses himself for listing animals in alphabetical order because this is not worthy of a philosopher, *hunc modum non proprium philosopho esse* (cited by Rouse and Rouse, "*Statim inveniri*," p. 211).

31. Like each of the new techniques which came together in the layout of the thirteenth century, introducing summaries too have a history. The so-called *accessus*, in which a commentator prefaces a text with tidbits about the author's life, the content of the work, and its utility to the reader, goes back to commentators on Greek philosophers. See Quain, "The Medieval *Accessus ad Auctores*." The new summaries, however, describe the outline of the book or chapter which they introduce.

ogy within which knowledge is henceforth pursued and which defines classes of scientific procedures is discontinuous to the space within which Hugh's mind still moves. From the teller of a story the author mutates into the creator of a text.

Author versus compiler, commentator, and scribe

It is not the twelfth-century Latin *corpus* that is changed or enlarged. Hugh and his contemporaries still worked on the premise that all books preserved from both pagan and Christian antiquity were known to them.[32] Those authors of antiquity who survived the dark ages in Arabic rather than in Latin were not yet available in translation to Hugh's contemporaries in Paris. Even by Hugh's pupils, the canonical authors were regarded with the deference he himself had shown them. But with the new ordering devices, they ceased to treat the old books as something simply reproduced or updated. Late twelfth-century writers digested them in a new way: no longer as fodder for their own meditative rumination, but as building materials that could be used in the construction of new mental edifices.

The Lombard, Gratian, and Benedictine *ordinatores glossae* were still driven by the ideal of simply reordering the Christian *corpus*.[33] The creators of indexes, who were overwhelmingly members of the new preaching orders, were intent on drawing preconceived "contents" from this *corpus* and making its gist, its subjects, accessible for the use of theological system builders, preachers, and lawyers.

Hugh teaches a way of reading so well ordered that his pupil, rather than "thumb through the pages," can use his recall as a finding device. The meditative reader discovers in the space of his own heart which thing or event refers by analogy to another. This is the reason why "we ought, in all that we learn, to gather brief and dependable abstracts to be stored in the little chest of our memory."[34] Only after Hugh's death, sounding lines on the page fade and the page becomes a screen for the order willed by the mind. Rather than a means to revive a *narratio,* the theological and philosophical book becomes the exteriorization of

---

32. Richard W. Southern, *The Making of the Middle Ages,* 16th printing (New Haven: Yale University Press, 1976 [orig. 1953]), p. 204: In the second generation of the twelfth century, with Bernard, Abaelard, and Hugh of St. Victor, "we come to a point where scholars begin to feel comfortable about their command of the achievements of the past. . . . Throughout the greater part of the twelfth century there was a confident sense that the steady mastery of works of the past was reaching its natural end."

33. Smalley, "La Glossa Ordinaria."

34. *DT,* III, 11, p. 94.

a *cogitatio,* of a thought structure. This *cogitatio* is not, primarily, the spoken memory of an event, but a thought-out outline of reasons. The layout of the page in turn impresses this outline on visual memory. The page is broken up into paragraphs, each of them corresponding to a *distinctio,* a distinct point of view. Markers call attention to the sequence of *distinctiones.* Titles had been used occasionally in antiquity. After Isidore, they became uncommon. In the thirteenth century they return with a vengeance: In the *summa* of that century, the references to the author's intent, such as the *quaestio, obicitur, respondeo dicendum est,* hold the exposition itself in their grip. Dictation becomes almost impossible for the theologian unless he refers to his notes.

Only a century later Bonaventure explicitly defines or discovers the distinct tasks that enter in the authorship of a book.

> There are four ways of making a book. There are some who write down the words of others, without adding or changing a thing, and he who does so is a scribe (*scriptor*). There are those who write down others' words, and add something, however not their own additions. One who does this is a compiler (*compilator*). Then, there are those who write down both others' and their own things, but material of others predominates, and their own is added like an annex for clarification. Who does this is called a commentator (*commentator*), rather than an author. But he who writes both what comes from himself and from others, with the material of others annexed for the purpose of confirming his own, ought to be called author (*auctor*).[35]

Layout

The ear, so far, had distinguished the voice of the dead author from the voice of the reader. Now the visual articulation of the page called

35. "Prooemium," *Commentarium in libris sententiarum,* in *Opera omnia* (Claras Aquas, 1882–1902), I, 14–15. Here, the modern concept of the author as the authentic is taking shape. Marie-Dominique Chenu, "Auctor, Actor, Autor," *Bulletin du Cange* 3 (1927): 81–86: Sallust and Suetonius occasionally designate the person who dictates a book both as *auctor* (from *augere* in the sense of "bringing forth" something like a statue, building, or writ) and as *actor,* like the agent, the "maker." During the next thousand years one Author, the Author of Holy Writ, namely God, gave this word a transcendent meaning. Simultaneously *auctoritas,* the dignity which a statement carries because of its intrinsic worthiness, reflected some of its meaning back to *auctor-actor.* By the end of the thirteenth century, "author" stresses the *authenticity* (p. 83) of the originator. See A. J. Minnis, *Medieval Theory of Authorship: Scholastic Literary Attitudes in the Later Middle Ages* (London: Scolar Press, 1984); and Neil Hathaway, "Compilatio: From Plagiarism to Compiling," *Viator* 20 (1989): 19–44.

for a new distinction between kinds of persons each of whom contributes a special feature to the texture of the page. The new layout not only reflected the will to use visual articulation as a means of interpretation; it also led to the first attempts at textual criticism. Three hundred years before printing made it possible to "establish" a critical edition, attempts became common to untangle the threads from which the visible text was woven. That which comes from the author who writes "his own" is distinguished from its shaping and ordering by other clerks. Inexorably "the" text of a book comes to be distinguished from the version in this or that other manuscript. This distinction became important long before the technology of printing would make it possible to establish and fix this text in a critical edition.

Illuminatio versus *illustratio*

The meaningful layout which addresses the eye has to compete for attention with the illustration on the same page.[36] Five functions which have been attributed to the ornamentation of Christian manuscripts can be distinguished.

For Cassiodorus (ca. 485–580) what the monk does in the scriptorium is all a kind of silent preaching of the word.[37] Illustrations are like the solemn vestments that by their beauty provide the word incarnate on the page with a setting worthy of its dignity.[38] The monk is used to the book as a sacred object that during the liturgy is carried around with great solemnity, is honored with incense, illuminated by a special candle, and kissed on the painted initials before and after the loud reading of the passage these pictures mark off.[39] The book is an

36. Christel Meier and Uwe Ruberg, eds., *Text and Bild: Aspekte des Zusammenwirkens zweier Künste in Mittelalter und früher Neuzeit* (Wiesbaden: Reichert, 1980), publishes the papers from a symposium on the history of the synergy between letters and pictures on the late medieval page.

37. L. Gougaud, "Muta praedicatio," *Revue bénédictine,* 42 (1930): 170.

38. For Cassiodorus, the whole body of the scribe preaches. What a happy invention, *felix inventio:* "to preach to people with one's hands, to open their tongues with one's fingers, silently to mediate salvation to mortals, and to struggle against the surreptitious attacks of the devil with a writing cane and ink." . . . *manu hominibus praedicare, digitis linguas aperire, salutem mortalibus tacitam dare et contra diaboli subreptiones illicitas calamo atramentoque pugnare* (ibid., p. 169; *PL* 70, 1144D–1145A). See also Leslie Webber Jones, trans., *An Introduction to Divine and Human Readings: Cassiodorus Senator* (New York: Octagon Books, Inc., 1966).

39. Jonathan James Graham Alexander, *The Decorated Letter* (New York: Braziller, 1978); H. Hermann, "The Bible in Art: Miniature, Paintings, Drawings, and Sculpture Inspired by the Old Testament," *Sacris Erudiri* 6 (1954): 189–281.

object of worship. Just as gold and gems are used to embellish its covers, its pages are covered with colors.

Besides honoring the word with clothes that befit it, the illustration had a didactic purpose. Just as the preacher enlivens his words by gestures, so the figure illuminates the meaning of the written word. It was meant to show to the bodily eye of the simple-minded what exceeded their intellectual grasp. While "listening" to the written word, one's imagination is nourished by the picture.[40] A technique used for this purpose was the so-called *Exultet Rolls,*[41] originating in Apulia, named after the *exultet,* a long solemn chant sung by the deacon during the Easter Vigil. Its haunting unforgettable melody, still heard today, is close to old synagogue patterns. The deacon stands behind a lectern while the Easter candle is blessed, intones Bible verses with their commentaries from Greek Church Fathers, and retells the story of salvation from the Jews' flight out of Egypt to the resurrection of Christ. And as he sings he unwinds a roll on which text and pictures follow each other. When you look at the roll, the pictures are upside down, and their subject precedes the story by many lines. The reason for this curious feature is a simple one: the deacon is supposed to unroll the scroll of parchment over the lectern so that, while he tells the story, the people who listen in front of him can contemplate the illustrations.

But illustrations are not only meant to adorn a sacred object and to help with instructions for the simple-minded.[42] As a third function they

40. Venerable Bede (A.D. 735): We make images for those who cannot read "so that they may learn about the works of our Lord and Saviour by the contemplation [of their picture]"—*possent opera Domini et Salvatoris nostri per ipsarum contuitum discere* (Gougaud, "Muta praedicatio," p. 168; *PL* 94, 228A. The Synod of Arras (A.D. 1025) orders the use of pictures so that those who cannot see the Lord in the Scriptures may contemplate him in the outline of pictures: *illiterati, quod per scripturas non possunt intueri, hoc per quaedam picturae lineamenta contemplantur.* The stress lies on the two distinct ways of being illuminated, by "seeing" in the letters and "contemplating" in the painting (Gougaud, p. 169).

41. Gerhart Ladner, "The Commemoration Pictures of the Exultet Roll Barberinus Latinus," in his book, *Images and Ideas in the Middle Ages: Selected Studies in History and Art* (Rome, 1983), vol. 1, pp. 283–426. See also H. Douteil, ed., *Exultet Rolle: Easter Preconium. MS Biblioteca Vaticana 9820* (Graz: Akademische Druck- und Verlagsanstalt, 1975). Guigues Cartusian (A.D. 1136): *Si ore non possumus dei verbum manibus praedicamus.* "If we cannot speak, we should preach the word of God with our hands." Honorius Augustodunensis (A.D. 1130): *Ob tres autem causas fit pictura: primo quia est laicorum litteratura.* "For three reasons, a picture should be made: first, because it is the literature of lay persons." See Gougaud, "Muta praedicatio," p. 169.

42. S. Lewis, "Sacred Calligraphy. The Chi-Rho Page in the Book of Kells," *Traditio* 36 (1980): 139–59: "The page [is] intended to confront the eye with an awesome array

are meant as exegetical and heuristic cues to prompt the monastic reader. They are intended as nonverbal vehicles for the same revelation which letters transmit as sounds. *Hoc visibile imaginatum figurat illud invisible verum* stands in the caption of one of these miniatures: "this visible image represents that invisible truth." Another caption is an even more explicit admonition: "here you should contemplate, that ...," *hic erat contemplandum.* An Irish codex of the twelfth century suggests the method that connects word and image: "What this picture allows you to grasp with the bodily senses is that which you should bring forth spiritually."[43]

Fourth, the early medieval miniature is conceived as an accompaniment that supports the sound given off by the lines when the reader moves through them. The miniature is meant to bring out the sparkle of the page's voices. It does not have in any way the purpose of the graphs or charts in a modern textbook where these devices reduce the subject matter to an abstract clarity for which language is too clumsy. Medieval illuminations invite the mumbler to fall silent adoring what no word could express. Nor are the pictures like photographs, meant to document a fact or provide evidence for the matter discussed in the text. Miniature and lines interlace ear and eye in the perception of the same delightful symphony which Dante calls the seductive "smile of the pages" (*ridon le carte*).[44]

Finally, the illustration of books before the thirteenth century has a practical—now often forgotten—mnemonic purpose. Hugh speaks of reading as a journey. He advances physically from page to page. The ornaments that line the rows of letters place the words into the landscape through which this journey leads.[45] On no two lines does the reader meet up with the same view, no two pages look alike, no two initial "A"s are identically colored. The foliage and grotesques in combination with the lines reenforce the power of remembrance; they sup-

of Christological and Eucharistic allusions consonant with the liturgical usage of the book. . . . An enormous erudition underlies each illumination" (p. 141). Christel Meier, "Zum Verhältnis von Text und Illustration bei Hildegard von Bingen," in *Hildegard von Bingen 1179–1979. Festschrift zum 800. Todestag,* ed. A. Brück (Mainz, 1979), pp. 159–69.

43. For references see M. Smeyers, *La Miniature.* Typologie des sources du moyen âge occidental, fasciculum 8 (Turnhout: Brepols, 1974); see esp. pp. 96–101.

44. Dante, *Divina comedia, Purgatorio* 11, 82. See also commentary by James Thomas Chiampi, "From Unlikeness to Writing: Dante's 'Visible Speech' in Canto Ten, Purgatorio," *Medievalia* 5 (1982): 97–112.

45. H. Jantzen, "Das Wort als Bild in der Frühmittelalterlichen Buchmalerei," in *Über den gotischen Kirchenraum und andere Aufsätze* (Berlin, 1951), pp. 53–60.

port the reader's recall of the *voces paginarum* in analogy to the scenery of the road that brings back the conversation which took place on the stroll.

Modern reading, especially of the academic and professional type, is an activity performed by commuters or tourists; it is no longer that of pedestrians and pilgrims. The speed of the car and the dullness of the road and the distraction of billboards put the driver into a state of sensory deprivation that continues when he hurries through manuals and journals once he arrives at his desk. Like the tourist equipped with a camera, so today's student reaches for the photocopy to keep a souvenir snapshot. He is in a world of photographs, illustrations, and graphs which put the memory of illuminated letter-landscapes beyond his reach.

During the twelfth century the intrinsic coherence of the line and its illumination dissolves.[46] As the line is made into a building element of paragraphs, the miniature turns into a circus of fantasy creatures, often a jungle which threatens to invade and to overpower the alphabetic component of the page.[47] Bernard of Clairvaux in several sermons attempts to exorcise this sensual intrusion of spirits gone wild. He recognizes that illuminations have their place in the prayer books provided

46. In the thirteenth century, the picture no longer addresses the onlooker by speaking to him about the *littera* that he is being read. It is now conceived of as a parallel kind of narration, a literature in its own right for the illiterate. Thomas Aquinas, *Scriptum super IV Sententiis,* bk. 1, dist. 3, ch. 1. *Fuit autem . . . ratio institutionis imaginis in Ecclesia. Primo, ad instructionem rudium, qui eis quasi quibusdam libris edocentur.* "This was the reason for using images in churches, namely, for the instruction of the illiterate who might learn from them as if they were books." The metaphor of the book is now so dominant, that the picture itself is conceived as a "book" for the instruction of those who cannot read.

47. For an introduction to the history of illuminated manuscripts, treated as an art form *sui generis,* see David M. Robb, *The Art of the Illuminated Manuscript* (South Brunswick and New York: Barnes, 1973). H. Focillon (*L'Art d'Occident, le moyen âge roman et gothique* [Paris, 1938]) discusses the opposition between the style of balance and integration in the ornamentation and sculptural composition of the early (still Romanesque) twelfth century and the later (already Gothic) period, especially in the country north of the Loire. Jurgis Baltrušaitis's *La Stylistique ornamentale dans la sculpture romane* (Paris, 1931) contains many illustrations of eleventh-century style. The book has been followed by two further studies by the same author: *Réveils et prodiges: le gothique fantastique* (Paris: Colin, 1960) deals with the continuity of theme and faith between Romanesque and Gothic fantasy. Here the sixth chapter (pp. 195–234), "Le réveil fantastique dans le décor du livre," illustrates the explosion of the new Gothic style in manuscript marginalia, mostly from examples conserved at the Bibliothèque Nationale in Paris. The second volume, *Le moyen âge fantastique* (Paris: Colin, 1955) focuses more on the influence of classical and oriental themes on the fantastic creatures generated by the medieval imagination.

by bishops in the pastoral care of lay people. But he insists that flam-
boyant ornaments addressing the senses foster a sensual devotion or
piety in people whose spirit has not been awakened. And he strongly
objects to the illustration of manuscripts meant for the spiritual readings of monks, whose entry into the cloister has led them beyond the
this-worldly crowd.[48] In 1134 a general chapter of Cistercians demands that even initial letters be written plainly and with one color
only.[49] This veto went unobserved; it was too starkly in contradiction
to the trends of the times.

The portable book

The miniature of the late Gothic manuscript frequently is an independent work of art. Sometimes the letters seem to be the mere frame for
the pictures. The book, in an age of growing urban wealth, becomes
an object of private ownership: its miniature paintings enhance the
status of one's own wealth.[50] But this privatization of the "book" as
a physical entity could not have happened without a further set of
technological breakthroughs.

The Bible as one single bulky object was unknown in the twelfth
century: it was still, as it had always been, a collection of separate
tomes. More often than not, the tomes were of different size, written
for different usages, and assembled only occasionally as the canonical
collection of sacred books. The Gospel lay on the ambon to the north
of the celebrant so that the deacon would face the region of darkness
and cold and paganism when reading it, and the Epistle on the opposite side, to be read by the lector. Thus, as a matter of course, these

48. *Scimus namque quod illi* [the bishops] . . . *carnalis populi devotionem, quia spiritualibus non possunt, corporalibus excitant ornamentis. Nos vero, qui iam de populo
exivimus* . . . "For we know that they [the bishops] . . . encourage the devotion of the
people, who are more carnal, with physical illustrations since they cannot do so by
spiritual means. But we, who have left the people . . ." (Bernard of Clairvaux, *Apologia
ad Guillelmum abbatem* 12, 28; in *Sancti Bernardi opera*, ed. J. Leclercq, vol. 3, pp.
104–5).

49. *Litterae unius coloris fiant et non depictae.* "The letters should be made with only
one color and no ornamentation." J. M. Canivez, ed., *Status Capitulorum Generalium
Ordinis Cisterciensis ab anno 1116 ad annum 1786,* vol. 1 (Louvain, 1933), stat.
80, p. 31.

50. Paradoxically, new wealth and a new spirit of voluntary poverty converged in
their demand for portable books: C. H. Talbot, ("The Universities and the Medieval
Library," in *The English Library before 1700,* ed. by F. Wormland and C. E. Wright
[London: The Athlone Press, 1958], pp. 76–79) suggests that the mendicant friars were
a major force behind the reduction of book size. They wanted to carry them on their
constant travels.

were separate volumes. The Psalter was open on a lectern in the middle of the choir. The Pentateuch was usually under separate covers from the Prophets.

Two merely technical reasons supported this functional division of the Bible into differently bound and differently ornamented objects. Available page materials were too bulky and heavy to enable the binding together of a complete Bible, and the letters used were too large to fit the text onto pages that might be bound into a single volume. Only during the thirteenth century were handwritten letters shrunk to a size that made it possible to fit all of the Bible into one volume. The intensive use of word abbreviations contributed to this compression of script. Even so, a thirteenth-century Bible rarely weighs less than ten pounds. Other techniques had to be created to transform the luggable into a truly portable Bible.

Throughout the Middle Ages, parchment was the standard surface for writing meant to last. Unlike leather, parchment is not from tanned, but from washed, shaved, cleaned-of-grease, and dry-stretched, hides. The smoothed skins of calves, goats, lambs, or sheep are then cut into strips. In antiquity these strips were rolled up and the parchment was inscribed in vertical columns, of which just a couple were unfurled by the reader. These rolls were sometimes kept in cylindrical containers. In the Middle Ages, for certain legal and liturgical purposes these rolls were kept intact; but already by the second century parchment had begun to be cut into rectangles, folded once or twice and bound into a codex—what we would call a book.

The quality of parchment depends on the age of the animal used, the slowness of the washing and drying process, and the delicacy of the scraping of the stretched pelt with a semilunar or circular knife.[51] Crucial to the twelfth-century advance toward the manageable book was the preparation of a new, thinner "virgin" parchment. It was made from the skin of unborn sheep, carefully tanned by using alum and delicately smoothed with finely grained pumice stone. The technique was costly and the result fit to receive many jewels.

51. See R. J. Forbes, *Studies in Ancient Technology,* 9 vols. (Leiden: Brill, 1966), vol. 5, passim, on papyrus and parchment; L. Santinfaller, *Beiträge zur Geschichte der Beschreibstoffe im Mittelalter, mit besonderer Berücksichtigung der päpstlichen Kanzlei,* 1. Untersuchungen. Mitteilungen des Institutes für österreichische Geschichtsforschung. Eränzungsband 16 (Graz, 1953); D. V. Thompson, "Medieval Parchment Making," *Library,* 4th ser., 16 (1935): 113–17. A delightful and complete description of parchment-making, which reflects the techniques used in the eighteenth century, can be found in "Parchemin, en commerce, etc. . . . ," in Denis Diderot and Jean Le Rond d'Alembert, *Encyclopédie ou Dictionnaire raisonnée des sciences, des arts et des métiers,* vol. 11, pp. 929–31 (Paris: Briasson, 1765).

This new technology had barely become known when paper reappeared in Europe. Egyptians had used papyrus, a plait of carefully prepared reed fibers. It is the result of manual layering, not of sedimentation.[52] It must not be confused with the material obtained by sedimenting a suspension of pulped cellulose, optimally rags, which creates a plastic, namely paper. The process of papermaking was invented by the Chinese sometime between 100 B.C. and A.D. 100. Koreans and Japanese acquired the skill around A.D. 600. Arabic traders, whose caravans ventured into Transoxania, learned the art of papermaking from Chinese artisans.[53] They carried the art to North Africa, and then to Spain, where the first European paper mill was established, in Xátvia, about 1100. The first extant European document on paper is a letter of Countess Adelaide written in 1109 to her son, Roger, later King of Sicily. The letter was dictated in Spain, but is written in Greek and Arabic letters. This new competitor for parchment reached Paris, via Spain, just in time for the opening of its university.

Ink also contributed to the new fluency in note-taking. Antique Egyptian and traditional Chinese inks were made not unlike our watercolors: vegetal pigments or lampsoot were suspended in gumwater, and when they dried, they simply stuck to the surface. During the fourth century before Christ metal-based ink was invented: it is a solution of metal salt (generally iron or copper) and tannin that was obtained by boiling the bark or the galls from oak trees. Upon drying on the paper, the tannin acts as a mordant, and through a chemical reaction the traces are fixed into the writing surface. Scholastic studies could hardly have come into vogue without the new, cheap, light writing surface, nor without the general availability of mordant ink.[54]

But the reduction of letter size and page weight, and new abbreviations were still insufficient to make the book portable.[55] A new way had to be found to stitch small paper sheets so that they open fully in the hand of the reader. Also, a new flexible cover had to be engineered

52. Theodor Birt, *Das antike Buchwesen in seinem Verhältnis zur Literatur, mit Beiträgen zur Textgeschichte des Theokrit, Catull, Properz und anderer Autoren* (Berlin: W. Herz, 1882 [reprint 1959] pp. 223–85, deals with papermaking in antiquity.

53. On the interrelationship of (al-)chemical studies and papermaking, see M. Levy, *Medieval Arabic Bookmaking and Its Relation to Early Chemistry and Pharmacology.* Transactions of the American Philosophical Society 52 (New York, 1962).

54. For details on the history of ink, see R. J. Forbes, *Studies in Ancient Technology,* vol. 3 (Leiden: Brill, 1965), pp. 236–39 (some good bibliography).

55. Graham Pollard, "Describing Medieval Bookbinding," in *Medieval Learning and Literature: Essays presented to R. W. Hunt,* ed. Jonathan James Graham Alexander and M. T. Gibson (Oxford: Clarendon, 1976), pp. 50–65. The influence of the commercial reproduction of manuscripts by extra-monastic scriptoria on the physical appearance of

❦ SEVEN

From Book to Text

By the end of the twelfth century, the book takes on a symbolism which it retained until our time. It becomes the symbol for an unprecedented kind of object, visible but intangible, which I shall call the *bookish text*.[1] In the long social history of the alphabet, the impact of this development can be compared with only two other events: the introduction of full phonetic script, which occurred around 400 B.C., making Greek a language upon which the speaker could reflect,[2] and the diffusion of printing in the fifteenth century, which made the *text* into a powerful mold for a new literary and scientific worldview.

The historian of technology who is concerned with the symbolic rather than the intended instrumental effect of technique, and who studies the technology of the alphabet, must carefully distinguish between manual techniques around 1150 creating the text as object, and mechanical techniques around 1460 reifying this object as a stamp. With this in mind, it appears that a very humble aggregate of scribal techniques, working in a highly sophisticated manner, effected a kind

1. I am now preparing some papers on the medieval beginning and the present eclipse of the "Text as Object par excellence."

2. Eric A. Havelock, *The Literate Revolution in Greece and Its Cultural Consequences* (Princeton: Princeton University Press, 1982). In this collection of controversial articles written shortly before the author's death, the alphabet is understood as a device, "a system of small shapes in an endless variety of linear arrangements which, when seen [read], trigger an acoustic memory of the complete spoken speech that is indexed by these shapes. . . . It became the means of introducing a new state of mind, the alphabetic mind . . . [and] furnished a necessary conceptual foundation to build the structure of science and philosophies. It converted the Greek spoken tongue into an artifact, thereby separating it from the speaker and making it into a language" (pp. 6–7).

of change in the mind-set of European culture clearly distinct from the transition of script to print. The history of the text as the object par excellence during the following centuries demands a clear distinction between these two early moments.

The page became a bookish text, this latter shaped the scholastic mind, and the text-mind relationship was as necessary a foundation for print culture as alphabetic recording had been for the culture of literature and philosophy in ancient Greece. So far this point has not been made. Not a single book, nor a sizable article deals ex professo with the hypothesis that it was a scribal revolution that created the object which, three hundred years later, was fit for print. The present essay aims to remedy this lacuna.

If my view is substantially correct, several things follow. The materialization of abstraction in the form of the bookish text can be taken as the hidden root metaphor giving unity to the mental space of this long period, which we might also call the "Epoch of the University," or the "Epoch of Bookish Reading." With the invention and diffusion of printing, this era of the book—initiated in the thirteenth century by the creation of the bookish text—was given a set of additional characteristics, making the bookish text as root metaphor a powerful determinant of a new worldview.[3] This is one era with two major parts: in the first, the book was the result of scribes writing by hand, in the second, that of a mechanical reproduction of a handset prototype.[4]

Toward a history of the text as object

In the social history of the alphabet, a mountain range separates pre-textual and text-molded reading, writing, speaking, and thinking. The

3. A select and annotated bibliography to support this opinion will be found in Ivan Illich and Barry Sanders, *ABC: The Alphabetization of the Popular Mind* (San Francisco: North Point Press, 1988), pp. 128–66.

4. This essay has been concerned directly with the art of reading, not that of writing. It calls for a parallel history of the psychomotor *ars scribendi*, on which I am working. As long as we lack a historical perspective on the ethology and symbolism of the dictating tongue, the hand, and writing postures, the mind-shaping significance of the text as object will remain as hidden as the moon in its second quarter. For instance, the shift from the monastic scriptorium to the commercial stationer (*pecia*), and then from the manuscript to the printed page, runs parallel with a new cult of the author's *chirograph*. Dictation declined, and the author's composition only now became typically a hand craft, since the printed text was more likely to be taken from the author's autograph rather than from the writ taken down by his scribe. The bookish text as a mental object is detached from the page through the hand of the author who crafts it.

watershed between these two sets of mental and behavioral patterns has been the theme of this essay. The distinction does not coincide with others to which we have become accustomed since Millman Parry opened the debate on Homer's orality in 1926—for example, between oral and written history, epic and literate tradition, ideographic versus alphabetic notation, ornamentation versus illustration. Emphatically, it ought not to be confused with scribal versus print-defined science.

It now becomes necessary to rethink what happened in the fifteenth century. Under the leadership of Elizabeth Eisenstein, the transition to print was commonly seen as the major turning point in the social history of the alphabet.[5] According to her view, typography was a necessary precondition for a text made so that it could be trusted for the transmission of poetry, prose, astronomical tables, and anatomical designs. Without the standardized characteristics of the printed text, and the updating and indexing it made possible, neither the humanities nor the sciences could have acquired the characteristics which distinguish them from learned endeavors in earlier epochs. All this is certain. The interpretation I propose does not challenge this view, but places it in a different perspective, thereby enriching it. If I am right, then the invention of movable letters was the outstanding event *within* the history of an overarching epoch, the age of the bookish text. The proposed shift in historiographic emphasis not only opens new insights into past mental configurations, but it also enables us to speak in a new way about another epochal turn in the social history of the alphabet that is happening within our lifetime: the dissolution of alphabetic technique into the miasma of communication.[6]

The reason no attention has been focused on the history of the text as object is to be sought precisely here: the humanist tradition that brought forth generations of historians is a phenomenon within the matrix of the text itself. With the detachment of the text from the physical object, the *Schriftstück,* nature itself ceased to be an object to be read and became the object to be described. Exegesis and hermeneutics became operations on the text, rather than on the world. Only now,

5. Elizabeth Eisenstein, *The Printing Press as an Agent of Change: Communications and Cultural Transformations in Early-Modern Europe,* 2 vols. (Cambridge: Cambridge University Press, 1979). See also by the same author, *The Printing Revolution in Early Modern Europe* (London: Cambridge University Press, 1984), which is less encyclopaedic, and easy to read.

6. This point is stressed by Vilèm Flusser in *Die Schrift. Hat Schreiben eine Zukunft?* (Göttingen: Immatrix Publications, 1987). Consult the important review of this book by Aleida Assmann, in *Poetica* 20 (1988): 284–88.

with nature re-conceived as encoded information, can the history of the "readability of the world" become an issue for study.[7]

In the *Didascalicon* it is still the *lumen* of the reader's eye that lights up the text on the surface of the parchment. A hundred years later, when Bonaventure comments on his admired predecessor, Hugh, the text has already begun to float above the page. It is on its way to becoming a kind of vessel that ferries meaningful signs through the space separating the copy from the original; it drops anchor here or there. However, in spite of this dissociation of the text from the page, the text maintains its port in the book. The book, in turn, metaphorically stands as a harbor for the text where it unloads sense and reveals its treasures. As the monastery had been the world for the culture of the sacred book, the university came into existence as the institutional framework and symbolic tutor for the new bookish text.

For some twenty generations, we were nourished under its aegis. I for one am irremediably rooted in the soil of the bookish book. Monastic experience has given me a sense of *lectio divina*. But reflection on a lifetime of reading inclines me to believe that most of my attempts to let one of the early Christian masters take me by the hand for a pilgrimage through the page have at best engaged me in a *lectio spiritualis* as textual as the *lectio scholastica* practiced not at the prie-dieu but at the desk. The bookish text is my home, and the community of bookish readers are those included in my "we."

This home is now as outmoded as the house into which I was born, when a few light bulbs began to replace the candle. A bulldozer lurks in every computer with a promise to open new highways to data, replacements, inversions, and instant print. A new kind of text shapes the mind-set of my students, a printout which has no anchor, which can make no claim to be either a metaphor, or an original from the author's hand. Like the signals from a phantom schooner, its digital strings form arbitrary font-shapes on the screen, ghosts which appear and then vanish. Ever fewer people come to the book as a harbor of meaning. No doubt, for some it still leads to wonder and joy, puzzlement and bitter regret, but for more—I fear—its legitimacy consists in being little more than a metaphor pointing toward *information*.

Those before us, who lived securely embedded in the epoch of the

---

7. The outstanding achievement in the pursuit of this history is Hans Blumenberg, *Die Lesbarkeit der Welt* (Frankfurt am Main: Suhrkamp, 1986). Of special relevance to my argument is chapter 22, pp. 372–409, on the construction of the "genetic code" as "text" since Erwin Schrödinger's Trinity College lectures in 1944. The new "text" has no meaning, no sense, and no author; it is conceived of as a command sequence, and upsets the meaning of reading.

bookish text, had no need to investigate its historical beginnings. Their security, in fact, was bolstered by the structuralist assumption that whatever there is, is in some way a *text*. This is no longer true for those who are aware that their feet rest one on each side of a new watershed. They cannot avoid turning back to the remnants of bookishness to explore the archaeology of the library of certainties in which they were brought up. Bookish readers have a historical beginning and their survival can now be recognized as a moral task that is intellectually based on understanding the historical fragility of the bookish text.

The abstraction of the text

The conversion of the book from a pointer to *nature* to a pointer to *mind* is due in great part to two distinct but subtly related innovations: on one hand, the uprooting of the text from the pages of the manuscript and, on the other, the detachment of the letter from its millennial bondage to Latin.

The text could now be seen as something distinct from the book. It was an object that could be visualized even with closed eyes. And the pen in the hand of the scribe rather than the font moved by the printer created this new entity. A set of about two dozen new graphic conventions used the old set of two dozen letters as building blocks for an unprecedented construct. The application of these twelfth-century scribal rules meant that strings of letters—words or lines—would henceforth generate an abstract architectural phantom on the emptiness represented by the page. The page lost the quality of soil in which words are rooted. The new text was a figment on the face of the book that lifted off into autonomous existence. This new bookish text did have material existence, but it was not the existence of ordinary things: it was *literally* neither here nor there. Only its shadow appeared on the page of this or that concrete book. As a result, the book was no longer the window onto nature or God; it was no longer the transparent optical device through which the reader gains access to creatures or the transcendent. Insofar as it remained an optical instrument, the book had turned around 180 degrees, as if a convex lens had been replaced by a concave one. Out of the symbol for cosmic reality had arisen a symbol for thought. The text, rather than the book, became the object in which thought is gathered and mirrored.

This cerebral revolution did not happen in a vacuum. It happened precisely in those Cistercian monasteries and canonical urban schools in which—exactly during these decades—the hotly disputed theme was the nature of universals. The *dictator* had landscaped the parchment as a garden of words. The new kind of thinker and *auctor*, with his own hand and in quick, cursive letters, cleared a building lot for the cathedral of a *summa*. He took up pen and ink and paper to materialize a process of abstraction which was analogous to what was discussed in the schools of the time. The bookish text—both in the way it was written and in the way it was read—reflects, articulates, reenforces, and legitimates the mental topology which the new approach to law, philosophy, and theology presupposes.

Chenu has called the twelfth century the *aetas boetiana*.[8] He reminds us that during this time the Greek philosophers were received in the cloister through the hands of the late Roman sage. But, writing in Latin, Boethius confused what Aristotle had distinguished. Two words in Aristotle were both translated by Boethius as *abstractio*. The first word is *chorízein* which means "to separate." It is used by Aristotle as a technical term and refers, usually in a critical way, to the separateness of Platonic ideas from reality. The other word translated as *abstractio* is *aphairesis,* which in Aristotelian terminology means something like "sequestration" or "bracketing."[9] It is consistently used to designate the mental process by which the material object is set apart by the categorizing mind. For instance, the foot is put into parentheses by a mathematician who considers it only as a measure of length. It took early scholastic philosophers more than a generation to reintroduce this distinction, and to understand conceptual thought as a process of formal sequestration.

Abstraction is not an issue for most of the early twelfth-century thinkers. The term does not even occur in the modern index of the works of Anselm of Canterbury.[10] When he has to explain how insight comes about, Anselm quotes one or the other passage from Augustine which tell of the mind's divine illumination, thus making God's ideas about nature intelligible to man. Later medieval Boethians, Abaelard[11] just as much as Hugh, take it for granted that concept formation has something to do with *abstractio*. However, they too are still under the spell of the Boethian confusion of *the separate* with that which is *put into parentheses*. They, like Hugh, are born into the meagre light of a predawn. Hugh, in spite of contrary evidence from the page, knew that

8. Marie-Dominique Chenu, "La Théologie au XIIᵉ siècle," in *Études de philosophie médiévale,* ed. Étienne Gilson (Paris: Vrin, 1957), p. 142.

9. M. D. Philippe, "*Aphaíresis próthesis, chorízen* dans la philosophie d'Aristote," *Revue Thomiste* 49 (1948): 461–79.

10. *Opera omnia,* ed. F. S. Schmitt, vol. 6, *Index rerum,* p. 28.

11. J. F. Boler, "Abaelard and the Problem of Universals," *Journal of the History of Philosophy* 1 (1963): 37–51.

there had to be a third way of reading, not for my ear or your ear but for our eyes. Thus, without insisting on it, he was already committed to a new way of explaining cognition by abstraction, adumbrating what would become common doctrine once Arabic and Byzantine manuscripts helped the Scholastics gain access to Aristotle's Greek thought. In this, Hugh's analysis of thinking is consistent with his analysis of reading.

Lingua and *textus*

One more point to be kept in mind when discussing the shift in the metaphor of the book: at the same time that the text takes off from the page, letters also break their traditional bondage to Latin. At the same moment when the twenty-four letters are used for one construct that is primarily visible, they also, finally, are used for that purpose for which in the mind of the modern reader they must have been made— for recording the sound of a living, spoken language. Too easily one forgets that throughout their existence, Latin letters connoted one and only one *lingua,* the Latin one. The letter "L" referred approximately to the first sound in *lingua, liber,* or *lumen,* but never to an utterance in vernacular speech. By the middle of the twelfth century, the letter "L" can just as well connote the beginning of *Liebe, love,* or *lust.* The detachment of the text from the materiality of the parchment "silenced" the page. The letters ceased to be those touches by the scribe which bring forth sound from the lines. Thus silenced on the page, the letters become available for the routine recording of non-Latin utterances. The proliferation of vernacular records, at least those written in the Roman alphabet, coincides with the prevalence of a bookish attitude toward the page. The book, taken as symbol, has ceased, simultaneously, to point unambiguously toward nature as a book and Latin as the language. It is within this twofold framework that the inversion of the book's symbolic vector after 1200 must be understood.

"All things are pregnant"

This vectorial inversion of the *Schriftstück* as symbol calls attention to a long, complex, and manifold metaphorical tradition. Since antiquity, the book was used as an ideogram, an attribute, and a cipher.[12] Al-

---

12. Leo Koep, *Das himmlische Buch in Antike und Christentum: eine religions-geschichtliche Untersuchung zur altchristlichen Bildersprache,* Theophaneia: Beiträge zur Religions- und Kirchengeschichte des Altertums 8 (Bonn: Hanstein, 1952).

ready in Mesopotamia the scroll was a metaphor for destiny, and this figure migrated westward, to Greece. In the *Greek Anthology,* life is compared with a scroll that unrolls to the scribe's ornate curlicue at the end of the last line.[13] In the Etruscan center of Italy, destiny was the work of the Parcae, three subterranean hags. Atropos spins out human destiny, Clotho takes up the yarn, Lachesis measures it out and irrevocably cuts the thread when a life has come to an end. In later antiquity this cavernous workroom is represented as a secretariat, where one beautiful woman dictates the horoscope, a second takes notes, and a third reads out the lot of each mortal.[14] The Parcae are no longer fate's rulers; they have become its bureaucratic administrators.

This "book of destiny" or "life as a book" must be distinguished from the "book of life," which is of Babylonian origin. This latter functions as a heavenly census, listing those chosen to survive. Occasionally this list contains scribal annotations, and becomes a record of debts that accompanies each one to the nether world.[15] Bas-reliefs show the scroll as the attribute of the otherworldly magistrate.[16]

The scroll in antiquity is thus not only metaphor but attribute. It labels the ruler. Like the law that he dictates, the scroll is in the hand of the king. Here the book is the sign of this-worldly rather than divine power. The Old Testament uses the book as a metaphor for destiny, roll call, and debt registry, but not as an attribute. Not a single pre-Christian god of Mediterranean antiquity has the book or a scroll in his hands. In this, Christ is unique. He alone has divine attributes, *and* wields a scroll. He both *is* the word and *reveals* the book. The Word becomes Flesh in the Book. Writing becomes an allegory for the Incarnation in the Womb of the Virgin. Hence the liturgical reverence for the book as object.

13. Cited in Ernst Robert Curtius, *Europäische Literatur und lateinisches Mittelalter,* 7th ed. (Bern and Munich: Francke, 1969), p. 311.

14. Otto J. Brendel, "The Celestial Sphere of the Moirai," in *Symbolism of the Sphere. A Contribution to the History of Earlier Greek Philosophy. Études préliminaires aux Religions Orientales dans L'Empire Romain,* vol. 67 (Leiden: E. J. Brill, 1977). "The Parcae are shown as casting the horoscope: Atropos, after reading the exact time from a sundial, turns to Lachesis in order to impart it to her who takes note of it in ink. The spinner, now superfluous, is missing. The ancient concept of the spinning sisters and subterranean sorceresses was so completely absorbed and digested. . . . The Moirae observe and write down what must happen according to elementary laws. As a group they form a transcription, as it were, of the horoscope under which all that comes into existence lives and dies" (pp. 81–83).

15. Ibid., pp. 26–28.

16. See Gottlieb Schrenk, "Bíblos, biblíon," in *Theologisches Wörterbuch zum NT,* vol. 1, pp. 613–20 (Stuttgart: Kohlhammer, 1933).

Augustine further enriched the metaphor. He goes beyond the three meanings of fate, roll call, and debt registry, and makes an unprecedented distinction. He makes the book into a symbol of God's twofold revelation. "God has written two books, the book of creation and the book of redemption."[17] By his time, the physical appearance of the book had already metamorphosed from the scroll to the *codex,* the stack of cut and bound pages that is still familiar to us. It is in this guise that for the Middle Ages it became the cipher for God's twofold gift, the two distinct sources of all knowledge. Throughout his writings Hugh constantly comes back to Augustine's sentence.

From this Augustinian passage, Hugh spins one of his loveliest expressions: *Omnis natura rationem parit, et nihil in universitate infecundum est.*[18] "All nature is pregnant with sense, and nothing in all of the universe is sterile." In this sentence, Hugh brings centuries of Christian metaphor to their full maturity. In the lines of the page, the reader enlightened by God encounters creatures who wait there to give birth to meaning. This ontological status of the book yields the key to an understanding of Christian monasticism as a life of reading. The reason why the *studium legendi* is an effective and infallible search for wisdom is founded in the fact that all things are impregnated with sense, and this sense only waits to be brought to light by the reader. Nature is not just like a book; nature itself is a book, and the man-made book is its analogue. Reading the man-made book is an act of midwifery. Reading, far from being an act of abstraction, is an act of incarnation. Reading is a somatic, bodily act of birth attendance witnessing the sense brought forth by all things encountered by the pilgrim through the pages.

In the earlier twelfth century, *librum manu factum* is but the third kind of book, ranged after the book of our salvation, the Redeemer, and the book of creation, tracings from the finger of God.

> *omnis mundi creatura*
> *quasi liber, et pictura*
> *nobis est, et speculum.*[19]

All of creation is given to us as a book, a picture, and a mirror.[20]

17. Augustine, *De Genesi ad Litteram; PL* 34, 245.

18. *DB* VI, 5, p. 123.

19. Alanus ab Insulis (Alain of Lille, 1120–1202): *Magistri Alani Rhythmus alter, quo graphice natura hominis fluxa et caduca depingitur* (*PL* 210, 579). See also Frank Olaf Büttner, "*Mens divina liber grandis est:* zu einigen Darstellungen des Lesens in spätmittelalterlichen Handschriften," *Philobiblon,* Vienna, 16 (1972): 92–126.

20. A magnificent and thorough study of the complex transformations of "image" and "likeness" during this one generation is Robert Javelet's *Image et ressemblance au XIIᵉ siècle de St. Anselme à Alain de Lille,* 2 vols. (Paris: Letouzey, 1967).

The book as symbol, analogue, and metaphor in Hugh's time is, above all, a symbol for *reading,* conceptualized and experienced as meiotic decipherment of reality by which the reader, like the midwife, brings forth—in God's invisible light—the sense with which all things are impregnated, God's Word.

> *Tres sunt libri: primus est quem fecit homo de aliquo, se-cundus quem creavit Deus de nihilo, tertius quem Deus genuit: Deum de se Deo. Primus est opus hominis corrupti-bile; secundus est opus Dei quod numquam desinit esse, in quo opere visibili invisibilis sapientia creatoris visibiliter scripta est; tertius, non opus Dei sed sapientia, per quam fecit omnia opera sua Deus.*[21]

There are three books. The first is the book that man makes out of something, the second that which God created out of nothing, the third that which God begat from Himself, God of God. The first is the corruptible work of man, the second is the work of God that never ceases to exist, in which visible work is written visibly the invisible wisdom of the Creator. The third is not the work of God, but the Wisdom by which God made all his works.[22]

21. Hugh of St. Victor, *De arca Noe morali* II, 12; *PL* 176, 643D–644A.

22. Translation from *Hugh of Saint-Victor. Selected Spiritual Writings,* trans. by a Religious of C.S.M.V., with an introduction by Aelred Squire, O.P. (New York: Harper and Row, 1962).

Bibliography

Adamson, J. W. "'The Illiterate Anglo-Saxon.'" In *"The Illiterate Anglo-Saxon" and Other Essays on Education Medieval and Modern*, ed. J. W. Adamson. Cambridge: Cambridge University Press, 1946. Pp. 1–20.

Aelred of Rievaulx. *Opera omnia*. A. Hoste, O. S. B., and C. H. Talbot, eds. Turnhout: Brepols, 1971.

Albino, Diana. "La divisione in capitoli nelle opere degli antichi." *Annali della Facolta di lettere e filosofia dell'Università di Napoli* 10 (1962–63): 219–34.

Alexander, Jonathan James Graham. *The Decorated Letter*. New York: Braziller, 1978.

———. "Scribes as Artists: The Arabesque Initial in Twelfth-Century English Manuscripts." In *Medieval Scribes, Manuscripts, and Libraries*, ed. M. B. Parkes and A. G. Watson. London: Scolar Press, 1978. Vol. 2, pp. 87–116.

Alexander, Jonathan James Graham, and Gibson, M. T., eds. *Medieval Learning and Literature: Essays Presented to R. W. Hunt*. London: Oxford University Press, 1976.

Allard, Grey H. "Vocabulaire érigénien relatif à la représentation de l'écriture." In *Drittes Internationales Eriugena Colloquium, 1979,* ed. Werner Beierswaltes. Freiburg: C. Winter, 1980. Pp. 16–32.

Alverny, Marie-Thérèse de. "Astrologues et théologiens au XIIᵉ siècle." In *Mélanges offerts à Marie-Dominique Chenu*. Bibliothèque Thomistique 37. Paris: Vrin, 1967. Pp. 31–50.

———. "Le Cosmos symbolique du XIIᵉ siècle." *Recherches de théologie ancienne et médiévale* 20 (1953): 31–81.

———. "L'Homme comme symbole. Le microcosme." In *Simboli e simbologia nell'alto Medioevo, 3–9 aprile, 1975.* Settimana di Studio 26, 1. Spoleto: Centro Italiano per i studi sull' Alto Medio Evo, 1976. Pp. 123–83.

———. "La Sagesse et ses sept filles. Recherches sur les allégories de la philosophie et des arts libéraux du IXᵉ siècle." In *Mélanges F. Grat*, vol 1. Paris, 1946. Pp. 245–278.

Andersen, Oivind. "Mündlichkeit und Schriftlichkeit im frühen Griechen-tum." *Antike und Abendland,* vol. 33, no. 1 (1987): 29–44.

Apel, Willi. *Gregorian Chant.* Champaign: University of Illinois Press, 1958.

Armbuster, Ludwig. "Zur Bienenkunde frühchristlicher Zeiten." *Archiv für Bienenkunde,* vol 16 (1936), pp. 177–208.

Armknecht, W. *Geschichte des Wortes "süß"; bis zum Ausgang des Mittelal-ters.* Germanische Studien 171. Berlin: Ebering, 1936.

Assmann, Aleida. Review of *Die Schrift. Hat Schreiben eine Zukunft?* by V. Flusser. *Poetica* 20 (1988): 284–88.

Assmann, Aleida; Assmann, Jan; and Hardmeier, Christof, eds. *Schrift und Gedächtnis: Beiträge zur Archäologie der literarischen Kommunikation.* Munich: Fink, 1983.

Auden, W. H. *About the House.* New York: Random House, 1965.

Auerbach, Erich. *Dante: Poet of the Secular World.* Chicago: University of Chicago Press, 1961.

———. "Dante's Address to the Reader." *Romance Philology* 7 (1954): 268–78.

———. *Literary Language and Its Public in Late Latin Antiquity and in the Middle Ages.* Princeton: Princeton University Press, 1965.

———. *Literatursprache und Publikum in der lateinischen Spätantike und im Mittelalter.* Bern: Franke, 1958.

———. *Typologische Motive in der mittelalterlichen Literatur.* Krefeld, 1964.

———. *Mimesis: Dargestellte Wirklichkeit in der abendländischen Literatur.* 7th ed. Munich: Franke, 1987. (Orig. publ. Istanbul, 1946; English transla-tion: *Mimesis: The Representation of Reality in Western Literature* [Princeton: Princeton University Press, 1953].)

Balogh, Joseph. "Voces Paginarum." *Philologus* 82 (1926–27): 84–109 and 202–40.

Balthasar, Hans Urs von. "Sehen, Hören und Lesen im Raum der Kirche." In *Sponsa Verbi.* Einsiedeln: Johannes Verlag, 1961. Pp. 484–501.

Baltrušaitis, Jurgis. *Essai sur une légende scientifique: le miroir. Révélations, science-fiction et fallacies.* Paris: Elmayan-Seuil, 1978.

———. *Le Moyen Âge fantastique.* Paris: Colin, 1955.

———. *Réveils et prodiges: le Gothique fantastique.* Paris: Colin, 1960.

———. *La Stylistique ornamentale dans la sculpture romane.* Paris: Librarie Ernest Leroux, 1931.

———. "Une Survivance médiévale: 'La Plante à têtes.'" *Revue des arts* 4 (1954): 81–92.

Barakat, Robert Z. *The Cistercian Sign Language: A Study in Non-Verbal Communications.* Cistercian Studies Series No. 11. Kalamazoo, Mich.: Cis-tercian Publications, 1975.

Baron, Hans. "The *Querelle* of the Ancients and the Moderns as a Problem for Renaissance Scholarship." *Journal of the History of Ideas* 20 (1959): 3–22.

Baron, Roger. "L'authenticité de l'oeuvre de Hugues de Saint-Victor." *Revue des sciences religieuses* 36 (1962): 48–58.

———. "Études sur l'authenticité de l'oeuvre de Hugues de Saint-Victor d'après les mss. Paris Maz., 717, BN 14506 et Douai 360–6." *Scriptorium* 10 (1956): 182–220.

———. *Hugonis de Sancto Victore Opera Propaedeutica: Practica geometriae, De grammatica, Epitome Dindimi in Philosophiam.* Publications in Medieval Studies, ed. Philip S. Moore. Notre Dame, Ind.: University of Notre Dame Press, 1966.

———."Hugues de Saint-Victor. Contribution à un nouvel examen de son oeuvre." *Traditio* 15 (1959): 223–97.

———. *Hugues de Saint-Victor. Six opuscules spirituels.* Paris: Les Éditions du Cerf, 1975.

———."L'Influence de Hugues de St.-Victor." *Recherches de théologie ancienne et médiévale* 22 (1955): 56–71.

———. "Note méthodologique sur la détermination d'authenticité pour l'oeuvre de Hugues de Saint-Victor." *Cahiers de civilisation médiévale* 9 (1966): 225–28.

———."Notes biographiques sur Hugues de Saint-Victor." *Revue d'histoire ecclésiastique* 51 (1956): 920–34.

———. "Le 'Sacrement de la Foi' selon Hugues de Saint-Victor." *Revue des sciences philosophiques et théologiques* 42 (1958): 50–78.

———. *Science et sagesse chez Hugues de Saint-Victor.* Paris: P. Lethielleux, 1986.

Bataillon, L. J.; Guyot, B.; and House, R., eds. *La Production du livre universitaire au moyen âge. Exemplar et pecia.* Paris: Edition du CNRS, 1988.

Battisti, Carlo. "Secoli illetterati. Appunti sulla crisi del latino prima della riforma carolingia." *Studi medievali* (1960): 369–396.

Bäuml, Franz. "Der Übergang mündlicher zur artes-bestimmten Literatur des Mittelalters. Gedanken und Bedenken." In *Fachliteratur des Mittelalters. Festschrift Gerhard Eis.* Stuttgart, 1968. Pp. 1–10.

———. "Varieties and Consequences of Medieval Literacy and Illiteracy." *Speculum* 55 (1980): 237–65.

———, ed. *From Symbol to Mimesis: the Generation of Walther von der Vogelweide.* Göppingen: Kümmerle, 1984.

Bäuml, Franz H., and Spielmann, Edda. "From Illiteracy to Literacy: Prologomena to a Study of the Nibelungenlied." In *Oral Literature. Seven Essays,* ed. Joseph J. Duggan. London: Scottish Academic Press, 1975. Pp. 62–73.

Bazan, B. C. "Les Questions disputées, principalement dans les facultés de Théologie." In L. Génicot, *Typologie des sources du moyen âge occidental.* Turnhout: Brepols, 1985.

Belting, Hans. *Bild und Kult: eine Geschichte des Bildes vor dem Zeitalter der Kunst.* Munich: Beck, 1990.

Benson, R. L., and Constable, G., eds. *Renaissance and Renewal in the Twelfth Century.* Cambridge, Mass.: Harvard University Press, 1982.

Benton, John F., ed. *Self and Society in Medieval France. The Memoirs of Abbot Guibert of Nogent (1064?-c. 1125).* The translation of C. C. Swinton Bland revised by the editor. New York: Harper, 1970.

Berkout, C. T., and Russell, J. B. *Medieval Heresies. A Bibliography 1960–1979.* Pontifical Institute of Medieval Studies. Subsidia Medievalia 2. Toronto, 1981.

Berlière, Ursmer. "Lectio divina." In *L'Ascèse bénédictine des origines à la fin du XIIe siècle.* Collection Pax. Maredsous, 1927.

Birt, Theodor. *Das antike Buchwesen in seinem Verhältnis zur Literatur, mit Beiträgen zur Textgeschichte des Theokrit, Catull, Properz und anderer Autoren.* Berlin: W. Herz, 1882. (Reprint Aalen: Scientia, 1959.)

———. *Die Buchrolle in der Kunst.* Leipzig: Teubner, 1907.

Bischoff, Bernhard. "Aus der Schule Hugos von St. Viktor." In *Aus der Geisteswelt des Mittelalters,* ed. A. Lang, J. Lecher, and M. Schmaus. Beiträge zur Geschichte der Philosophie und Theologie des Mittelalters, Supplementband 3, Halbband 1. Münster, 1935. pp. 246–50.

———."Elementarunterricht und *probationes pennae* in der erstern Hälfte des Mittelalters." *Mittelalterliche Studien* 1 (1966): 74–78.

———. "Die Gedächtniskunst im Bamberger Dom." In *Anecdota Novissima.* Stuttgart: Hiersemann, 1984. Pp. 204–11.

———. *Mittelalterliche Studien. Ausgewählte Aufsätze zur Schriftkunde und Literaturgeschichte.* 2 vols. Stuttgart: Hiersemann, 1966–67.

———. *Paläographie des römischen Altertums und des abendländischen Mittelalters.* Grundlagen der Germanistik 24. Berlin: E. Schmidt, 1980.

———. "Il ruolo del libro nella riforma di Carlo Magno." *Schede medievali* 2 (1982): 7–13.

———. "The Study of Foreign Languages in the Middle Ages." *Speculum* 36 (1961): 109–226.

———. *Die süddeutschen Schreibschulen und Bibliotheken in der Karolingerzeit.* 2 vols. Wiesbaden: Harrassowitz, 1980.

———. "Eine verschollene Einteilung der Wissenschaften." *Archives d'histoire doctrinale et littéraire du moyen âge* 33 (1958): 5–20.

Bischoff, B., and Hoffmann, J. *Libri Sancti Kyliani: die Würzburger Schreibschule und die Dombibliothek im 8. und 9. Jahrhundert.* Würzburg: Schönigh, 1952.

Bloch, P. "Autorenbildnis." In *Lexikon der christlichen Ikonographie,* vol. 1, cols. 232–34. Freiburg, Br.: Herder, 1968.

Blum, H. *Die antike Mnemotechnik, Spudasmata.* Studien zur klassischen Gesetzgebung 15. Hildesheim: Olms, 1969.

Blume, Karl. *Abbatia. Ein Beitrag zur Geschichte der kirchlichen Rechtssprache.* Stuttgart: Enke, 1941.

Blumenberg, Hans. *Die Lesbarkeit der Welt.* Frankfurt, Main: Suhrkamp, 1986.

Boblitz, Hartmut. "Die Allegorese der Arche Noah in der frühen Bibelauslegung." *Frühmittelalterliche Studien* 6 (1972). Pp. 159–70.

Boer, P. A. H. *Gedenken und Gedächtnis in der Welt des alten Testamentes.* Stuttgart: Kohlhammer, 1962.

Boler, J. F. "Abaelard and the Problem of the Universals." *Journal of the History of Philosophy* 1 (1963): 37–51.

Bonnard, Fourier. *Histoire de l'Abbaye Royale et de l'ordre des Chanoines Réguliers de St.-Victor de Paris. Première période: 1013–1500.* Paris: Savaète, 1907.

Borgolte, Michael. "Freigelassene im Dienst der Memoria. Kulttradition und Kultwandel zwischen Antike und Mittelalter." *Frühmittelalterliche Studien* 17 (1983): 234–50.

Borst, Arno. *Der Turmbau von Babel. Geschichte der Meinungen über Ursprung und Vielfalt der Sprachen und Völker.* Stuttgart: Hiersemann, 1963.

Bosse, Heinrich. "'Die Schüler müssen selber schreiben lernen' oder die Einrichtung der Schiefertafel." In *Schreiben — Schreiben lernen. Rolf Sanner zum 65. Geburtstag,* ed. D. Boueke and N. Hopster. Tübinger Beiträge zur Linguistik 249. Tübingen: Narr, 1985. Pp. 164–99.

Bottéro, Jean. *Mésopotamie. L'Écriture, la raison et les dieux.* Paris: Gallimard, 1987.

Boueke, D., and Hopster, N., eds. *Schreiben — Schreiben lernen. Festschrift Rolf Sanner zum 65. Geburtstag.* Tübinger Beiträge zur Linguistik 249. Tübingen: Narr, 1985.

Bourgain, Pascale. "L'Édition des manuscrits." In *L'Histoire de l'édition française,* ed. H. J. Martin and R. Chartier, vol. 1. Paris: Promodis, 1982. Pp. 48–75.

Brendel, Otto J. "The Celestial Sphere of the Moirai." In *Symbolism of the Sphere. A Contribution to the History of Earlier Greek Philosophy. Études préliminaires aux religions Orientales dans L'Empire Romain,* vol. 67. Leiden: E. J. Brill, 1977. Pp. 81–83.

Brincken, Anna Dorothea von den. "*Mappa Mundi* und Chronographie. Studien zur *imago mundi* des Mittelalters." *Deutsches Archiv für Erforschung des Mittelalters* 24 (1968): 118–86.

———. "*Tabula Alphabetica.* Von den Anfängen alphabetischer Registerarbeiten zu Geschichtswerken." In *Festschrift für Hermann Heimpel.* Veröfenlichungen des Max Planck Instituts für Geschichte. Göttingen: Vandenhoek, 1972. Pp. 900–923.

———. "*. . . ut describeretur universus orbis.* Zur Universalkarthographie des Mittelalters." *Miscellanea Medievalia* 7 (1970): 249–78.

Bruni, Francesco. "Traduzione, tradizione e diffusione della cultura: Contributo alla lingua dei semicolti." *Quaderni Storici* 38 (1978): 523–34.

Bultot, Robert. "Cosmologie et contemptus mundi." *Recherches de théologie ancienne et médiévale.* Numéro Special 1. Mélanges de théologie et de littérature médiévales offerts à Dom Hildebrand Bascuoa, O.S.B. Louvain, 1980.

Buttimer, Charles Henry. *Hugonis de Sancto Victore, Didascalicon. De Studio Legendi: A Critical Text.* Dissertation by Brother Charles Henry Buttimer, M.A. Washington, D.C.: Catholic University Press, 1939.

Büttner, Frank Olaf. "*Mens divina liber grandis est:* zu einigen Darstellungen des Lesens in spätmittelalterlichen Handschriften." *Philobiblon* (Vienna) 16 (1972): 92–126.

Bynum, Caroline Walker. "Did the Twelfth Century Discover the Individual?" *Journal of Ecclesiastical History* 31 (1980): 1–12.

——. *Docere verbo et exemplo: An Aspect of Twelfth-Century Spirituality.* Harvard Theological Studies 31. Missoula: Scholar Press, 1979.

——. "The Spirituality of Regular Canons in the Twelfth Century: A New Approach." *Medievalia et Humanistica*, n.s., 11 (1973): 3–24.

Calati, B. "La *lectio divina* nella tradizione monastica benedettina." *Benedictina* 28 (1981): 407–38.

Camille, Michael. "The Devil's Writing: Diabolic Literacy in Medieval Art." In *World Art: Themes of Unity in Diversity: Acts of the Twenty-sixth International Congress of Art,* ed. Irving Lavin. University Park: Pennsylvania State University Press, 1989.

——. "Seeing and Reading: Some Visual Implications of Medieval Literacy and Illiteracy." *Art History* 8 (1985): 26–49.

——. "Visual Signs of the Sacred Page: Books in the Bible Moralisee." *Word and Image,* vol. 5, no. 1 (Jan. 1989): 111–30.

Canivez, J. M., ed. *Status Capitulorum Generalium Ordinis Cisterciensis ab anno 1116 ad annum 1786,* vol. 1. Louvain, 1933.

Caplan, Harry. *Rhetorica ad Herennium. De ratione dicendi.* With an English translation. Cambridge, Mass.: Harvard University Press, 1954.

Capua, F. di. "Osservazioni sulla lettura e sulla preghiera ad alta voce presso gli antichi." *Rendiconti dell'Accademia di Archeologia, Lettere e Belle Arti di Napoli,* n.s., 28 (1953–54): 59–62.

Caruthers, Mary. *The Book of Memory: A Study of Memory in Medieval Culture.* Cambridge: Cambridge University Press, 1990.

Casel, Odo, O.S.B. *Vom Spiegel als Symbol.* Nachgelassene Schriften zusammengestellt von Julia Platz. Maria Laach: Ars Liturgica, 1961.

Charland, Thomas M. *Artes Praedicandi: Contributions à l'histoire de la rhétorique au moyen âge.* Publications de l'Institut d'Études médiévales d'Ottawa 7. Paris: Vrin, 1936.

Charpin, Dominique, ed. *Le Geste, la parole et l'écrit dans la vie juridique en Babylonie ancienne. Écriture, systèmes idéographiques et pratiques expressives.* Actes du colloque international de l'Université de Paris VII. Paris: Sycomore, 1982.

Chartier, Roger. *Lectures et lecteurs dans la France d'ancien régime.* Paris: Seuil, 1987.

Chastel, André, et al., eds. *La sculpture. Principes d'analyse scientifique: Méthode et vocabulaire.* Ministère de la Culture et de la Communication. Inventaire Général des Monuments . . . de la France. Paris: Imprimerie nationale, 1978.

Châtillon, Jean. "Le *Didascalicon* de Hugues de Saint-Victor." In *La Pensée encyclopédique au moyen âge.* Neuchâtel: Baconnière, 1966. Pp. 63–76.

——. "Une Ecclésiologie médiévale: L'Idée de l'Église dans la théologie de l'école de Saint-Victor au XIIe siècle." *Irénikon* 22 (1949): 115–38, 395–411.

——. "Les Écoles de Chartres et de Saint-Victor." In *La scuola nell' Occi-*

dente Latino nell' alto medio evo. 2 vols. Settimane di Studio 19. Spoleto: Centro Italiano per i studi sull' Alto Medio Evo, 1972. Pp. 795–839.

———. "De Guillaume de Champeaux à Thomas Gallus: Chronique littéraire et doctrinale de l'école de Saint-Victor." *Revue de moyen âge latin* 8 (1952): 139–62.

———. "Hugo von St. Viktor." In *Theologische Realenzyklopädie*, vol. 15. Berlin, 1986. Pp. 629–35.

———. "Hugues de Saint-Victor critique de Jean Scot." In: *Jean Scot Erigène et l'histoire de la philosophie*. Actes du Colloque international du Centre National de la Recherche scientifique, Laon 1975. Paris, 1977. Pp. 415–31.

Chaunu, Pierre. *Histoire science sociale. La Durée, l'espace et l'homme à l'époque moderne*. Paris: Soc. édit. d'Enseignement Supérieur, 1974.

Chaytor, H. J. *From Script to Print: An Introduction to Medieval Vernacular Literature*. Cambridge: Cambridge University Press, 1945.

———. "The Medieval Reader and Textual Criticism." *Bulletin of the John Rylands Library* 26 (1941): 49–56.

Chenu, Marie-Dominique. "Arts 'mécaniques' et oeuvres serviles." *Revue des sciences philosophiques et théologiques* 29 (1940): 313–15.

———. "Auctor, Actor, Autor." *Bulletin du Cange* 3 (1927): 81–86.

———. "Les Catégories affectives dans la langue de l'école." In *Le Coeur*. Études carmelitaines. Bruges: Desclée De Brouwer, 1950. Pp. 123–28.

———. "Civilisation urbaine et théologie. L'École de Saint-Victor au XIIᵉ siècle." *Annales: économies, sociétés, civilisations* 29 (1974): 1253–63.

———. "Conscience de l'histoire et théologie au XIIᵉ siècle." *Archives d'histoire doctrinale et littéraire du moyen âge* 21 (1954): 107–33.

———. "Cur homo? Le Sous-sol d'une controverse au XIIe siècle." *Mélanges de science religieuse* 10 (1953): 195–204.

———. "La Décadence de l'allégorisation. Un Témoin, Garnier de Rochefort." In *L'Homme devant Dieu. Mélanges offerts au père Henri de Lubac*, vol. 2. Paris: Aubier, 1964. Pp. 129–36.

———. "L'Éveil de la conscience dans la civilisation médiévale." In *Conférence Albert le Grand 1968*. Montréal: Institute d'Études Médiévales, 1969.

———. "Grammaire et théologie au XIIᵉ et XIIIᵉ siècles." *Archives d'histoire doctrinale et littéraire du moyen âge* 10–11 (1935–36): 5–28.

———. "*Involucrum*: Le Mythe selon les théologiens médiévaux." *Archives d'histoire doctrinale et littéraire du moyen âge* 30 (1955): 75–79.

———. "Les Masses pauvres." In G. Cottier; J.-C. Baumont, A. Chouraqui, et al. *Église et pauvreté*. Paris: Cerf, 1965. Pp. 169–76.

———. "Moines, clercs, et laïcs au carrefour de la vie évangélique." *Revue d'histoire ecclésiastique* 49 (1954): 59–89.

———. "La Nature et l'homme: La renaissance du XIIᵉ siècle." In *La Théologie au XIIᵉ Siècle*. Paris: Vrin, 1976. Pp. 19–51.

———. "Nature ou histoire? Une Controverse éxégétique sur la création au XIIᵉ siècle." *Archives d'histoire doctrinale et littéraire du moyen âge* 20 (1953): 25–30.

———. "Notes de lexicographie philosophique médiévale: *disciplina*." *Revue des sciences philosophiques et théologiques* 25 (1936): 686–92.

———. "Platon à Citeaux." *Archives d'histoire doctrinale et littéraire du moyen âge* 21 (1954): 99–106.

———. *Il risveglio della coscienza nella civilitá medievale*. Giá e Non Ancora 57. Milano: Jaca Book, 1982.

———. "*Spiritus:* Le Vocabulaire de l'âme au XIIe siècle." *Revue des sciences philosophiques et théologiques* 41 (1957): 209–32.

———. "La Théologie au XIIe siècle." In *Études de philosophie médiévale*, ed. Étienne Gilson. Paris: Vrin, 1957.

———. *La Théologie comme science au XIIIe siècle*. 3d rev. ed. Bibliothèque Thomistique. Paris: Vrin, 1957.

Chiampi, James Thomas. "From Unlikeness to Writing: Dante's 'Visible Speech' in Canto Ten, Purgatorio." *Medievalia* 5 (1982): 97–112.

Chiffoleau, J. "Perché cambia la morte nella regione di Avignone alla fine del Medioevo." *Quaderni Storici* 50 (1982): 449–65.

Christ, Karl. *The Handbook of Medieval Library History*, trans. and ed. by Theophil M. Otto. Metuchen, N.J.: The Scarecrow Press, Inc., 1984.

Clanchy, M. T. *From Memory to Written Record, England 1066–1307*. Cambridge, Mass.: Harvard University Press, 1979.

———. "Remembering the Past and the Good Old Law." *History* 40 (1970): 165–76.

Clapp, Vernon W. *The Story of Permanent Durable Book Paper, 1115–1970*. Toronto: University of Toronto Press, 1971.

Congar, Yves. "Modèle monastique et modèle sacerdotal en Occident, de Grégoire VII (1073–1085) à Innocent III (1198)." In *Études de civilisation médiévale (IXe–XIIe). Mélanges offerts à Edmond-René Labande*. Poitiers, 1973.

Constable, Giles. "Aelred of Rievaulx and the Nun of Watton: An Episode in the Early History of the Gilbertine Order." In *Medieval Women*, ed. Derek Baker. Studies in Church History, Subsidia 1. Oxford: Blackwell, 1978. Pp. 209–26.

———. *Attitudes toward Self-Inflicted Suffering in the Middle Ages*. Brookline, Mass.: Hellenic College Press, 1982.

———. *The Letters of Peter the Venerable*. Cambridge, Mass.: Harvard University Press, 1967.

———. *Medieval Monasticism. A Select Bibliography*. Toronto Medieval Bibliographies 6. Toronto: University of Toronto, 1976.

———. "Monachisme et pèlerinage du moyen âge." *Revue historique* 101 (1977): 3–27.

———. "*Nudus nudum Christum sequi* and Parallel Formulas in the Twelfth Century: A Supplementary Dossier." In *Continuity and Discontinuity in Church History. Festschrift J. H. Williams*, ed. E. F. Church, and T. George. Studies in Christian Thought 19. Leiden, 1981. Pp. 83–91.

———. "Opposition to Pilgrimage in the Middle Ages." In *Mélanges G. Fransen*. Studia Gratiana 19. Bologna, 1976. Pp. 125–46.

———. "The Popularity of Twelfth-Century Spiritual Writers in the Late Middle Ages." In *Religious Life and Thought*. London: Variorum, 1979.

———. "Resistance to the Tithes in the Middle Ages." *Journal of Ecclesiastic History* 13 (1962): 172–85.

Constable, Giles, and Smith, B. *Libellus de diversis ordinibus qui sunt in Ecclesia.* Oxford: Oxford University Press, 1972.

Corbier, M. "L'Écriture dans l'espace public romain." In Centre national de la récherche scientifique. *L'Urbs: Espace urbain et histoire.* Rome: École francaise de Rome, 1987. Pp. 583–95.

Corbin, Henry. "Les cités emblématiques." In *Les symboles du lieu, l'habitation de l'homme.* Le Cahiers de l'Herne, ed. Horia Damian and Jean-Pierre Raynaud. Paris: l'Herne, 1983. Pp. 47–54.

Corcoran, T. *Renatae Litterae, saeculo 16. in scholis societatis Iesu stabilitae. Ad usum academicum in collegio Dublinensi.* Dublin, 1927.

Courcelle, Pierre. *Connais-toi toi-même, de Socrate à Saint Bernard.* 3 vols. Paris: Études Augustiniennes, 1974.

———. "Étude critique sur le commentaire de la 'Consolation' de Boece (XIᵉ-XVᵉ siècles)." *Archives d'histoire doctrinale et littéraire du moyen âge* 12 (1939): 6–140.

Cremascoli, G. *Exire de saeculo. Esami di alcuni testi della spiritualitá benedettina e francescana (Sec. XIII-XIV).* Quaderni di Ricerche Storiche sul Primo Movimento Francescano e del Monachesimo Benedettino 3. Nantes, 1982.

Curshman, Michael. "The Concept of the Oral Formula as an Impediment to Our Understanding of Medieval Oral Poetry." *Medievalia Humanistica,* n.s., 8 (1977): 63–76.

Curtius, Ernst Robert. *Europäische Literatur und lateinisches Mittelalter.* 7th ed. Bern and Munich: Francke, 1969. (English translation: *European Literature and the Latin Middle Ages* [Princeton: Princeton University Press, 1953].)

Cusanus, Nicolaus. *De venatione sapientiae, Die Jagd nach Weisheit,* ed. P. Wilpert. Hamburg, 1964.

Damish, Hubert. "L'Alphabet des masques." *Nouvelle revue de psychoanalyse* 21 (1981): 123–31.

Décanet, J. M. "Amor ipse intellectus est." *Revue du moyen âge latin* 1945: 368.

Deferrari, Roy J., ed. *Hugh of St. Victor's 'On the Sacraments of the Christian Faith.'* Cambridge: Cambridge University Press, 1951.

Delaruelle, E. *La Piété populaire au moyen âge.* Turin: Botteghe Oscure, 1975.

Dereine, Charles. "Coutumiers et ordinaires de chanoines réguliers." *Scriptorium* 5 (1951): 107–17.

Destrez, Jean. *La 'Pecia' dans les manuscrits universitaires du XIIIᵉ et XIVᵉ siècles.* Paris: Vautrain, 1935.

Detienne, Marcel, ed. *Les Savoirs de l'écriture en Grèce ancienne.* Cahiers de Philologie. Série apparat critique 14. Lille: Centre de Recherche Philologique de l'Université de Lille 3, 1988.

Dewan, L. "*Obiectum.* Notes on the Invention of a Word." *Archives d'histoire doctrinale et littéraire du moyen âge* 48 (1981): 37–96.

Dickey, Mary. *Some Commentaries on the "De Inventione" and "Ad Heren-*

nium" of the Eleventh and Early Twelfth Century. Medieval and Renaissance Studies 1. London: Warburg Institute, 1968. Pp. 1–41.

Diringer, David. *The Alphabet: A Key to the History of Mankind*, vol. 1. 3d ed. New York: Funk and Wagnalls, 1968. (Orig. 1848.)

Douteil, H., ed. *Exultet Rolle: Easter Praeconium. MS Biblioteca Vaticana 9820.* Graz: Akademische Druck- und Verlagsanstalt, 1975.

Dragonetti, Roger. *Le Mirage des sources: l'art du faux dans le roman médiéval.* Paris: Seuil, 1987.

Dronke, Peter. *A History of Twelfth-Century Western Philosophy.* Cambridge: Cambridge University Press, 1988.

———. *Poetic Individuality in the Middle Ages. New Departures in Poetry 1000–1150.* Oxford: Clarendon Press, 1970.

———. *Women Writers of the Middle Ages: A Critical Study of Texts from Perpetua (230) to Marguerite Porete (1310).* Cambridge: Cambridge University Press, 1984.

Druce, G. C. "The Medieval Bestiaries and Their Influence on Ecclesiastical Decorative Art." *Journal of the British Architectural Association* 1919–20.

Du Cange, Charles Du Fresne Sieur. *Glossarium mediae et infirmae latinitatis.* Editio nova, aucta 1883–1887. Graz, reprint 1954. (Orig. 1678.)

Duhem, Pierre. *Medieval Cosmology: Theories of Infinity, Place, Time, Void, and the Plurality of Worlds.* Translated and ed. Roger Ariew. Chicago: University of Chicago Press, 1985.

Dumont, Louis. "A Modified View of Our Origins. The Christian Beginnings of Modern Individualism." *Religion* 12 (1982): 1–27.

Dunne, Carrol. "The Roots of Memory." *Spring* (1988): 113–18.

Ebeling, G. "Geist und Buchstabe." In *Religion in Geschichte und Gegenwart*, vol. 2, cols. 1290–96. Tübingen: Mohr, 1958.

———. *Kirchengeschichte als Geschichte der Auslegung der Heiligen Schrift.* Tübingen: Mohr, 1947.

Ehlers, Joachim. "*Arca significat ecclesiam:* ein theologisches Weltmodell aus der ersten Hälfte des 12. Jahrhunderts." In *Jahrbuch des Institutes für Frühmittelalterforschung der Universität Münster,* vol. 6. Münster, 1972. Pp. 121–87.

———. *Hugo von St. Victor: Studien zum Geschichtsdenken und zur Geschichtsschreibung des 12. Jahrhunderts.* Frankfurter historische Abhandlungen 1973. Wiesbaden: Steiner, 1972.

———. "Hugo von St. Victor und die Victoriner." In Martin Gerschat, *Gestalten der Kirchengeschichte,* vol. 3, pt. 1. Mittelalter 1. Pp. 192–204.

Eisenstein, Elizabeth. *The Printing Press as an Agent of Change: Communications and Cultural Transformations in Early-Modern Europe.* 2 vols. Cambridge: Cambridge University Press, 1979.

———. *The Printing Revolution in Early Modern Europe.* London: Cambridge University Press, 1984.

Elbern, Victor H. "Zisterziensische Handschriften des frühen Mittelalters als Zeichen sakraler Abrenzung." In *Der Begriff der Repraesentatio im Mittelalter: Stellvertretung, Symbol, Zeichen, Bild,* ed. Albert Zimmermann. Berlin: De Gruyter, 1971. Pp. 340–56.

Emery, K. "Reading the World Rightly and Squarely: Bonaventure's Doctrine of the Cardinal Virtues." *Traditio* 39 (1983): 183–218.

Endres, Joseph Anton. *Das Jakobsportal in Regensburg und Honorius August-odunensis. Ein Beitrag zur Ikonographie und Liturgiegeschichte des 12. Jahrhunderts.* Kempten: Kösel, 1903.

Ernout, A. "Dictare, dicter, allem dichten." *Revue des études latines* 29 (1951): 155–61.

Ernout, A., and Meillet, A. *Dictionnaire étymologique de la langue latine: histoire des mots.* Paris: Klincksieck, 1967.

Evans, Gillian R. "A Change of Mind in Some Scholars of the Eleventh and Early Twelfth Century." In *Religious Motivation: Biographical and Sociological Problems for the Church Historian,* ed. D. Baker. Oxford: Blackwell, 1978. Pp. 27–37.

———. "Hugh of St. Victor on History and the Meaning of Things." *Studia Monastica* 25 (1983): 223–34.

———. *Old Arts and New Theology: The Beginnings of Theology as an Academic Discipline.* Oxford: Clarendon, 1980.

———. "Two Aspects of *Memoria* in the Eleventh and Twelfth Century Writings." *Classica et medievalia* 32 (1971–1980): 263–78.

Faral, Edmond. "Le Manuscrit 511 du 'Hunterian Museum' de Glasgow." *Studi Medievali* 9 (1936): 106–7.

Faulhaber, Charles. *Latin Rhetorical Theory in Thirteenth and Fourteenth Century Castile.* University of California Publications on Modern Philology 103. Berkeley: University of California Press, 1972.

Finkenzeller, Joseph. *Die Lehre von den Sakramenten im Allgemeinen: Von der Schrift bis zur Scholastik.* Vol. 4 of *Handbuch der Dogmengeschichte.* Freiburg, Br.: Herder, 1980.

Fiske, Adèle M. *Friends and Friendship in the Monastic Tradition.* Presentation by Gerhart B. Ladner. CIDOC Cuaderno 51. Cuernavaca: CIDOC, 1970.

———. "Paradisus Homo amicus." *Speculum* 40 (1965): 426–59.

Flusser, Vilèm. *Die Schrift. Hat Schreiben eine Zukunft?* Göttingen: Immatrix Publications, 1987.

Focillon, H. *L'Art d'Occident, le moyen âge roman et gothique.* Paris, 1938.

Folliet, Georges. "*Deificare in otio*, Augustin, Epistula X, 2." In *Recherches augustiniennes, 2, Hommage au R. P. Fulbert Cayre.* Paris: Études augustiniennes, 1962. Pp. 225–36.

Forbes, R. J. *Studies in Ancient Technology.* 9 vols. Leiden: Brill, 1964–72.

Forcellini, Aegidio. *Lexicon totius latinitatis.* Josepho Perin, ed. Bologna: La casa editrie Arnoldo Forni, 1965. (Originally published 1864–1926.).

Foreville, Raymonde, ed. *Les Mutations socio-culturelles au tournant des XIᵉ-XIIᵉ siècles. Actes du colloque international du CNRS, le Bec-Hellouin, 11–16 juillet 1982.* Spicilegium Beccense 2. Paris: Éditions du Centre National de la Recherche Scientifique, 1984.

Fracheboud, M. André. "Le Problème action-contemplation au coeur de Saint Bernard: 'Je suis la chimère de mon siècle.'" *Collectanea Ordinis Cisterciensium Reformatorum* 16 (1954): 45–52, 128–36, 183–91.

Franklin, Alfred. *Histoire de la bibliothèque de l'abbaye de Saint-Victor à Paris.* Paris, 1865.

Franz, A. *Die Messe im deutschen Mittelalter. Beiträge zur Geschichte der Liturgie und des religiösen Volkslebens.* Freiburg, Br.: Herder, 1902.

Freundgen, Joseph. *Hugo von St. Viktor, Das Lehrbuch. Sammlung der bedeutendsten pädagogischen Schriften aus alter und neuer Zeit.* Paderborn: F. Schöningh, 1896.

Fuhrmann, Horst. "Die Fälschungen im Mittelalter. Überlegungen zum mittelalterlichen Wahrheitsbegriff." *Historische Zeitschrift* 197 (1963): 529–54, 580–601.

———. "Überlegungen eines Editors." In *Probleme der Edition mittel- und neulateinischer Texte,* ed. L. Hödl and D. Wuttke. Boppard: Verlags Gesellschaft mbH, 1978.

Funkenstein, Amos. *Heilsplan und natürliche Entwicklung. Formen der Gegenwartsbestimmung im Geschichtsdenken des hohen Mittelalters.* Munich, 1965.

Gadamer, H. G. "Unterwegs zur Schrift?" In *Schrift und Gedächtnis. Archäologie der literarischen Kommunikation,* ed. Aleida and Jan Assmann. Munich: Fink, 1983. Pp. 10–19.

Ganz, David. "The Preconditions of Caroline Minuscle." *Viator* 18 (1987): 23–43.

Ganz, Peter. *The Role of the Book in Medieval Culture.* 2 vols. Turnhout: Brepols, 1986.

Gardeil, A. "Dons du Saint Esprit." In *Dictionnaire de théologie catholique,* vol. 4, cols, 1728–81. Paris: Letouzey, 1939.

Gasparri, F., ed. "L'Enseignement de l'écriture a la fin du moyen âge: apropos du *tractatus in omnem modum scribendi,* MS 76 de l'abbaye de Krebsmünster." *Scrittura e civiltà* 3 (1979): 243–65.

Gatard, A. "Chant grégorien du 9ᵉ au 12ᵉ siècle." In *Dictionnaire d'archéologie chrétienne et de liturgie,* vol. 2, cols. 311–21. Paris: Letouzey, 1913.

Gaudemet, J. *La Société ecclésiastique dans l'Occident médiéval.* London: Variorum Reprints, 1980.

Gellrich, Jesse M. *The Idea of the Book in the Middle Ages: Language Theory, Mythology, and Fiction.* Ithaca: Cornell University Press, 1984.

Gerhardson, B. *Memory and Manuscript: Oral Tradition and Written Transmission in Rabbinic Judaism and Early Christianity.* Uppsala: Gleerup, 1961.

Ghellinck, Joseph de. "Les Bibliothèques médiévales." *Nouvelle revue de théologie* 65 (1939): 36–55.

———. *L'Essor de la littérature latine au XIIᵉ siècle.* Museum Lessianum. Paris: Desclée de Brouwer, 1957.

———. "Latin chrétien ou langue latine des chrétiens." *Les Études classiques* 8 (1939): 449–78.

———. *Le Mouvement théologique du XIIᵉ siècle.* Bruges: Éditions 'De Tempel,' 1948.

———. "Originale et originalia." *Bulletin du Cange* 14 (1939): 95.

———. *Patristique et moyen âge: études d'histoire littéraire et doctrinale.* 2 vols. Paris: Desclée de Brouwer, 1947.

———. "La Table des matières de la première édition des oeuvres de Hughes de St.-Victor." *Recherches des sciences religieuses* 1 (1910): 270–89 and 383–96.

Gilson, Étienne. *The Christian Philosophy of St. Augustine.* New York: Octagon Books, 1983.

———. *From Aristotle to Darwin and Back Again: A Journey in Final Causality, Species, and Evolution.* Indiana: University of Notre Dame Press, 1984.

———. *Heloise and Abaelard.* Ann Arbor: University of Michigan Press, 1960.

———. "Regio Dissimilitudinis de Platon à Saint Bernard de Clairvaux." *Medieval Studies* 9 (1947): 103–30.

———. *The Spirit of Medieval Philosophy.* New York: Charles Scribner's Sons, 1936. (Reprint: Norwood, Penn.: Telegraph Books, 1985.)

Gindele, C. "Bienen-, Waben- und Honigvergleiche in der frühen monastischen Literatur." *Review of Benedictine Studies* 6–7 (1977–78): 1–26.

———. "Die Strukturen der Nokturnen in den lateinischen Mönchsregeln vor und um St. Benedikt." *Revue bénédictine* 64 (1954): 9–27.

Giroud, Charles. *L'Ordre des Chanoines Réguliers de Saint-Augustin et ses diverses formes de régime interne.* Paris: Martigny, 1961.

Glorieux, Palémon. "Pour revaloriser Migne. Tables rectificatives." *Mélanges de sciences religieuses.* Vol. 9, *Cahier supplementaire.* Lille, 1952.

———. "Techniques et méthodes en usage à la Faculté de Théologie de Paris au XIIᵉ siècle." *Archives d'histoire doctrinale et littéraire du moyen âge* 35 (1968): 3–186.

Gode, P. K. "Some Notes on the History of Ink Manufacture in Ancient and Medieval India and Other Countries." Chap. 5 in *Studies in Indian Cultural History,* vol. 3. Hoshiarpur: Vishveshvaranand Vedic Research Institute, 1960; Poona: Shri S. R. Sardessi, 1969. Pp. 31–35.

Godefroy, L. "Lecteur." In *Dictionnaire de théologie catholique,* vol. 9, cols. 117–25. Paris: Letouzey, 1926.

Goetz, W. "Die Enzyklopädien des 13. Jahrhunderts." *Zeitschrift für die deutsche Rechtsgeschichte* 2 (1936): 227–50.

Goldbacher, Al., ed. *Epistolae Sancti Augustini.* Prague: Bibliopola academiae litterarum caesareae vindobonensis, 1895.

Goldman, E. "Cartam levare." *Mitteilungen des Institutes für Österreichische Geschichtsforschung* 35 (1914): 1–59.

Gossen, C.-Th. "Graphème et phonème: le problème central de l'étude des langues écrites du moyen âge." *Revue de linguistique romane* 32 (1968): 304–45.

Gougaud, L. "Muta praedicatio." *Revue bénédictine* 42 (1930): 168–71.

Goy, R. *Die Überlieferung der Werke Hugo von St. Viktor. Ein Beitrag zur Kommunikationsgeschichte des Mittelalters.* Monographien zur Geschichte des Mittelalters 14. Stuttgart, 1976.

Grabmann, M. *Die Geschichte der scholastischen Methode.* Vol. 1. 2d ed. Freiburg, Br.: Herder, 1957.

Green, William M., ed. "Hugo of St. Victor: *de tribus maximis circumstantiis gestorum.*" *Speculum* 18 (1943): 484–93.

Grégoire, R. "L'adage ascétique *Nudus nudum Christum sequi.*" In *Studi storici in onore di O. Bertolini.* Vol. 1. Pisa, 1975. Pp. 395–409.

——. "Scuola e educazione giovanile nei monasteri dal sec. IV al XII." *Esperienze di pedagogia cristiana nella storia* 1 (1983): 9–44.

Gregory the Great. *Morales sur Job.* Intro. by Robert Gillet, O.S.B. Paris: Les Éditions du Cerf, 1975.

Gregory, Tulio. "La Nouvelle idée de nature et de savoir scientifique au XII° siècle." In *The Cultural Context of the Middle Ages,* ed. John M. Murdoch and Edith D. Sylla. Boston Studies in the Philosophical Sciences 26. Boston: Reidel, 1978. Pp. 193–210.

Grove, George. *A Dictionary of Music and Musicians.* New York: Macmillan, 1880.

Grundmann, Herbert. *Geschichtsschreibung im Mittelalter.* Göttingen: Vandenhoeck, 1978.

——. "Die Grundlagen der mittelalterlichen Geschichtsanschauung." *Archiv für Kulturgeschichte* 24 (1934): 326–36.

——. "Jubel." In *Festschrift J. Trier.* Weissenheim a.d. Glan, 1954. Pp. 477–511.

——. "*Litteratus-illiteratus.* Der Wandel einer Bildungsnorm vom Altertum zum Mittelalter." *Archiv für Kulturgeschichte* 40 (1958): 1–65.

——. *Religiöse Bewegungen im Mittelalter.* Darmstadt: Wissenschaftliche Buchgesellschaft, 1970.

Guerreau-Jalabert, A. "La 'Renaissance carolingienne': modèles culturels, usages linguistiques et structures sociales." *Bibliothèque de l'École des Chartes* 139 (1981): 5–35.

Guichard, P. *Structures "orientales" et "occidentales" dans l'Espagne musulmane.* Paris: Mouton, 1977.

Haering, Nikolaus M. "*Charakter, Signum, Signaculum:* Die Entstehung bis nach der karolingischen Renaissance." *Scholastik* 30 (1955): 481–512.

——. "Commentary and Hermeneutics." In *Renaissance and Renewal in the Twelfth Century,* ed. R. L. Benson and Giles Constable. Cambridge, Mass.: Harvard University Press, 1982. Pp. 173–200.

Hajdu, Helga. *Das mnemotechnische Schrifttum des Mittelalters.* Amsterdam: E. J. Bonset, 1967. (Orig. Leipzig, 1936.)

Hajnal, Istvan. *L'Enseignement de l'écriture aux universités médiévales.* 2d ed. Budapest, 1959.

Harms, Wolfgang. *Homo viator in bivio: Studien zur Bildlichkeit des Weges.* Medium Aevum 21. Munich: Finck, 1970.

Harms, Wolfgang, and Reinitzer, Heimo. *Natura loquax: Naturkunde und allegorische Naturdeutung vom Mittelalter bis zur frühen Neuzeit.* Mikrokosmos: Beiträge zur Literaturwissenschaft und Bedeutungsforschung 7. Frankfurt, Main: Lang, 1981.

Hartlaub, G. F. *Zauber des Spiegels: Geschichte und Bedeutung des Spiegels in der Kunst*. Munich: Pieper, 1951.

Haskins, Charles H. "The Life of Medieval Students Illustrated by Their Letters." *The American Historical Review* 3 (1897–98): 203–29. (Reprinted in Charles H. Haskins, *Studies in Mediaeval Culture* [Oxford: Clarendon Press, 1929; New York: Ungar, 1958], pp. 1–35.)

Hathaway, Neil. "Compilatio: From Plagiarism to Compiling." *Viator* 20 (1989): 19–44.

Hausherr, Irénée. *The Name of Jesus*. Kalamazoo: Cistercian Publications, 1978.

Havelock, Eric A. *The Literate Revolution in Greece and Its Cultural Consequences*. Princeton Series of Collected Essays. Princeton: Princeton University Press, 1982.

Heer, Friedrich. *Der Aufgang Europas: Eine Studie zu den Zusammenhängen zwischen politischer Religiosität, Frömmigkeitstil und dem Werden Europas im 12. Jahrhundert*. Vienna: Europäische Verlagsanstalt, 1949.

Heisig, Karl, "Muttersprache: Ein romanistischer Beitrag zur Genesis eines deutschen Wortes und zur Entstehung der deutsch-französichen Sprachgrenze." *Muttersprache* 22 (1954): 144–74.

Helgeland, John. "The Symbolism of Death in the Later Middle Ages." *Omega* 15 (1984–85): 145–60.

Hendrickson, G. L. "Ancient Reading." *The Classical Journal* 25 (1929): 182–96.

Hermann, H. "The Bible in Art: Miniature, Paintings, Drawings, and Sculpture Inspired by the Old Testament." *Sacris Erudiri* 6 (1954): 189–281.

Heyneman, Martha. "Dante's Magical Memory Cathedral." *Parabola* 11 (1986): 36–45.

Hödl, Ludwig. "*Sacramentum et res*. Zeichen und Bezeichnung. Eine Begriffsgeschichtliche Arbeit zu frühneuzeitlichen Eucharistietraktaten." *Scholastik* 38 (1963): 161–82.

Hofmeier, Johann. *Die Trinitätslehre des Hugo von St. Viktor*. Munich, 1936.

Holman, J. "La Joie monastique chez Gilbert de Hoyland." *Collectanea Cisterciensia* 48 (1986): 279–96.

Hörm, O. *Schriftform und Schreibwerkzeug. Die Handhabung der Schreibwerkzeuge und ihr formbildender Einfluß auf die Antiqua bis zum Einsetzen der Gothik*. Vienna, 1918.

Howell, Wil Samuel. *The Rhetoric of Alcuin and Charlemagne: A Translation with an Introduction, the Latin Text, and Notes*. New York: Russell and Russell, 1965.

Hunt, Richard W. "The Introduction to the '*artes*' in the Twelfth Century." In *Studia Medievalia in honorem R. J. Martin*. Bruges, 1948. Pp. 85–112.

———. "Manuscripts Containing the Indexing Symbols of Robert Grosseteste." *Bodleian Library Record* 4 (1953): 241–55.

Hunt, T., ed. "Vernacular Glosses in Medieval Manuscripts." *Church History* 39 (1979): 9–37.

Illich, Ivan. "Computer Literacy and the Cybernetic Dream." *STS Bulletin*,

Pennsylvania State University, 1987. (Reprinted in Illich, *In the Mirror of the Past.*)

———. *In the Mirror of the Past.* London: Marion Boyars, 1992.

———. "A Plea for Lay Literacy." *Interchange* 18 (1987): 9–22. (Reprinted in Illich, *In the Mirror of the Past.*)

———. *Schule ins Museum: Phaidros und die Folgen.* Introduction by Ruth Kriss-Rettenbeck and Ludolf Kuchenbuch. Bad Heilbrunn: Klinkhardt, 1984.

———. *Shadow Work.* London: Boyars, 1981.

Illich, Ivan, and Sanders, Barry. *ABC: The Alphabetization of the Popular Mind.* San Francisco: North Point Press, 1988.

Jantzen, H. "Das Wort als Bild in der frühmittelalterlichen Buchmalerei." In *Über den gotischen Kirchenraum und andere Aufsätze,* ed. H. Jantzen. Berlin, 1951. Pp. 53–60.

Javelet, Robert. "Considérations sur les arts libéraux chez Hugues et Richard de Saint Victor." In *Actes du 6ème Congrès International de Philosophie médiévale. Université de Montréal 1967.* Paris, 1969. Pp. 557–68.

———. *Image et ressemblance au XII° siècle de St. Anselm à Alain de Lille.* 2 vols. Paris: Letouzey, 1967.

———. "Psychologie des auteurs spirituels du 12e siècle." *Revue des sciences religeuses* 33 (1959): 18–64, 97–164, 209–93.

———. "Sens et réalité ultime selon Hugues de Saint-Victor." *Ultimate Reality and Meaning* 3, no. 2 (1980): 84–113.

Jeauneau, Edouard. "Simples notes sur la cosmogonie de Thierry de Chartres." *Sophia* 23 (1955): 172–83.

———. "L'Usage de la notion d'integumentum à travers les gloses de Guillaume des Conches." *Archives d'histoire doctrinale et littéraire du moyen âge* 24 (1957): 35–100.

Jocqué, Lucas, and Milis, Ludovicus, eds. *Liber ordinis Sancti Victoris Parisiensis.* Corpus Christianorum: Continuatio Medievalis 41. Turnhout: Brepols, 1984.

Jolivet, Jean. "The Arabic Inheritance." In *A History of Twelfth-Century Western Philosophy,* ed. Peter Dronke. Cambridge: Cambridge University Press, 1988. Pp. 113–14.

———, ed. *Oeuvres de Saint Augustin.* Paris: Desclée de Brouwer, 1948.

Jousse, Marcel. *L'Anthropologie du geste.* Paris: Gallimard, 1974.

———. "Le Bilatéralisme humain et l'anthropologie du langage." *Revue anthropologique,* Aug.–Sept., 1940, pp. 1–30.

———. *La Manducation de la parole.* Paris: Gallimard, 1975.

———. "Le Style oral rythmique et mnémotechnique chez les verbo-moteurs." *Archives de philosophie* 2 (1924): 1–240.

Jungmann, Josef A. *Christian Prayer through the Centuries.* New York: Paulist Press, 1978.

———. *The Mass of the Roman Rite: Its Origin and Development (Missarum Solemnia).* 2 vols. Trans. F. A. Brunner. New York: Christian Classics, 1955.

Kiessling, Nicolas. *The Library of Robert Burton.* Oxford: Oxford Bibliographical Society, 1987.

Kittel, G. "Akouo." In *Theologisches Wörterbuch zum Neuen Testament,* vol. 1, pp. 216–25. Stuttgart: W. Kohlhammer, 1933.

Klauser, Renate. "Ein Beutelbuch aus Isny." *Joost* (1963): 139–46.

Kleinz, John P. *The Theory of Knowledge of Hugh of Saint Victor.* Washington, D.C.: Catholic University of American Press, 1944.

Klink, B. *Die lateinische Etymologie des Mittelalters.* Medium Aevum 17. Munich: Finck, 1970.

Kluge, F. *Etymologisches Wörterbuch der deutschen Sprache.* 18th ed. Berlin: De Gruyter, 1960.

Knox, R. "Finding the Law. Developments in Canon Law during the Gregorian Reform." *Studi Gregoriani* 9 (1972): 421–66.

Koep, Leo. *Das himmlische Buch in Antike und Christentum: eine religionsgeschichtliche Untersuchung zur altchristlichen Bildersprache.* Theophaneia: Beiträge zur Religions- und Kirchengeschichte des Altertums 8. Bonn: Hanstein, 1952.

Kohlenberger, H. K. "Zur Metaphysik des Visuellen bei Anselm von Canterbury." *Analecta Anselmiana* 1 (1969): 11–37.

Köpf, U. *Die Anfäge der theologischen Wissenschaftstheorie im 13. Jahrhundert.* Beiträge zur historischen Theologie 49. Tübingen: J. C. B. Mohr, 1974.

Kos, M. "Carta sine litteris." *Mitteilungen der Österreichischen Gesellschaft für Geschichtsforschung* 62 (1954): 97–100.

Kriss-Rettenbeck, Lenz. "Zur Bedeutungsgeschichte der Devotionalien." *Umgang mit Sachen. Zur Kulturgeschichte des Dinggebrauchs.* Vol. 23. *Deutscher Volkskunde-Kongress in Regensburg, Oct. 1981,* ed. Konrad Köstlin und Hermann Bausinger. Regensburg, 1983. Pp. 213–39.

Kuchenbuch, Ludolf. *Schriftlichkeitsgeschichte als methodischer Zugang: das Prümer Urbar 893–1983.* Einführung in die Ältere Geschichte. Kurseinheit 2. Hagen: Fernuniversität, 1990.

Kunze, Horst. *Über das Registermachen.* Munich, 1964.

Kutzelnigg, Artur. "Die Verarmung des Geruchswortschatzes seit dem Mittelalter." *Muttersprache* 94 (1983–84): 328–46.

Ladner, Gerhart H. "The Concept of the Image in the Greek Fathers and the Byzantine Iconoclastic Controversy." In *Dumbarton Oaks Papers,* vol. 7. 1953. Pp. 1–34. (German translation in *Der Mensch als Bild Gottes,* ed. Leo Scheffczyk. Darmstadt: Wissenschaftliche Buchgesellschaft, 1969. Pp. 144–92.)

———. "*Homo viator:* Medieval Ideas on Alienation and Order." *Speculum* 42 (1967): 233–59.

———. *The Idea of Reform: Its Impact on Christian Thought and Action in the Age of the Fathers.* Part 1. Cambridge, Mass.: Harvard University Press, 1961.

———. *Images and Ideas in the Middle Ages: Selected Studies in History and Art.* Rome: Edizioni di Storia e Litteratura, 1983.

———. "Medieval and Modern Understanding of Symbolism: A Comparison." *Speculum* 54 (1979): 223–56.

———. "Terms and Ideas of Renewal." In *Renaissance and Renewal in the*

Twelfth Century, ed. R. L. Benson and Giles Constable. Cambridge, Mass.: Harvard University Press, 1982. Pp. 1–33.

——. "Vegetation Symbolism and the Concept of the Renaissance." In *De Artibus Opuscula. Forty Essays in Honor of Erwin Panofski.* New York, 1961. Pp. 303–22.

Larkin, Philip. *High Windows.* New York: Farrar Straus and Giroux, 1974.

Larsen, Steen F. "Remembering and the Archaeology Metaphor." *Metaphor and Symbolic Activity* 2 (1987): 187–99.

Lasić, Dionysius. *Hugonis de S. Victore theologia perfectiva.* Studia Antoniana 7. Rome: Pontificium Athenaeum Antonianum, 1956.

Lauwers, M. "Religion populaire, culture folklorique, mentalités." *Revue d'histoire écclesiastique* 82 (1987): 221–58.

Le Brun, Jacques. "De l'antique textuelle à la lecture du texte." *Le Débat* 1988: 84–121.

Leclercq, Henry. "Bréviaire." In *Dictionnaire d'archéologie chrétienne et de liturgie,* vol. 2, cols. 1262–1316. Paris: Letouzey, 1925.

——. "Chant romaine et grégorien." Ibid., vol. 3, cols. 256–311. Paris: Letouzey, 1913.

Leclercq, Jean. *L'Amour des lettres et le désir de Dieu: initiation aux auteurs monastiques du moyen âge.* Paris: Cerf, 1957. (English translation: *The Love of Learning and the Desire for God* [New York: Fordham University Press, 1982].)

——. "Aspects spirituels de la symbolique du livre au XIIᵉ siècle." In *L'Homme devant Dieu. Mélanges offerts au père Henri de Lubac,* vol. 2. Paris: Aubier, 1964. Pp. 62–72.

——. "Les Caractères traditionels de la lectio divina." In *La Liturgie et les paradoxes chrétiens,* ed. J. Leclercq. Paris, 1963. Pp. 243–57.

——. *Études sur le vocabulaire monastique du moyen âge.* Studia Anselmiana Fasciculum 48. Rome: St. Anselmo, 1961.

——. "Exercices spirituels; antiquité et haut moyen âge." In *Dictionnaire de spiritualité,* vol. 4, cols. 1903–1908. Paris: Beauchesne, 1960.

——. "Monachisme et pérégrination du IX au XII siècle." *Studia Monastica* 3, 1 (1960): 33–52.

——. *Otia Monastica.* Rome: Studia Anselmiana, 1959.

——. "Saint Bernard et ses secrétaires." *Revue bénédictine* 61 (1951): 208–29.

Leclercq, Jean, ed. "Le De grammatica de Hugues de Saint-Victor." *Archives d'histoire doctrinale et littéraire du moyen âge* 15 (1943–45): 263–322.

Lemay, R. "Dans l'Espagne du XIIe siècle. Les Traductions de l'arabe au latin." *Annales: économies, sociétés, civilisations* 18 (1963): 639–65.

Lemoine, Michel. *Hugo a Sancto Victore. L'art de lire: Didascalicon.* Paris: Éditions du Cerf, 1991.

Levy, M. *Medieval Arabic Bookmaking and Its Relation to Early Chemistry and Pharmacology.* Transactions of the American Philosophical Society 52. New York, 1962.

Lewis, S. "Sacred Calligraphy: The Chi-Rho Page in the Book of Kells." *Traditio* 36 (1980): 139–59.

Liccaro, V. "Ugo di San Vittore di fronte alla novitá delle traduzioni delle opere scientifiche greche ed arabe." In *Actas del 5. Congreso Internacional de Filosofía Medieval*, vol. 2. Madrid. 1979. Pp. 919–26.

Lord, Albert. "Perspectives on Recent Work on Oral Literature." In *Oral Literature: Seven Essays*, ed. J. Duggan. Edinburgh: Scottish Academic Press, 1975. Pp. 1–24.

Lubac, Henri de. *Exégèse médiévale: les quatre sens de l'écriture.* 4 vols. Paris: Aubier, 1964.

Maio, A. *Dalle scuola episcopali al seminario del duomo. Vicende, problemi, protagonisti.* Archivo Ambrosiano 36. Milan: Nuove Edizione Duomo, 1979.

Mâle, Émile. *L'Art religieux du 13ᵉ siècle en France.* 4 vols. 5th ed. Paris: Armand Colin, 1923.

Manselli, Raoul. *La réligion populaire du Moyen Age: problèmes de méthode et d'histoire.* Montreal: Institut d'études médiévales Albert-le-Grand, 1975.

Mansi, Joannes Dominicus. *Sacrorum conciliorum nova et amplissima collectio.* Graz: Akademische Druck- und Verlagsanstalt, 1960.

Marietan, Josèphe. *Le Problème de la classification des sciences d'Aristote à St. Thomas.* Paris: Félix Alcan, 1901.

Marrou, Henri-Irénée. "*Doctrina* et *disciplina* dans la langue des pères de l'Église." *Bulletin du Cange* 10 (1934): 5–25.

———. *Saint Augustin et la fin de la culture antique.* 4th ed. Paris: Boccard, 1958.

Mattoso, J. "La *lectio divina* nos autores monásticos de alta Idade média." *Studia Monastica* 9 (1967): 167–87.

Mayer, A. L. "Die Liturgie und der Geist der Gotik." *Jahrbuch für Liturgiewissenschaft* 6 (1926): 68–95.

Mazal, Otto. *Europäische Einband Kunst: Mittelalter und Neuzeit.* Graz: Akademische Druck- und Verlagsanstall, 1970.

———. *Lehrbuch der Handschriftenkunde.* Elemente des Buch und Bibliothekwesens 10. Wiesbaden, 1986.

McCulloch, W. *Embodiments of Mind.* Cambridge: MIT Press, 1965.

McDonnell, E. W. "The Vita Apostolica: Diversity or Dissent." *Church History* 24 (1955): 15–31.

McGarry, Daniel. *The Metalogicon of John of Salisbury.* Berkeley: University of California Press, 1955.

McKeon, Richard. *Thought, Action, and Passion.* Midway Reprint Series. Chicago: University of Chicago Press, 1974.

———, ed. *The Basic Works of Aristotle.* Introduction by R. McKeon. New York: Random House, 1941.

McKitterick, Rosamond. *The Carolingians and the Written Word.* Cambridge: Cambridge University Press, 1989.

———, ed. *The Uses of Literacy in Early Medieval Europe.* Cambridge: Cambridge University Press, 1990.

Meier, Christel. "Vergessen, erinnern. Gedächtnis im Gott-Mensch-Bezug. Zu einem Grenzbereich der Allegorese bei Hildegard von Bingen und anderen

Autoren des Mittelalters." In *Verbum et Signum,* ed. M. Fromm et al. Munich: Fink, 1975. Pp. 143–94.

————. "Zum Verhältnis von Text und Illustration bei Hildegard von Bingen." In *Hildegard von Bingen 1179–1979. Festschrift zum 800. Todestag,* ed. A. Brück. Mainz, 1979. Pp. 159–69.

Meier, Christel, and Ruberg, Uwe, eds. *Text und Bild: Aspekte des Zusammenwirkens zweier Künste in Mittelalter und früher Neuzeit.* Wiesbaden: Reichert, 1980.

Mentz, A. "Die tironischen Noten. Eine Geschichte der römischen Kurzschrift." *Archiv für Urkundenforschung* 17 (1942): 222–35.

Michael, B. *Johannes Buridan: Studien zu seinem Leben, seinen Werken und zur Rezeption seiner Theorien im Europa des späten Mittelalters.* Phil. Diss. Berlin, 1985.

Michaud-Quantin, Pierre. "Aspects de la vie sociale chez les moralistes." In *Beiträge zum Berufsbewußtsein des mittelalterlichen Menschen,* ed. P. Wilpert. Berlin, 1964. Pp. 30–43.

————. "Collectivités médiévales et institutions antiques." *Miscellanea Medievalia* 1 (1962): 239–52.

————. *Études sur le vocabulaire philosophique du moyen âge.* Lesscio intellectuale europeo 5. Rome: Ateneo, 1970.

Miethke, Jürgen. "Die Mittelalterlichen Universitäten und das gesprochene Wort." *Historische Zeitschrift* 251 (1990): 1–44.

————. "Zur Herkunft Hugos von St. Viktor." *Archiv für Kulturgeschichte* 54 (1972): 241–65.

Minnis, A. J. *Medieval Theory of Authorship: Scholastic Literary Attitudes in the Later Middle Ages.* London: Scolar Press, 1984.

Mohrmann, Christine. "Comment St. Augustin s'est familiarisé avec le latin des chrétiens." In *Études sur le latin des chrétiens,* vol. 1, *Le latin des chrétiens.* Roma: Storia e Letteratura, 1958. Pp. 383–89.

————. "Le Dualisme de la latinité médiévale." *Revue des études latines,* vol. 29 (1952): 330–48.

————. *Études sur le latin des chrétiens,* vol. 3, *Latin chrétien et liturgique.* Rome: Storia e Letteratura, 1965.

————. "Die Rolle des Lateins in der Kirche des Westens." In *Études sur le latin de chrétiens,* vol. 2, *Latin chrétien et médiéval.* Rome: Storia e Letteratura, 1961. Pp. 35–62.

Mollard, A. "L'imitation de Quintilien dans Guibert de Nogent." *Le Moyen Âge* 3 (1934): 81–87.

Montelera, Ernesto Rossi de. "Tradition et connaissance chez Marcel Jousse." *Nova et Vetera* 64, no. 1 (1989): 53–67.

Moore, Walter J. *Schrödinger: Life and Thought.* Cambridge: Cambridge University Press, 1989.

Morris, Colin D. *The Discovery of the Individual 1050–1200.* London: Church Historical Society S.P.C.V., 1972.

————. "Individualism and Twelfth-Century Religion: Some Further Reflections." *Journal of Ecclesiastical History* 31 (1980): 195–206.

Morse, Jonathan. *Word by Word. The Language of Memory.* Ithaca: Cornell University Press, 1990.

Müri, W. *Symbolon: wort- und sachgeschichtliche Studie.* Beilage zum Jahresbericht über das Städtische Gymnasium in Bern. Bern, 1931.

Murphy, James, ed. *Medieval Eloquence: Studies on the Theory and Practice of Medieval Rhetoric.* Berkeley: University of California Press, 1978.

Murra, John V. "Current Research and Prospects in Andean Ethnohistory." *Latin American Research Review,* Spring 1970, pp. 3–36.

————. "La función del tejido en varios contextos sociales del estado Inca." In *Actas y trabajos. Segundo Congreso de Historia Nacional del Perú.* Vol. 2. Lima, 1958. Pp. 215–40.

Murray, Alexander. *Reason and Society in the Middle Ages.* New York: Oxford University Press, 1978.

Mus, Paul. *India Seen from the East: Indian and Indigenous Cults in Champa.* Monash Papers on South East Asia 3. Melbourne: Monash University Press, 1975.

————. "The Problematic of Self, West and East." In *Philosophy and Culture, East and West. 3e conférence internationale des philosophes occidentaux et orientaux, juillet 1959,* ed. L. A. Moore. Honolulu, 1959.

Mutschmann, Hermann. "Inhaltsangabe und Kapitelüberschrift im antiken Buch." *Hermes* 46 (1911): 93–107.

Nilgen, Ursula. "Evangelisten." In Engelbert Kirschbaum, S. J., ed., *Lexikon der christlichen Ikonographie,* vol. 1, cols. 696–713. Freiburg, Br.: Herder, 1968.

Nobis, H. M. "Buch der Natur." In *Historisches Wörtenbuch der Philosophie,* vol. 1, cols. 957–60. Darmstadt: Wissenschaftliche Buchgesellschaft, 1971.

————. "Die Umwandlung der mittelalterlichen Naturvorstellung. Ihre Ursachen und die wissenschaftsgeschichtlichen Folgen." *Archiv für Begriffsgeschichte* 13 (1969): 34–57.

Norberg, Dag. "À quelle époque a-t-on cessé de parler latin en Gaule?" *Annales: économies, sociétés, civilisations* 21 (1966): 346–55.

Notopoulos, James A. "Mnemosyne in Oral Literature." *Transactions of the American Philosophical Association* 69 (1938): 465–93.

Oehl, Wilhelm, ed. *Deutsche Mystikerbriefe des Mittelalters 1100–1550.* Darmstadt: Wissenshaftliche Buchgesellschaft, 1972.

Ohly, Friedrich. "Das Buch der Natur bei Jean Paul." In *Studien zur Goethezeit. E. Trunz zum 75. Geburtstag.* Beihefte zur Euphorion 18. Heidelberg, 1981. Pp. 177–232.

————. "Geistige Süße bei Otfried." In Ohly, *Schriften zur mittelalterlichen Bedeutungsforschung.* Pp. 93–127.

————. *Hohelied-Studien: Grundzüge einer Geschichte der Hohenliedauslegung des Abendlandes bis um 1200.* Schriften der Wissenschaftlichen Gesellschaft an der Johann-Wolfgang-Goethe-Universität Frankfurt/ M.; Geisteswissenschaftliche Reihe 1. Wiesbaden: Steiner, 1958.

————. "Die Kathedrale als Zeitraum: zum Dom von Siena." In Ohly, *Schriften zur mittelalterlichen Bedeutungsforschung.* Pp. 171–273.

————. Schriften zur mitellalterlichen Bedeutungsforschung. Darmstadt: Wissenschaftliche Buchgesellschaft, 1977.

————. "Die Suche in der Dichtungen des Mittelalters." Zeitschrift für deutsche Altertumskunde 94 (1965): 171–84.

————. "Vom Sprichwort im Leben eines Dorfes" In Volk, Sprache, Dichtung. Festgabe für Kurt Wagner, ed. K. Bischoff and L. Röhrich. Beiträge zur deutschen Philologie 28. Gießen, 1960. Pp. 276–93.

Olson, David R. "The Cognitive Consequences of Literacy." Canadian Psychology 27 (1986): 109–21.

Ong, Walter J. Orality and Literacy: The Technologization of the Word. London: Methuen, 1982.

————. The Presence of the Word. Some Prolegomena for Cultural and Religious History. The Terry Lectures. New Haven: Yale University Press, 1967.

Onions, C. T. The Oxford Dictionary of English Etymology. New York: Oxford University Press, 1966.

Önnerfors, Alf, ed. Mittelalterliche Philologie. Beiträge zur Erforschung der Mittellateinischen Latinität. Darmstadt: Wissenschaftliche Buchgesellschaft, 1975.

Ossola, C. " 'Un Oeil immense artificiel': Il sogno pineale della scritura da Baudelaire d'Annunzio e a Zanzotto." Letteratura italiana 35 (1983): 457–79.

Ott, Ludwig. "Hugo von St. Viktor und die Kirchenväter." Divus Thomas 3 (1949): 180–200 and 293–332.

————. Untersuchungen zur theologischen Briefliteratur der Frühscholastik unter besonderer Berücksichtigung des Viktorinischen Kreises. Münster: Aschendorff, 1932.

Ouspensky, L. La Théologie de l'icône dans l'Église Orthodoxe. Paris: Cerf, 1980.

Palmer, Nigel F. "Kapitel und Buch: zu den Gliederungsprinzipien mittelalterlicher Bücher." Frühmittelalterliche Studien 23 (1989): 43–88.

"Parchemin, en commerce, etc. . . ." In Diderot, Denis, and d'Alembert, Jean Le Rond. Encyclopédie ou dictionnaire raisonné des sciences, des arts et des métiers, vol. 11, pp. 929–31. Paris: Briasson, 1765.

Parkes, Malcolm B. "The Impact of Punctuation: Punctuation or Pause and Effect." In Medieval Eloquence: Studies on the Theory and Practice of Medieval Rhetoric, ed. James Murphy. Berkeley: University of California Press, 1978. Pp. 127–42.

————. "The Influence of the Concepts of Ordinatio and Compilatio on the Development of the Book." In Medieval Learning and Literature. Essays presented to Richard William Hunt, ed. Jonathan James Graham Alexander and M. T. Gibson. Oxford: Clarendon, 1976. Pp. 115–41.

Patt, W. D. "The Early 'Ars dictaminis' as Response to a Changing Society." Viator 9 (1978): 133–35.

Payne, Robert O. The Key of Remembrance: A Study of Chaucer's Poetics. New Haven and London: Yale University Press, 1963.

Peabody, B. The Winged Word: A Study in the Technique of Ancient Greek

Oral Composition as Seen Principally through Hesiod's "Works and Days."
Albany: State University of New York Press, 1975.

Pedersen, J. "La Recherche de la sagesse d'après Hugues de St.-Victor." *Classica et medievalia* 16 (1955): 91–133.

Petrucci, A., and Romeo, C. "Scrittura e alfabetismo nella Salerno del IX secolo." *Scrittura e civiltá* 7 (1983): 51–112.

Pfaff, C. *Scriptorium und Bibliothek des Klosters Mondsee im Hohen Mittelalter.* Veröffentlichungen der Kommission für die Geschichte Österreichs, ed. A. Lhorsky, fasc. 2. Vienna, 1967.

Pfander, Homer G. "The Medieval Friars and Some Alphabetical Reference-Books for Sermons." *Medium Aevum* (Oxford) 3 (1934): 19–29.

Philippe, M. D. "*Aphaíresis próthesis, chorízen* dans la philosophie d'Aristote." *Revue Thomiste* 49 (1948): 461–79.

Piazzoni, A. M., ed. "Il *De unione spiritus et corporis* di Ugo di San Vittore." *Studi Medievali* 21 (1980): 861–88.

———, ed. "Ugo di San Vittore *auctor* delle *Sententiae de divinitate.*" *Studi Medievali* 23 (1982): 861–955.

Picard, J.-C. "L'Éducation dans le haut moyen âge. (A propos d'un livre de Pierre Riché)." *Histoire de l'éducation* 6 (1980): 1–8.

Pinborg, Jan. *Die Entwicklung der Sprachtheorie im Mittelalter.* Beiträge zur Geschichte der Philosophie und Theologie des Mittelalters 42, 2. Münster: Aschendorfsche Verlagsbuchhandlung, 1979.

———. *Medieval Semantics. Selected Studies on Medieval Logic and Grammar.* Collected Studies Series 195, ed. Sten Ebbesen. London: Variorum Reprints, 1984.

Pollard, Graham. "Describing Medieval Bookbinding." In *Medieval Learning and Literature: Essays presented to R. W. Hunt,* ed. Jonathan James Graham Alexander and M. T. Gibson. Oxford: Clarendon, 1976. Pp. 50–65.

———. "The Pecia System in the Medieval Universities." In *Medieval Scribes, Manuscripts, and Libraries: Essays presented to N. R. Ker,* ed. M. B. Parkes and A. G. Watson. London; Scolar Press, 1978. Pp. 145–61.

Poole, Reginald L. *Lectures on the History of the Papal Chancery Down to the Time of Innocent III.* Cambridge, England: Cambridge University Press, 1915.

Pörksen, Uwe. *Der Erzähler im mittelhochdeutschen Epos. Formen seines Hervortretens bei Lamprecht, Konrad, Hartmann, in Wolframs Willehalm und in den Spielmannsepen.* Berlin: Schmidt, 1972.

Powitz, Gerhard. "Textus cum commento in codices manuscripti." *Zeitschrift für Handschriftenkunde* 5, 3 (1979): 80–89.

Pross, Harry. "Fernsehen als Symbolsehen." *Symbolon,* n.s., 7 (1984): 153–60.

Pulgram, E. "Spoken and Written Latin." *Language* 26 (1950): 458–66.

Quain, Edwin A. "The Medieval *Accessus ad Auctores.*" *Traditio* 3 (1945): 215–64.

Rahner, Karl. "Le Début d'une doctrine des cinq sens spirituels, chez Origène." *Revue d'ascétique et de mystique* 13 (1932): 113–45.

————. "La Doctrine des sens spirituels au moyen âge, en particulier chez Saint Bonaventure." Ibid., 263–99.

Rasmussen, Holger. "Der schreibende Teufel in Nordeuropa." In *Festschrift Mathias Zender,* ed. E. Ennen et al. Bonn, 1972. Pp. 455–64.

Rassow, P. "Die Kanzlei St. Bernhards von Clairvaux." *Studien und Mitteilungen zur Geschichte des Benediktinerordens und seiner Zweige* 34 (1913): 63–103 and 243–93.

Rauch, W. *Das Buch Gottes. Eine systematische Untersuchung des Buchbegriffes bei Bonaventura.* Münchner Theologische Schriften 2. Munich, 1961.

Resnik, I. M. "*Risus monasticus.* Laughter in Medieval Monastic Literature." *Révue bénédictine* 97 (1987): 90–100.

Richard, J. "Voyages réels et voyages imaginaires, instruments de la conaissance géographique au moyen âge." *Culture et travail intellectuel dans l'Occident médiéval. Bilan des colloques d'humanisme médiéval.* Paris: Centre National de Recherche Scientifique, 1981.

Riché, P. "L'Étude du vocabulaire latin dans les écoles anglo-saxonnes au début du Xe siècle." In *La Lexicographie du latin médiéval et ses rapports avec les recherches actuelles sur la civilisation du moyen âge.* Colloques internationaux du Centre national de la recherche scientifique 589. Paris, 1981. Pp. 115–23.

————. "La Formation des scribes dans le monde mérovingien et carolingien." In *Instruction et vie religieuse dans le haut moyen âge."* London, 1981. Pp. 161–71.

————. "La Vie quotidienne dans les écoles monastiques d'après les colloques scolaires." In *Sous le règle de Saint Benoit. Structures monastiques et sociétés en France du moyen âge à l'époche moderne.* Hautes études médiévales et modernes 47. Geneva, 1981. Pp. 417–26.

Richter, D. "Die Allegorie der Pergamentbearbeitung. 1. Beziehungen zwischen handwerklichen Vorgängen und der geistlichen Bildsprache des Mittelalters." In *Fachliteratur des Mittelalters. Festschrift für Gerhard Eis,* ed. G. Keil, R. Rudolf, W. Schmidt, and H. J. Nermeer. Stuttgart, 1968. Pp. 83–92.

Robb, David M. *The Art of the Illuminated Manuscript.* South Brunswick and New York: Barnes, 1973.

Rouche, Michael. "Des origines à la Renaissance." In *Histoire générale de l'enseignement et de l'éducation en France,* ed. L.-H. Parias, vol. 1. Paris: Nouvelle Librairie de France, 1983.

Rouse, M. A., and Rouse, R. H. "Alphabetization." In *Dictionary of the Middle Ages,* vol. 1, pp. 204–7. New York: Macmillan, 1982.

Rouse, Richard. "Concordances et index." In *Mise en page et mise en texte du livre manuscrit,* ed. Henri-Jean Martin and Jean Vézin. Paris. Éditions du Cercle de la Librarie-Promodis, 1990. Pp. 219–28.

————. "L'Évolution des attitudes envers l'autorité écrite: le développement des instruments de travail au XIIIᵉ siècle." In *Culture et travail intellectuel dans l'Occident médiéval. Bilan des colloques d'humanisme médiéval.* Paris: Centre National de la Recherche Scientifique, 1981. Pp. 115–44.

——. "La naissance des index." In *Histoire de l'édition francaise,* ed. Henri-Jean Martin. Paris: Promodis, 1983. Pp. 77–85.

Rouse, R. H., and Rouse, M. A. "*Statim inveniri.* Schools, Preachers, and New Attitudes to the Page." In *Renaissance and Renewal in the Twelfth Century,* ed. R. L. Benson and Giles Constable. Cambridge, Mass.: Harvard University Press, 1982. Pp. 201–25.

——. "The Verbal Concordance of the Scriptures." *Archivum Fratrum Praedicatorum* 44 (1974): 5–30.

Rousse, Jacques, and Sieben, Herman Joseph. "*Lectio divina* et lecture spirituelle." In *Dictionnaire de spiritualité,* vol. 9, cols. 470–87. Paris: Beauchesne, 1975.

Ruberg, Uwe. "Allegorisches im 'Buch des Natur' Konrads von Megenberg." *Frühmittelalterliche Studien* 12 (1978): 310–25.

Rupert of Deutz. *Commentaria in evangelium sancti Johannis.* Rhabanus Haacke, O.S.B., ed. Turnhout: Brepols, 1969.

Saenger, Paul, "Physiologie de la lecture et separation des mots." *Annales E.S.C.* 1 (1989): 939–52.

——. "Silent Reading: Its Impact on Late Medieval Script and Society." *Viator* 113 (1982): 367–414.

Santiago Otero, Horacio. "*Esse et habere* en Hugo de San Victor." In *L'Homme et son univers au moyen âge. Acte du 7ème Congrès International de Philosophie Médiévale, 1982.* Coll. Philosophes Médiévaux 16 and 17, ed. Christian Wenin. Louvain la Neuve, 1986. Pp. 427–31.

Santifaller, L. *Beiträge zur Geschichte der Beschreibstoffe im Mittelalter, mit besonderer Berücksichtigung der päpstlichen Kanzlei. 1. Untersuchungen.* Mitteilungen des Instituts für österreichische Geschichtsforschung. Ergänzungsband 16. Graz, 1953.

Sayce, Olive. "Prolog, Epilog und das Problem des Erzählers." In *Probleme mittelalterlicher Erzählforschung,* ed. Peter Ganz et al. Berlin: Schmidt, 1972. Pp. 63–71.

Schilling, Michael. "*Imagines Mundi.* Metaphorische Darstellung der Welt in der Emblematik." In *Mikrokosmos 4. Beiträge zur Literaturwissenschaft und Bedeutungsforschung,* ed. W. Harms. Frankfurt am Main: Lang, 1979. Pp. 71–81.

Schleusener-Eichholz, Gudrun. *Das Auge im Mittelalter.* 2 vols. Münsterische Mittelalterschriften 35. Munich: Fink, 1985.

Schlögl, W. *Die Unterfertigung deutscher Könige von der Karolingerzeit bis zum Interregnum durch Kreuz und Unterschrift. Beiträge zur Geschichte und zur Technik der Unterfertigung in Mittelalter.* Münchener Historische Studien, Abt. Geschichtliche Hilfswissenschaften 16. Kallmünz: Michael Lassleben, 1978.

Schlosser, "A History of Paper." In *Paper — Art and Technology,* ed. Paulette Long. San Francisco: World Print Council, 1979. Pp. 1–19.

Schneider, W. A. *Geschichte und Geschichtsphilosophie bei Hugo von St. Victor.* Münster, 1933.

Schönborn, C. von. *L'Icône du Christ. Fondements théologiques élaborés entre le 1ᵉ et le 2ᵉ Concile de Nicée (325–987).* 2d ed. Collection Paradosis. Fribourg: Éditions de l'Université de Fribourg, 1976.

Schöne, Wolfgang. *Das Gottesbild im Abendland.* Berlin: Eckart, 1959.

———. *Über das Licht in der Malerei.* Berlin: Mann, 1954.

Schreiner, Klaus. "Bücher, Bibliotheken und 'Gemeiner Nutzen' im Spätmittelalter und in der frühen Neuzeit: Geistes- und sozialgeschichtliche Beiträge zur Frage nach der *utilitas librorum.*" *Bibliothek und Wissenschaft* 9 (1975): 202–49.

———. "*Discrimen veri ac falsi:* Ansätze und Formen der Kritik in der Heiligen- und Reliquienverehrung des Mittelalters." *Archiv für Kulturgeschichte* 48 (1966): 1–53.

———. "Laienbildung als Herausforderung für Kirche und Gesellschaft: religiöse Vorbehalte und soziale Widerstände gegen die Verbreitung von Wissen im späten Mittelalter und in der Reformation." *Zeitschrift für historische Forschung* 11 (1984): 257–354.

Schreiner, Rudolf. "Marienverehrung, Lesekultur, Schriftlichkeit. Bildungs- und frömmigkeitsgeschichtliche Studien zur Auslegung und Darstellung von Mariä Verkündigung im Mittelalter." *Frühmittelalterliche Studien* 24 (1990): 314–64.

Schrenk, Gottlieb. "Bíblos, biblíon." In *Theologisches Wörterbuch zum Neuen Testament,* vol. 1, pp. 613–20. Stuttgart: Kohlhammer, 1933.

Schuman, J. C. G. *Hugo von Sankt Viktor als Pädagog.* Kleinere Schriften über pädagogische und kulturgeschichtliche Fragen. 2 vols. Hannover, 1878.

Schüssler-Fiorenza, Elisabeth. *In Memory of Her: A Feminist Theological Reconstruction of Christian Origins.* New York: Crossroad, 1986.

Scribner, Sylvia, and Cole, Michael. *The Psychology of Literacy.* Cambridge: Harvard University Press, 1981.

Segal, C. "Otium and Eros: Catullus, Sappho, and Euripides' Hippolytus." *Latomus,* vol. 48, no. 4 (1989): 817–22.

Severino, Emanuele. "Temporalité et aliénation." In *Temporalité et aliénation. Actes du colloque, Rome, 3–8 janvier, 1975,* ed. Enrico Castelli. Paris: Aubier, 1975. Pp. 303–12.

Severino, G. "La discussione degli *ordines* di Anselmo de Havelberg." *Bolletino dell'Istituto Storico Italiano per il Medioevo e Archivo Muratoriano* 78 (1967): 75–122.

Sirat, Colette. "La Morphologie humaine et la direction des écritures." *Académie des Inscriptions et Belles Lettres,* Sept., 1987, pp. 135–67.

Skeat, T. C. "The Use of Dictation in Ancient Book Production." *Proceedings of the British Academy* 42 (1956): 179–208.

Smalley, Beryl. "La Glossa Ordinaria." *Recherches de théologie ancienne et médiévale* 9 (1937): 365–400.

———. *The Study of the Bible in the Middle Ages.* South Bend: University of Notre Dame Press, 1964.

Smeyers, M. *La Miniature*. Typologie des sources du moyen âge occidental 8. Turnhout: Brepols, 1974.

Southern, Richard W. "Beryl Smalley and the Place of the Bible in Medieval Studies 1927–1984." In *The Bible in the Medieval World: Essays in Memory of Beryl Smalley*, ed. K. Walsh and D. Wood. Oxford: Blackwell, 1985. Pp. 1–16.

————. *The Making of the Middle Ages*. 16th printing. New Haven: Yale University Press, 1976. (Orig. 1953.)

————. "The Schools of Paris and the School of Chartres." In *Renaissance and Renewal in the Twelfth Century*, ed. R. L. Benson and Giles Constable. Cambridge, Mass.: Harvard University Press, 1982. Pp. 113–37.

Spaemann, R. "Genetisches zum Naturbegriff des 18. Jahrhunderts." *Archiv für Begriffsgeschichte* 11 (1967): 59–74.

Spahr, P. C. "Die *lectio divina* bei den alten Cisterciensern. Eine Grundlage des cisterciensischen Geisteslebens." *Analecta Cisterciensia* 34 (1978): 27–39.

Spicq, P. C. *Esquisse d'une histoire de l'exégèse au moyen âge*. Paris, 1946.

Spitz, H. J. "Schilfrohr und Binse als Sinnträger in der lateinischen Bibelexegese." *Frühmittelalterliche Studien* 12 (1978): 230–57.

Stadelhuber, J. "Das Laienstundengebet vom Leiden Christi in seinem mittelalterlichen Fortleben." *Zeitschrift für Katholische Theologie* 71 (1949): 129–83; 72 (1950): 282–322.

Steinen, Wolfram von den. "Das mittelalterliche Latein als historisches Phänomen." *Schweizer Zeitschrift für Geschichte* 7 (1957): 1–27.

Steiner, George. "The End of Bookishness." *Times Literary Supplement*, vol. 8, 16 July, 1988, p. 754.

————. "Our Homeland the Text." *Salmagundi* 66 (1985): 4–25.

Sternagel, Peter. *Die Artes Mechanicae im Mittelalter: Begriffs- und Bedeutungsgeschichte bis zum Ende des 13. Jahrhundert*. Münchener Historische Studien. Abt. Mittelalterliche Geschichte, ed. J. Spörl, vol. 2. Kallmünz: Michel Lassleben, 1966.

Stock, Brian. "Experience, Praxis, Work, and Planning in Bernard of Clairvaux: Observations on the Sermones and Cantica." In *The Cultural Context of Medieval Learning. Proceedings of the First International Colloquium in Philosophy, Science, and Technology in the Middle Ages, Sept. 1973*. Boston Studies in the Philosophy of Science 26, ed. Robert S. Cohen and M. W. Wartofsky. Boston, 1973. Pp. 219–68.

————. *The Implications of Literacy: Written Language and Models of Interpretation in the Eleventh and Twelfth Centuries*. Princeton: Princeton University Press, 1983.

Table Ronde de École Française de Rome. *Faire croire. Modalités de la diffusion et de la réception des messages religieux du XIIe au XVe siècle. 22–23 juin, 1979*. Rome and Paris, 1981.

Talbot, C. H. "The Universities and the Medieval Library." In *The English Library before 1700*, ed. F. Wormland and C. E. Wright. London: Athlone Press, 1958. Pp. 76–79.

Taylor, Jerome. *The Didascalicon of Hugh of St. Victor. A Medieval Guide to the Arts*. Translated from the Latin with an Introduction and Notes. New York and London: Columbia University Press, 1961.

Teicher, J. L. "The Latin-Hebrew School of Translators in Spain in the Twelfth Century." In *Homenaje à Millas Vallicrosa*, vol. 2. Barcelona, 1956. Pp. 425–40.

Thesaurus linguae latinae. Editus auctoritate et consilio academiarum quinque germanicarum. Leipzig: Teubner, 1909–34.

Thompson, D. V. "Medieval Parchment Making." *Library*, 4th ser., 16 (1935): 113–17.

Van Aasche, M. "Divinae vacari lectioni." *Sacris Erudiri* 1 (1948): 13–14.

Van Buuren, Maarten. "Witold Gombrowisz et le grotesque." *Littérature* 48 (1982): 52–73.

Van den Eynde, Damian. "Chronologie des écrits d'Abélard a Héloise." *Antonianum* 37 (1962): 337–49.

——. "Détails biographiques sur Pierre Abélard."*Antonianum* 38 (1963): 217–23.

——. "Les Écrits perdus d'Abélard." *Antonianum* 37 (1962): 467–80.

——. *Essai sur la succession et la date des écrits de Hugues de Saint-Victor*. Studia Antoniana 13. Rome: Pontificium Athenaeum Antonianum, 1960.

Vauchez, A. *La Spiritualité du moyen âge occidental, 7è-12è siècles*. Collection SUP, L'Historien 19. Paris, 1975.

Verbeke, Werner, et al., eds. *The Use and Abuse of Eschatology in the Middle Ages*. Mediaevalia Lovaniensia 1, Studia 15. Louvain, 1988.

Verheijen, Melchoire. *Praeceptum*. Paris, 1967.

Vernet, F. "Hugues de Saint-Victor." In *Dictionnaire de théologie catholique*, vol. 7, cols. 240–308. Paris: Letouzey, 1930.

Veyne, Paul. *Writing History*. New York: Wesleyan University Press, 1987.

Vezin, J. "La Fabrication du manuscrit." In *Histoire de l'édition française*, ed. H. J. Martin and R. Chartier. Paris: Promodis, 1982. Pp. 25–48.

——. "L'Organisation matérielle du travail dans les scriptoria du haut moyen âge." In *Sous la règle de Saint Benoit. Structures monastiques et sociétés en France du moyen âge à l'époque moderne*. École pratique des Hautes Études. Hautes Études médiévales et modernes 47. Geneva, 1982. Pp. 427–31.

——. *Les 'scriptoria' d'Angers au 11ᵉ siècle*. Paris: H. Champian, 1974.

Wackernagel, Wilhelm. "Über den Spiegel im Mittelalter." In *Kleinere Schriften*, vol. 1, ed. W. Wackernagel. Leipzig, 1872. Pp. 128–42.

Waller, Katherine. "Rochester Cathedral Library: An English Book Collection Based on Norman Models." In *Les Mutations socio-culturelles au tournant des XIᵉ-XIIᵉ siècles. Études anselmiennes. 4ᵉ session. Abbaye N. D. du Bec. Juillet, 1982*. Paris: CNRS, 1983. Pp. 237–52.

Wathen, A. "Monastic Lectio: Some Clues from Terminology." *Monastic Studies* 12 (1976): 207–16.

Webber Jones, Leslie, trans. *An Introduction to Divine and Human Readings: Cassiodorus Senator*. New York: Octagon Books, Inc., 1966.

Weckwerth, Alfred. "Das altchristliche und das frühchristliche Kirchengebäude—ein Bild des Gottesreiches." *Zeitschrift für Kirchengeschichte* 4 (1958): 26–78.

Weijers, O. "Collège, une institution avant la lettre." *Vivarium* 21 (1983): 73–82.

Weimar, Peter. "Die legistische Literatur und die Methode des Rechtsunterrichtes der Glossatorenzeit." *Jus commune* 2 (1969): 41–83.

Weinrich, H. "Typen der Gedächtnismetaphorik." *Archiv für Begriffsgeschichte* (1946): 106–19.

Weisweiler, Heinrich. "Die Arbeitsmethode Hugos von St. Viktor. Ein Beitrag zum Entstehen seines Hauptwerkes '*De sacramentis*.'" *Scholastik* 20–24 (1949): 59–87 and 232–67.

———. "Die Einflußsphäre der 'Vorlesungen' Hugos von St. Viktor." In *Mélanges J. de Ghellinck*, vol. 2. Museum Lessianum, sect. hist. 14. Gembloux, 1951. Pp. 527–81.

———. "Sacrament als Symbol und Teilhabe. Der Einfluß des Ps.-Dionysius auf die allegemeine Sakramentenlehre Hugos von San Victor." *Scholastik* 27 (1952): 321–43.

Weitzmann, K. *Illustrations in Roll and Codex. A Study of the Origin and Method of Text Illustration.* Princeton: Princeton University Press, 1970.

Weyrauch, Erdmann. *Nach der Erfindung des Buchdruckes: Bücher, Bürger und Reformation in Strasburg 1521–1534.* Einführung in die Ältere Geschichte. Kurseinheit 7. Hagen: Fernuniversität, 1987.

———. "Überlegungen zur Bedeutung des Buches im Jahrhundert der Reformation." In *Flugschriften als Massenmedium der Reformationszeit*, vol. 7, ed. H. J. Köhler. Stuttgart, 1981. Pp. 243–60.

Wienbruch, Ulrich. "*Signum, significatio* und *illuminatio* bei Augustin." In *Der Begriff der Repraesentatio im Mittelalter: Stellvertretung, Symbol, Zeichen, Bild.* Miscellanea Medievalia 8, ed. Albert Zimmermann. Berlin: De Gruyter, 1971. Pp. 76–93.

Wiesehöfer, Joseph. *Ausbau des Schriftbezuges als Fortschritt der Wissenschaft. Die Entzifferung der Keilschrift.* Einführung in die Ältere Geschichte. Kurseinheit 9. Hagen: Fernuniversität, 1987.

Wildhaber, Robert. "Formen der Besitzergreifung im Volksrecht, im Volksglauben und in der Volksdichtung." *Narodno Stvaralostvo Folklor* (Belgrade) 1965: 1227–39.

———. *Das Sündenregister auf der Kuhhaut.* FF Communications 163. Helsinki: Academia Scientiarum Fennica, 1955.

Wright, Roger. "Speaking, Reading and Writing Late Latin and Early Romance." *Neophilologus* 60 (1976): 178–89.

Yates, Frances. *The Art of Memory.* Chicago and London: University of Chicago Press, 1966.

Ziegler, Joseph. *Dulcedo Dei. Ein Beitrag zur Theologie der griechischen und lateinischen Bibel.* Alttestamentliche Abhandlungen, Band 13, Heft 2. Münster: Aschendorfsche Verlagsbuchhandlung, 1937.

Zinn, G. A., Jr. "*Historia fundamentum est:* The Role of History in the Contemplative Life According to Hugh of St. Victor." In *Contemporary Reflec-*

tions on the Medieval Christian Tradition. Essays in Honor of Ray C. Petry, ed. G. H. Shriver. Durham, N.C.: Duke University Press, 1974. Pp. 135–58.

————. "Hugh of St. Victor and the Ark of Noah: A New Look." *Church History* 40 (1971): 261–72.

————. "Hugh of St. Victor and the Art of Memory." *Viator* 5 (1974): 211–34.

————. "The Influence of Hugh of St. Victor's *Chronicon* on the *Abreviationes Chronicorum* by Ralph of Diceto." *Speculum* 52 (1977): 38–61.

Zumthor, Paul. *La Lettre et la voix de la "littérature" médiévale.* Paris: Seuil, 1987.